Annabel Crabb is one of Australia's most popular political commentators, a Walkley-awarded writer, and the host of Australia's first dedicated political cooking show, ABC TV's *Kitchen Cabinet*. She writes for ABC Online's *The Drum* and has worked extensively in TV and radio. She is a columnist for the *Sunday Age*, *Sun-Herald* and Canberra's *Sunday Times*, and has worked as a political correspondent and sketchwriter for titles including the *Advertiser*, the *Age* and the *Sydney Morning Herald*, and as London correspondent for Fairfax's Sunday papers. She won a Walkley Award for her 2009 essay on Malcolm Turnbull, and was Australia's 2011 Eisenhower Fellow.

Annabel is an enthusiastic social media user and tweets about politics and food as @annabelcrabb. She lives in Sydney with her partner, Jeremy, and their three children.

Praise for *The Wife Drought*

'Crabb is an excellent writer, and the book is neither a polemical rant nor a statement of the bleeding obvious. She has presented the facts – the Australian economy is being held back by the rigid gender roles of its employees – in a new and interesting way, penned with the wry wit for which she is famous' Margot Saville, *Crikey*

'In a refreshing change of tack, Crabb doesn't just focus on the obstacles women, particularly mothers, face in pursuing a career but also the barriers men confront in trying to leave the workforce and stay at home . . . In her trademark witty style, Crabb chooses not to fire another bitter broadside in the gender wars' Sam de Brito, *Sydney Morning Herald*

'Though Crabb writes with her characteristic impish wit and flair, her central thesis is nonetheless a serious one. Having a "wife", Crabb argues, is an extraordinary advantage. She is right . . . [*The Wife Drought*] is an extremely useful invitation to do some serious thinking, from economics to ethics, not only about how women need wives, as Crabb suggests, but also more deeply about how we devalue care and penalise those who do it' Anne Manne, *The Monthly*

'What a joy to read *The Wife Drought* by Annabel Crabb, who usually makes words and ideas dance on a page. There are so many gems in this book and many new lines for today's conversations about gender. This is not small stuff, and Crabb treats the issue with the scholarship and attention it deserves . . . [the book] made me smile, chuckle and feel poignant and furious that we are still writing about the same issues forty years later' Wendy McCarthy, *Anne Summers Reports*

'[Crabb] is keen to speak *to* rather than *at*, and takes care to give the human aspect to the statistics she draws forth, often through wry stories honed from her years as a political correspondent and as host of the ABC's *Kitchen Cabinet* . . . *The Wife Drought* is both an attempt to laugh with the weary and to speak frankly to the circumspect' Jessica Au, *Financial Review*

'Packed with data yet impishly written, *The Wife Drought* dissects the gender dynamics bedeviling Australia's labour force in a way that is both serious and seriously funny' *The Interpreter*

Also by Annabel Crabb

*Losing it: The Inside Story of the Labor Party
in Opposition*

*Quarterly Essay 34. Stop at Nothing: The Life and
Adventures of Malcolm Turnbull*

Rise of the Ruddbot: Observations from the Gallery

THE
WIFE
DROUGHT

Why Women Need Wives
and Men Need Lives

Annabel Crabb

EBURY
PRESS

An Ebury Press book
Published by Random House Australia Pty Ltd
Level 3, 100 Pacific Highway, North Sydney NSW 2060
www.randomhouse.com.au

Penguin
Random House
Australia

First published by Ebury Press in 2014

Random House Books is part of the Penguin Random House group of
companies whose addresses can be found at global.penguinrandomhouse.
com.

National Library of Australia
Cataloguing-in-Publication Entry

Crabb, Annabel, author
The wife drought/Annabel Crabb

ISBN 9780857984289 (paperback)

Wives – Social conditions
Work and family
Women executives – Social conditions
Women in public life – Social conditions
Husbands – Effect of wife's employment on

306.8723

Cover design by Josh Durham, Design by Committee
Internal design by Midland Typesetters
Typeset in Sabon by Midland Typesetters, Australia
Printed in Australia by Griffin Press, an accredited ISO AS/NZS 14001:2004
Environmental Management System printer

CONTENTS

To Audrey, Elliott and Kate

PREFACE

Just over a year ago, when I finished writing *The Wife Drought*, I was all the things authors usually are at the end of a project: sick of the sound of my own typing, convinced the thing was terrible, and simultaneously extremely pleased to have it finished. The question of whether anyone would ever read it was, by that stage of the enterprise, a low-order issue – for me, at least, though I concede my publisher might differ on that point.

What has thrilled me since the book's publication is not that a lot of people have read it (though of course I found that both mildly surprising and intensely gratifying); it is, more specifically, that so many men have read it.

And of all the letters and emails and tweets I've received, and conversations I've had at writers' festivals and forums and when I bump into people in the street or sit next to them on a train, it's men I've loved hearing from the most. Because I love men being in this conversation, and it strikes me as incredibly weird when they're not.

I can narrow it right down for you, actually. The single best exchange I've had since the book was published was with a guy who wrote to me on Twitter asking for specific instructions on how to jelly his wife's breast milk.

Now, I hear what you're thinking. This sounds like a piece of correspondence best forwarded to the nearest law enforcement agency. But this chap was for real: he'd read one of my more exotic tips (see page 22) for juggling work and young children and had written to me for further instruction, as his wife was about to go back to work, and their baby – an extremely single-minded young lady – would not take fluids from a bottle.

For a couple of weeks, we corresponded. The day of his wife's return to work came and went, and I heard nothing. When eventually I inquired, his response made me punch the air: 'Won't have a bar of the bottle. Loves the jelly!' Much more recently, I heard from him again – he sent a photo of his child, happy and chubby and covered with what looked like Bolognese sauce. All is well with them.

Everything about that exchange made me happy. The knowledge that somewhere there was a woman going back to work who might be infinitesimally less likely to sob in the toilets was part of it. But mainly it was that this guy had looked at the situation his family was in and seen it as his problem, not just his wife's. And he'd rolled up his sleeves and sent a freaky message to a total stranger in an attempt to sort it out.

I know there are men like that everywhere, and what I always hoped in writing this book was that our society could change a little bit to encourage their involvement in the domestic sphere, or at any rate not make it so hard, or not be quite so gobsmacked when they do it off their own bat.

So every time a big company announces it's introducing a fully-fledged paid paternity leave scheme, or I hear a politician or commentator talk about work–life balance without assuming that work–life balance is a women's issue, or I hear a high-profile bloke talking about how he 'does it all', I celebrate another tiny step forward.

I've signed copies of this book for countless political wives, for husbands who have been told to read it, and (encouragingly) for many executives and managers. I hope they – and you, if you've just picked it up – read the book in the spirit in which it was written. Which is to say, in good humour and in fervent hope that the statistics it contains will very soon be hopelessly out of date.

I'm often asked what policy steps the Government can take to address the sorts of issues I raise in *The Wife Drought*, and my honest response is that in the main, it's not governments who need to change. It's us, women and men, checking the assumptions we often make – sometimes carelessly, sometimes at unbelievably busy times of our lives – about who will do what, or who *wants* to do what. Tiny steps. But significant ones.

Annabel Crabb

Introduction

THE WIFE DROUGHT

It was a funny sort of setting for a personal light-bulb moment. I was interstate at a 'summit' – one of those networking events at which various professionals and public policy experts waft about politely waiting for each other to finish before sharing their own views. I was already in a bit of an ill temper about it. Having accepted the invitation to attend, I belatedly opened the conference programme and immediately experienced a familiar, sinking feeling as I scanned the columns and columns of male names – economists, business figures, foreign policy experts – and realised that I had very likely been invited to chock up the event's skirt-rate.

All the signs were there. The morning involved a series of panels in which the panellists were all blokes and my job – as moderator – was to provide some sort of perky connective tissue. I noticed with particular horror that the following day I was scheduled to cross-examine, for sixty minutes, a chap who was a world expert in some sort of climatology in which I was significantly less expert. Of course, these things usually turn out to be interesting and worthwhile, and so indeed did this one, but as I headed to lunch on that first day I could not quite subdue the plaintive little voice in the back of my skull asking why I had abandoned my children for this.

As luck would have it, I ran into an old pal at lunch: a fellow who had been a ministerial adviser in Canberra but was now doing less, for more, in the private sector. We exchanged enthusiastic greetings and sat down. 'What's new with you?' I asked.

'I'm married! And we have a toddler!' he announced. Much mutual agreement ensued about how lovely children are, and so on.

'Yes, life is great,' he continued, digging with gusto into his French-trimmed lamb cutlets. 'My wife has quit her job, so I can be absolutely confident our child's getting the best of care. It's all worked out really well.'

Now, I like this bloke. I really do. And I wish him nothing but happiness. But why did I suddenly want to push his smiling face into the Potatoes Dauphinoise? Was it just because I was in a huff after spending the morning trying to make a group of economists sound interesting, while back in Sydney my own children nosed through rubbish bins for sustenance?

It's all worked out really well. I looked around the room, and I recognised what was going on. How many of these blokes had wives at home – picking up kids from school, digging Play-Doh out of the cracks in the floorboards for

2

the gazillionth time, taking Nanna to the doctor, waiting around for the phone guy to turn up 'between the hours of eight and twelve', which, as any veteran of the game will tell you, actually means 'thirty seconds after you have disappeared round the corner for a quick sortie to school to deliver the lunch bag that was left on the table this morning'.

The hour of 2.45 pm would never, for these men, bring that faint but always perceptible neural pressure. They had wives. I looked at the women I could see in the room. Was it my imagination or did they look kind of distracted?

I glanced back at my companion, chomping obliviously through his delicious lunch. He didn't even realise how fortunate he was; what a lucky door prize he'd won. What a weird and – for him – wonderful crimp in the sociological evolution of humanity it was that allowed him to walk out the door at 8 am, work a full and rewarding day, eat a nice lunch with both his hands, and come home – or so I imagined – to a newly bathed baby poised for bed.

He thought that was just how things worked. And the worst thing of all? He was right. Men get wives, and women don't. That *is* how it works.

I had wife envy, and I had it bad.

Bouts of wife envy strike me periodically. Sometimes it happens in airports, where I see squads of booming businessmen flocking together into the Qantas Club, while I am skulking by, possibly with a nipper strapped to my chest who has just observed the baby's prerogative to go what Martin Amis once termed 'super-void' in an already spongy nappy just as the final-call sign starts flashing. The resultant reproachful personal paging and walk of shame on to the flight, to be confronted by the politely horrified eyes of my seat neighbour, only exacerbates my envy. 'Well, yes,' I want to say to the guy I'm sitting next to. 'I find this a bit confronting as well, just so you know.'

I, too, want to go over that report while enjoying a complimentary Crown Lager. I, too, want to talk genially about what a little tiger my young son is, while peacefully completing my meeting presentation, safe in the knowledge that his every need is being met by my beautiful wife. Why am I writing this peering round an infant who is intently stuffing Cheerios up my nose? I want a wife, damn it. And I don't see how all these bozos get one, when I don't.

If you are working full-time, and your spouse is working either part-time or not at all, then – congratulations! You have a 'wife'. A wife, traditionally, is a person who pulls back on paid work in order to do more of the unpaid work that accumulates around the home (cleaning, fixing stuff, being around for when the plumber doesn't turn up, spending a subsequent hour on hold to find out why the plumber didn't turn up, and so on). This sort of work goes into overdrive once you add children to the equation, and the list of household jobs grows exponentially to include quite specialised work such as raising respectful, pleasant young people, and getting stains off things with a paste of vinegar and sodium bicarbonate.

A 'wife' can be male or female. Whether they're men or women, though, the main thing wives are is a cracking professional asset. They enable the busy full-time worker to experience the joy and fulfilment of children, without the considerable inconvenience of having to pick them up from school at 3 pm, which – in one of the human experience's wittier little jokes – is the time that school ends, a time that is convenient for pretty much no one. Having a wife means that if you get caught up at work, or want to stay later, either to get some urgent job finished or to frown at your desktop computer in a plausible simulacrum of working in order to impress a new boss while actually reading Buzzfeed, it can be done. Many wives work, but they do jobs that are either part-time or offer sufficient flexibility for the accommodation of late-breaking debacles.

In the olden days, wives were usually women. Which is funny, because nowadays wives are usually women too.

I first started thinking seriously about the significance of wives back in 2013, when Tony Abbott named a federal Cabinet with only one woman in it and the nation went into one of its periodic fits of self-examination as to why there aren't more women in federal politics. I wrote a column expressing my view that if women MPs were blessed with wives in the same way that male MPs frequently are, you might get quite a noticeable participatory uptick, because that way women wouldn't have to choose between having a career in politics and having a family. Many women have had to do that over the years, while male politicians breed like hamsters while in office and nobody even notices.

I was left in no doubt, by the resultant stream of correspondence, that asymmetric rates of wife-having are a disparity not restricted to MPs. Businesswomen, executives, academics, journalists and lawyers wrote to me with spookily similar experiences. All of them watched their male contemporaries and competitors start families, and noticed how fatherhood made barely any difference to the way those guys worked; they still worked long hours, travelled at the drop of a hat, or had no difficulty making work functions after-hours. Usually it was because they had wives who either stayed at home full-time or worked fewer hours in order to manage child care. But my correspondents didn't have wives, and all of them thought life would be easier if they did.

Right then, I thought. Just out of curiosity, how many working fathers have 'wives' in Australia, compared to working mothers? What exactly, in other words, is the comparative national rate of wife-having, expressed as a ratio between women and men? Ascertaining how many working dads have part-time or stay-at-home partners, compared to the other way around, should be a relatively easy business, I assumed. Surely some statistics nut must have had a gander at it at some stage.

My search for this information began blithely, with a few confident Google key-strokes, but quickly degenerated into a horrifying snarl-up involving the 2011 Census data, much back-of-the-envelope calculation, reams and reams of almost-helpful Australian Bureau of Statistics tables, and some heroic assumptions on my part that would offend any serious statistician. There was plenty of data on fathers' employment, and mothers' employment. But that was no use to me; I wanted to join them together, and find out which dads and which mums lived together, and how they managed things between them.

Eventually, I did what many a statistical fraud would do in my position: I telephoned the Australian Institute of Family Studies, and asked to speak to Jennifer Baxter. I didn't know Jenny, but her name was on all the most interesting reports I'd read about patterns in male and female employment, especially in relation to families. If anyone could yank the figures I was after, I was fairly confident it would be Jenny. And when I finally ran her to earth, after dealing with the traditional public-relations maze that most agencies have now installed to shield their employees from the horror of journalists cold-calling them, she was pleasantly receptive.

I explained my problem: what I really wanted was a wife-count. Who had wives? Was it still just a bloke thing? Or were ladies getting them too these days?

Jenny was exceedingly helpful, and her voice had the rich, reassuring cadence of the super-numerate. Just as I'd hoped. But she warned me not to get too excited. 'I get a lot of journalists ringing me about stay-at-home dads,' she said, kindly. 'Everybody wants a story about how they're on the rise. But they're not, really. You look at the data, and it's just not there.'

A day or two later, Jenny emailed me an exciting little package of data, which she had tickled out of the 2011 Census data with the assistance of her data-crunching software and her brain; always likely to be a better bet, I guess, than *my* brain, a pencil, and forty-eight cups of tea, which is what I'd used.

And here's the story. Of Australian couple families with kids under the age of fifteen, 60 per cent have a dad who works full-time, and a mum who works either part-time or not at all. How many families have a mum who works full-time, and a dad who is at home or works part-time? Three per cent.[1]

Who gets wives? Dads do. Most mums have to make do with alternative arrangements.

Only one in four mothers with children under the age of fifteen work full-time. These are the women who – in all sorts of lines of work – find themselves in open competition in the full-time workplace. What interests me is: how do their circumstances compare against the dads who are doing similar jobs? How many of the full-time working mothers have 'wives', compared with the full-time working dads?

It turns out that in Australian workplaces, 76 per cent of full-time working dads have a 'wife'. Three out of four. But among the mothers who work full-time, the rate of wife-having is much, much lower: only 15 per cent.[2] Working fathers, in other words, are five times as likely to have a 'wife' as working mothers. As I suspected: Australian working women are in an advanced, sustained and chronically under-reported state of wife drought, and there is no sign of rain.

Not everyone gets married, obviously. Not everyone has children. And not every relationship is a male–female affair. Humanity is a broad church, full of endless fascinating combinations and permutations. But when Australian men and women settle down, buy a fridge and have children together, the patterns are much more pronounced than you might think. This is free-and-easy, egalitarian Australia's intriguing little secret; our attachment to the male-breadwinner model is deep and robust.

Not having a wife is an urgent practical disadvantage. If two employees, both parents, are to compete with each other for advancement and promotion, what attributes could they invoke? Natural aptitude, intelligence, rigour, leadership – so far, so good. But what about the ability to work extra hours? To do the networking that in many white-collar industries is central to success, or the long hours and absences from home that are necessary in blue-collar fields?

If one of those employees has a wife, that employee has an immediate and distinct economic advantage so significant as to be positively anti-competitive. Being able to go to your job and concentrate on your work to the absolute exclusion of all else is something that our system assumes men and women are able to do equally. But that assumption is far from the truth.

Imagine an industrial system in which 76 per cent of male employees were given cars, but the vast majority of women were obliged to catch the bus. Imagine a system in which white employees got free child care, but black employees didn't. We would be pretty shocked by either of those arrangements, because our view of fairness is that people shouldn't miss out on economic privileges just because of their race or gender.

Well, having a wife *is* an economic privilege. A privilege that far more men enjoy than women. But it's a state of affairs so broadly accepted as to be barely mentioned.

Terrance Fitzsimmons, a researcher from the University of Queensland, wrote a doctoral thesis in 2011 comparing the experiences of male and female CEOs.[3] He interviewed about thirty of each in great depth, discovering in the process that men and women who get to the top tend to be different in many ways. But the baldest difference between Fitzsimmons' CEOs was the way they organised their domestic lives. Of the thirty men he interviewed, twenty-eight had children. And all twenty-eight of those had a stay-at-home wife. Of the thirty-one women he interviewed, only two had stay-at-home husbands, and in both those cases the men were self-employed. The men had wives, and the women didn't – simple as that. Of the female CEOs who had children (about two-thirds of them, the rest having decided against it or, as is often the case, simply got to the point in their lives and careers where they realised it wasn't going to happen) *every single one* of them identified herself as the primary caregiver.

Of his interviews with CEOs, Fitzsimmons observes that 'Many male respondents noted that being a "family man" had made a significant positive contribution to their career progression and ultimate selection as CEO. No female respondents made this connection.'[4]

None of this is exactly rocket science. Of course a person with a spouse who takes care of stuff at home will be more free to prosper in the workplace. Yet the weird thing is that among all the reasons we traditionally proffer for women's under-representation in politics, company boards and so on – blokey culture, bosses who don't promote women, women who don't lean in, and so on – the factor of 'no one at home remembering whether it's damn mufti day or not' gets mentioned surprisingly infrequently.

'Oh, but things are changing,' you might think. 'I saw that *House Husbands* show on the telly. I know some hands-on dads.' And you probably do. But they are unusual – trust me; if you look at the statistics, things aren't budging much. Over the last twenty years, the proportion of fathers who work has actually gone up – from 86 per cent to 90 per cent. The proportion of fathers who are not working has gone down.[5]

Greater flexibility for women? Better support in the workplace? Better mentoring systems? Quotas for boards? Cultural education? Yes, yes, yes. But as the daughters of the 1970s feminists get older, have children later, and cluster together to talk – not about sex and art, but about the challenges of doing a good job of both work and family – and they joke to each other 'What I really need is a wife!', we need to understand that it's not actually a joke.

It's not a joke, because women who work full-time are not only statistically less likely to *have* a wife; they're still fairly likely to *be* a wife. Even when mothers work full-time, they still do more than twice as much household work as their full-time working husbands: forty-one hours a week compared to twenty.[6]

The last five decades might feel as though they have brought about a gender revolution, but the most revolutionary aspects have been contained largely to one side of the ledger: women taking on more paid work. To a great extent, women have maintained their unpaid jobs at home too, and men have not filled the breach. The obligation that evolves for working mothers, in particular, is a very precise one; the feeling that one ought to work as if one did not have children, while raising one's children as if one did not have a job. To do any less feels like failing at both. This explains the constant state of tension and anxiety widely reported by working mothers.

I think of a *Candid Camera* show I once saw where applicants for a job in a doughnut factory were told they needed to do a trial shift on the boxing line. Secretly filmed, the candidates donned their hairnets and sat down at a conveyor belt, stacking freshly made doughnuts neatly into boxes. But as they worked, the conveyor belt got faster and faster. The piles of doughnuts got messier and messier as the poor victims tried to keep up. Eventually, they were just chucking the things into the boxes any which way, as more and more doughnuts relentlessly poured forth from the maw of the machine. It was – in the classic manner of such TV shows – utterly unbearable to watch.

That segment summarises to me what juggling work and family feels like. You start off all right, and all your doughnuts are going where they are supposed to go. But as more jobs materialise, and more deadlines bob up, and freakishly unexpected developments arrive (your child comes down with gastro; the hot water tap in the bathroom inexplicably gets jammed at full-bore; your boss announces that now would be a good time for you to deliver a formal progress report on your project to the board; suddenly the prime minister's on the TV announcing a snap Royal Commission into something; everyone gets nits), everything has to be done just that little bit faster, and the faster you go the more the panic rises, as does the guilt about doing everything just that little bit worse. You're just hurling the damn doughnuts now, hating doughnuts and wondering why anyone would ever bother eating the stupid things anyway. Generally, it's at this point that you'll realise that you forgot it was your mother's birthday yesterday. Or you'll stub your toe, and dissolve into a wail of entirely disproportionate self-pity.

It's not just about the work hours involved. Paid work can be demanding, stressful and exacting. But work in the home can consume a huge amount of emotional bandwidth, in which failure brings a sense of guilt and self-recrimination far more tearing and existential than what you feel when you bugger something up mildly at work.

For example: I am fast approaching the deadline for finishing this book. In the last twelve weeks, I've written eighty thousand words. In the weeks to come, there are dense weeks of parliamentary drama, the planning of a new *Kitchen Cabinet* series, several speeches and God knows what else. But the only thing that has actually reduced me to tears is Chiquita, a foot-tall stuffed kangaroo.

Chiquita lives at the childcare centre my four-year-old son attends twice a week. Every holiday, a lucky child gets to take Chiquita home and show her a good time. Chiquita travels with her own scrapbook, and the idea is that parents will capture action shots of Chiquita's adventures with her juvenile escort, then paste them into the book to create a permanent marsupial travel diary. At Easter, it was our turn.

Chiquita had a quiet holiday. We forgot to take her to the Easter Show. We forgot to take her to the pool. We forgot to take her to the museum. Any outing we actually achieved was undertaken in Chiquita's absence; she spent most of Easter perched hopefully on the dinner table. It was only at the eleventh hour of the Easter egg hunt, when the children were half-heartedly poking through undergrowth for any overlooked goodies, that anyone remembered to get a snap of Chiquita even vaguely near the action. The day before Chiquita was due back, the task of printing out the lame Chiquita pictures drummed at the back of my skull. I had a column and two speeches to write. Three o'clock was fast approaching. I had just enough time to get to the photo shop, if I hustled. The discovery that the photo shop had gone out of business the day before very nearly finished me. With Herculean restraint, I did not actually claw hysterically at the expressionless roller door securing the defunct shop's dim interior. But I wanted to.

Sticking pictures of a nomadic stuffed kangaroo in a book is – in economic terms – an insignificant piece of work, of no interest to national productivity, immaterial to the formal prosperity of my household. But the emotional exposure is considerable, and this is at the heart of the Chiquita Syndrome: I do not want my son to be the kid who brings the Chiquita book back blank because his mum was too busy to organise it. Failing Chiquita isn't like failing as an employee; it feels like failing as a person, which cuts much deeper, notwithstanding the triviality of the enterprise itself.

Chiquita is a small but typical example of 'wife work' – utterly invisible to the national economy, but significant to the wellbeing of a family. She fits beautifully into the job specifications for the position of 'wife', which might look something like this:

Opening exists for leader of a small, spirited team in a vibrant but often chaotic environment. Applicant must be mature and patient, as team members may at times be prone to sudden mood swings, unorthodox social techniques, strategic tunnel vision and outright insubordination.

Applicant will have responsibility for cleaning, laundering, tutoring, light maintenance, heavy maintenance, procurement, occupational health and safety, occupational therapy, nutrition, ethical guidance counselling, transport, skills training, intra-team human resource management, outsourcing, mentoring, mediation, education and sanitation.

Fine motor control and calm temperament a must. Creative experience and demonstrated innovation strong advantages, esp. capacity to construct, for example, a plausible bat costume from basic household items in under ten minutes.

Some tasks may be repetitive. Formal performance assessment very limited, though applicant may self-assess regularly in bleaker moments.

Salary nominal.

If you look at this gig through the eyes of a conventional job-seeker, it's pretty obvious why blokes do not regularly apply. The signposts of success in the workplace – the clear milestones and targets, the achievement of which might earn you backslaps or bonuses or both – are nowhere to be seen. You don't get paid, which I guess is sort of a deal-breaker for some people straight up. Achievements may frequently prove fleeting, and soon forgotten. Washed clothes get dirty again. A perfectly balanced, home-cooked dinner still gets eaten, and will encounter exactly the same digestive fate as frozen pizza. Toys, blocks and general filth will quickly reclaim any territory cleared by even quite concerted parental effort. Some of the key performance indicators – looking at you, Chiquita – are so random as to be ridiculous.

If you do well at this job, the returns are hugely significant: good relationships with your children, a balanced approach to life, probably a happy retirement in which you will be able to enjoy yourself with gentle pursuits, rather than working till you're seventy and then dropping dead. But we're talking some pretty long-tail business there. In the meantime maybe someone will thank you for it. Or maybe they won't.

Paid work is hard, but it offers predictability. Anyone who – dressed, clean, showered and ready for the day – has ever clicked the front door shut at 8.30 am on a scene of roiling domestic chaos within will be familiar with the rich sense of possibility and calm available to the escaping parent. Perhaps a cup of coffee at the train station? One that can be procured with newspaper in hand, and no accompanying small people demanding a biscuit? To the non-primary carer spouse, a cup of coffee in a shop is nothing – a mere bagatelle. To a person lugging small children about, a cup of coffee in a shop can be a space mission requiring considerable equipment, detailed advance site knowledge (can I even get this damn pram in there?) and the ever-present spectre of social humiliation.

So, yes, recruitment for male wives is a tricky thing. So tricky, in fact, that many women in particularly demanding jobs just give up looking.

A brief word to male readers. I do not propose to spend the entire length of these pages smouldering away in a fit of impotent rage next to innocent chaps happily eating French-trimmed lamb cutlets. And I am more than aware that if you are a man reading this book you have either A) an already evolved appreciation of work–life responsibility and are propping the pages up as you complete a large batch of bolognese sauce for the freezer or B) a wife with a .22 rifle trained at your temple. I shall have some very nice things to say about you at various points.

This is not a book of rage, on the whole. And – more importantly – it's not just a book about women. Because in all the research and argument and thought that's been expended over the past five decades on the question of why women don't succeed at work like men do there's a great, gaping hole. It's a man-shaped hole.

What I can't believe is this: why, after all these decades of campaign, reform, research and thought about how we can best get women into the workplace, are we so slow to pick up that the most important next step is how to get men out of it?

I don't mean that in a 'burn their punch cards and barricade the corner office' way, either. I mean that if we are serious about equality, we should stop worrying so exclusively about women's ease of access to the workplace and start worrying more about men's ease of egress from it.

'Women have trouble asking for pay rises, and men have trouble asking for time off,' is how my sagacious friend and colleague, the writer George Megalogenis, once put it to me.

And I wonder if we are perhaps looking at things the wrong way up. So much has changed for women, even over my lifetime. The year before I was born just north of Adelaide, women in my home state of South Australia were still obliged to resign from their state public service jobs when they got married. In the forty-one years since, women have surged into the workforce at a considerable clip. They've overtaken men in tertiary education.

And yet, for men, weirdly little has changed. While the horizons for women have opened right up, the baseline expectations of men are pretty much what they were when I was born: grow up, get a job, have children (an event which will make little discernible difference to your working life apart from probably making you a better bet for a pay rise), retire and expire. Fathers are expected to be more involved with their children than their own fathers were, certainly. But they are expected to do that in their own spare time; while the workplace has changed hugely to accommodate women over the last half-century, it still takes a largely dim view of men who want to work flexibly so they can pick up their kids from school.

What would happen if we stopped looking at this situation as one in which women are the victims, and started looking at what men miss out on? For example, Australia has one of the highest rates of part-time work in the OECD; nearly twice the rate in the United States.[7] (The vast majority of part-time workers are women; that's the compromise we have reached, wordlessly, as a nation, to the great industrial thumbscrew of women who want to do more work and men who don't want to do any less.)

We often look at part-time work as inferior to full-time work. But to have flexibility at work is quite a marvellous thing. Working part-time has a range of drawbacks, but it can be a superb and workable solution to different phases of the life cycle, as human beings respond to the needs of others, be they children, ageing relatives, or sick friends and family. That is a normal, human thing to do. But somewhere along the way, we've settled on the idea that this is a normal, *lady* thing to do. Forty-three per cent of Australian mothers with primary school children work part-time, for example, but only 5 per cent of fathers do.[8]

Surveys regularly find that Australian men – especially fathers – would prefer to work fewer hours. But lots of them never ask. Why? Are they fibbing about wanting to see more of their kids? Or are they genuinely concerned that doing so would damage their standing at work?

And let's not shy away from the difficult questions here: Could it also be because the world of 'home' has as many intricate secret handshakes and baffling key performance indicators today as the world of 'work' had when women first started turning up? Could the one man showing up for school reading or canteen duty possibly feel just as exposed and uncomfortable as the one woman showing up to the board meeting might?

The soft, redeeming glow of gender-neutral language (*parenting*, it's now called, not mothering) bathes everything in the presumption of neutrality, but the truth is that Australia still has some pretty rigorous expectations about who is likely to do which jobs. Niggly little bat-signals tell mothers they would be more normal if they didn't work. 'Aren't you exhausted?' or 'Who's looking after the children?' the working mother is often asked, though nobody would ask her husband the same question. The prime minister's 2013 campaign reference to 'the house-wives of Australia . . . as they do their ironing' articulated the presumption clearly. And niggly little signals tell fathers they would be more normal if they didn't look after their kids ('Off to be Mr Mum, are you?').

Obviously, this is a big country and there are innumerable exceptions. The hardest thing about writing a book like this is the knowledge that it'll be read one person at a time. Every person is different; every family, too. You might split everything evenly in your house, or have a best mate who is a blissful home dad. I don't dispute that. All I'm saying is that, by and large, you are in a minority.

And it's awkward – awkward! – talking about this stuff even at the best of times. Every decision people make about how to manage working with having a family is haunted by the ghosts of the paths unchosen. Parents who work worry that they are short-changing their kids. Parents who don't work feel they are invisible to the rest of society. As a result, the levels of defensiveness around this subject are sky high. If I offend you with my generalisations, I apologise; I generalise only, I hope, when the evidence warrants it.

Just by the way, I will regularly use the word 'husband' and 'wife' when talking about any heterosexual, live-in partnership, regardless of whether rings are on fingers. I think this is fair enough, given the modern popularity of de facto relationships, but I am also aware that many families do not conform to this formula in any event; they might be childless, or same-sex, or single-parent. Obviously, any broad conclusions about the typical domestic arrangements of a heterosexual couple family with children will not apply to those families. This doesn't mean those people are insignificant, unworthy of discussion or don't have their problems. But this is a book about women and men, and the big patterns that still emerge – stubbornly, undeniably – across this country when women and men get together and make a family.

A personal disclosure, at this point, seems fair. I have three small children, and a full-time job. I have a partner who also works full-time. Our families live mostly interstate. I do not have a wife (poor me), and neither does he (poor him).

I get asked all the time, 'How do you do it all?' No one ever asks my partner that, which is kind of unfair, seeing as he does a lot of juggling too. But the answer is: I don't. Do it all, that is. Not at the same time, anyway. No one does. You get all the help you can, whenever you can, and the rest you squish into the time you have available. My partner, Jeremy, works flexibly one day a week. The little children are in day care two days a week. For the last six years, we have hosted, off and on, a series of live-in au pairs. Because I work weird hours, often starting early or finishing late, there is pretty much no childcare centre that would fully meet our needs; the last-minute radio interviews, the travel, the speaking engagements, the days on which all hell breaks loose and suddenly federal politics becomes a rolling story. Having a third person around to pick up unexpected slack is an incredible advantage, without which our place would not be able to function. It also means that the children are near to where I am working. I see them all the time, even when I am working flat out, and that is a piece of good fortune for which I am grateful every day.

Because I work online a lot, I can write and file copy much more flexibly than newspaper writers can. I cram it into times when children are sleeping, or at school, or at child care, or when I have a babysitter in place. I go back to work once they're in bed. I catch the bus so I can work on the way to work. I time my shower to coincide with the broadcast of the morning radio current affairs show *AM*, so that I don't waste any time. I use every scrap of the day like an Italian farmer uses all of the pig.

At times, I have done ridiculous things. We started making the third series of *Kitchen Cabinet* when my youngest daughter, Kate, was about ten weeks old. So she came with me to work, in a baby sling. I wrote standing up, at a Rumsfeldesque work-desk composed of the dining room table, eight cookbooks and a laptop, so that she could sleep on me while I worked. (She decided against sleeping in cots. Tried it once, didn't like it.) When we shot episodes of the show at a politician's house, our series producer Madeleine walked around outside with my baby strapped to her chest and a remote earpiece in her ear, listening to the action on set. (Madeleine also researched this book. I hope, in time, she may agree to marry me, but I don't want to rush her.)

I have changed that baby on Jenny Macklin's floor, in Craig Emerson's bedroom, in Malcolm Turnbull's farm library, and at one point – starved of alternative child-care options – I got Bill Heffernan to hold her. My parents drove from their Adelaide Plains farm to Broken Hill to serve as on-set nannies.

When it turned out that Kate had a permanent aversion to bottles of any kind, we racked our brains to think of ways to get milk into her as an alternative to the most obvious way. Reader: there is no other way to tell you this. For a time, I jellied my own breastmilk so she could eat it off a spoon. (Sorry. I hope you're still there.)

Women swap stories like this all the time. In the modern pentathlon that is wifeless working, tales of debacle are hard currency. And I will happily confess that for all my periodic wife envy, I would not like to miss out on that debacle. It feels messy and alive and real. It makes for excellent comedy. And as much as the juggling life is not easy, I think it's a tragedy – a proper tragedy – that men are encouraged to miss out on it, every day. It feels like a universe of experience from which fathers are disproportionately excluded, and that's a sad thing.

I wrote this book because, in our long and vexed national discussion about gender and work, it feels to me that we miss something quite big. We focus our attention on who wins and loses at work, but we don't join it up with what's happening at home.

As long as we assume women are the only losers in this situation, nothing will change. Because the truth is that everybody loses in a system like this. Women who feel hard done by, men who feel trapped at work, children who don't see enough of their fathers.

Australia's twenty-eighth prime minister, Tony Abbott, took office in 2013 promising to help marginalised Australians, including 'women struggling to combine career and family'.[9] (He was immediately as good as his word, appointing a Cabinet that did not create work–family issues for a single Coalition woman.) His words were meant honourably. But this shouldn't be a struggle for women. It should be a struggle for people.

1

AWFUL MEN,
HOPELESS WOMEN

At a media Christmas party in 2011, I found myself in an especially happy state; just convivial enough to approach a very senior colleague from a rival media company to address a question that had long been troubling me.

'Tell me,' I inquired, with a smile to indicate that I came in peace (it was an ABC party, and my target was in hostile territory). 'Why is it that there are so few women in your opinion pages?'

It wasn't an attack – I did genuinely wonder – and to his credit, he replied honestly.

'Yes, there aren't enough,' he said. 'The thing is, we really struggle to find female columnists. I'm a firm believer that women are equal; it's just that they haven't really been equal for long enough to create a pool of women who have the breadth of experience to write really authoritative columns on the subjects we cover in our opinion page.'

We looked at each other for a bit; I digesting his answer, he no doubt waiting for me to throw my glass of riesling at him.

I didn't do that. And I don't name him here because I liked the fact that he answered genuinely, rather than trying to fob me off by listing the handful of women who in fact appear regularly on the bloke-infested opinion page in question.

But his response told me a couple of things. One – he probably hadn't been asked the question many times. Two – these things are incredibly subjective, even in the most visible of workplaces. When *I* looked at his publication, I saw a sea of male faces so comprehensive as to seem weird. When *he* looked at his publication, he saw a field of excellence to which – owing to a certain regrettable tardiness in the natural evolution of things – only a few women at this stage qualified for admission, notwithstanding the warmly accepted principle that in all general respects blokes and chicks should be equal.

This is not an uncommon crossroads for men and women to find themselves loitering awkwardly upon. Why aren't there more female CEOs? Why aren't there more women on boards? Why aren't there more women in Cabinet?

These questions surface with all the rehearsed and seasonal regularity of a Nativity play. Some report will come out confirming that there are more ASX companies with communications directors who are left-handed than there are organisations with a majority of women on their boards. A brief round of national hand-wringing may then ensue.

Someone will say, 'The problem is, there just aren't enough women with experience. Things will straighten out once equality works its way through the system.' Someone else will say, 'Are you kidding? Why don't we just introduce a damn quota system and fix it?' And then someone else will say: 'Because it's unfair. Horrible to imagine perfectly good blokes being thrown over for token women who will no doubt be annoyed to be picked for their gender rather than on merit.' And then some footballer will be caught injecting horse blood or something, and we will all move on to the next subject.

The 'experience' thing comes up again and again. And folded into the experience argument is the notion that things will get better, gradually, as that lovely equality just oozes its way through the system, with women steadily getting more excellent and men finally declaring, 'Whoa, ladies! Point taken! Help yourselves to half this loot!'

But how much does 'lack of experience' actually explain, anyway?

For example, let's look at the gender pay gap in Australia. Women constitute almost half of the workforce, but get paid on average 17 per cent less than men.[1] Now, there are plenty of people who will tell you that the pay gap is imaginary – that women are paid less because they tend to take lower-paid jobs, because they move in and out of the work force, or because they have fewer qualifications, or less *experience*. The thing is, when researchers – and there is plenty of research on this particular topic – dig down and compare male and female workers with comparable levels of experience and qualifications, there remains a stubborn 60 per cent or so of the gender pay gap which cannot be explained by anything apart from the presence or absence of certain dangly bits.[2]

And though we think of the gender pay gap – or I always have, at any rate – as a sort of blanket layer of disadvantage, a generalised GST-style penalty that is lopped off as soon as you get to the pay window and they realise you're a chick – the truth is it doesn't work like that at all. Actually, the gender gap is much smaller among lower-paid workers, and much bigger among the higher-paid.

When Melbourne University researcher Deborah Cobb-Clark and her colleague Juan Barón examined in close detail the pay discrepancies between private sector employees, they found that the gap between low-paid men and low-paid women was about 8 per cent, which could indeed be explained away by productivity factors, experience and so on. But up among the high-income earners, the lawyers and executives, the pay gap blew out to 28 per cent, and only about a quarter of that could be explained by anything other than gender.[3]

As Catherine Fox dryly observed, after a long passage in her book *Seven Myths about Women and Work* in which she canvassed all the other potential contributing factors considered and dismissed by researchers looking at this area: 'The most important element in equalising the differential is for a woman to become a man.'[4]

The higher up the food chain you go as a woman, therefore, not only does it become more likely that you will be paid less than the identically qualified chap who sits opposite you, but it simultaneously becomes less likely that that disparity will be explicable on any other grounds apart from the fact that you are a dame and he is a fella. Now – this bunching-up of the gender pay gap towards the top of the tree does make a certain rudimentary amount of horse sense. Lower-paid people are more likely to be on bands or awards, which are visible to everybody and from which formal bias should long ago have been eliminated. But higher wages are far less likely to be accountable in the same way – the better paid you get, the more likely that your salary becomes a 'package', with all sorts of bonuses and fringe benefits that are the discretionary gift of employers and not necessarily handed out in an equal way.

'I don't know what they get paid. They don't know what I get paid,' wrote *Sunrise* presenter Natalie Barr of her male colleagues in her widely circulated 2014 column advising women to 'stop blaming men' for their failures in the workplace.[5] She is correct – at her level in her industry, contracts are top secret. But I'd bet that if Ms Barr and her male colleagues played a little show-and-tell, she'd be more surprised than they would be.

The high-paid bracket is the cohort to which – the argument has regularly been made – the pipeline of qualified and 'experienced' women, flowing through university degrees and middle management and then triumphantly into senior executive positions, would eventually deliver equality, like the floodwaters arriving at the Serengeti Plain.

But that's not what's happened. The surge of women into tertiary qualifications has happened, all right. For nearly two decades now, women have graduated from university in greater numbers than men. They took the lead in 1985, and now represent 60 per cent of graduates.[6] And women persist strongly to a certain point about halfway up the professional ladder, constituting 45 per cent of middle managers.[7] But they only occupy 10 per cent of executive positions. And only 2 to 3 per cent of CEO positions in the

ASX200, depending on whether Gail Kelly is on holidays or not.[8]

This is what University of Queensland researcher Terrance Fitzsimmons calls the 'Stupid Curve' – the arc described by the numbers of women as they swan-dive away to virtually nothing when plotted against seniority in the workplace. The Stupid Curve is the visual representation of all the education, work and experience that women en masse collect up until a certain point, whereupon much of it seems just to evaporate, or at least run out of northward puff.

Meaning – and this is amusing, in a despairing sort of a way – that the problem really isn't, at heart, that there aren't enough experienced women around; it's that very few enterprises seem capable of capitalising fully on all the experience that's currently going to waste.

And it's an extraordinarily expensive piece of wastefulness. Not only the cost of teaching and training all those women, but the productivity forgone. When Goldman Sachs and JBWere teamed up in 2009 to investigate the cost to Australia of women's under-representation, they worked out that if women's workforce participation rates became more like men's, it would add 11 per cent to gross domestic product.[9] Think of an Australia with a whole extra mining sector added on. That's what we're missing out on.

Australian working women get a rougher deal than many of their colleagues in comparable Western economies; we rank 24th in the world for pay equality, and are nowhere near the top ten, which is dominated of course by Euro-smoothies like Iceland, Sweden, Norway and

Switzerland.[10] According to the World Economic Forum, countries where the gender gap has been all but eliminated also tend to do better economically overall – although that reasoning seems a little clunky in the case of the world number one, Iceland; possibly a statistical aberration brought on by excessive consumption of fermented shark meat.

Being undervalued is a pricey business for women personally, too. Thanks to the magic made available to us by the University of Canberra's National Centre for Social and Economic Modelling (NATSEM), we can actually predict and compare the likely parallel courses of men and women just starting out on their careers today. Let's take a woman, and make her twenty-five years old and give her a postgraduate education. Let's call her 'Jane'. If she works for forty years, Jane is likely – if things go according to the average experience – to earn a lifetime total of $2.49 million. But if you take a second graduate, and call him 'Jeff', and give him exactly the same qualifications as Jane and bless him with the same degree of averageness, he ends his forty-year career with a lifetime total of $3.78 million.[11] That amounts to, as Anne Summers pointed out in her book *The Misogyny Factor*, 'a million dollar penalty for being a young woman in Australia today'.[12]

Over the decades that have elapsed since anyone started caring to any noticeable extent, the question of why women don't get to the top so much has collected a sprawling tangle of answers.

They are extensive and time-consuming, and if you listen to enough daytime radio and read enough management journals you will hear them all in the fullness of time: Male bosses are sexist. Women don't want the top jobs. Men are naturally more ambitious. Men promote men. Women have kids and drop out. Men are better at self-promotion. Women aren't aggressive enough. Workplaces are structured to suit men. Women are no good at leadership – look at Julia Gillard. Men think they know everything – look at Kevin Rudd. Women aren't good enough for the first eleven – just ask Tony Abbott.

If you take all these arguments, theories, studies, hypotheses, things you saw on the Internet and everything starting with 'I'm not sexist but' and threw them into a giant cement mixer and tumbled them free of their outer casings of assumptions and prejudices, you would find that they can be sorted into two broad categories, which I – for convenience – will call 'men are awful' and 'women are hopeless'.

The first group of reasons centre formally around the fact that the decision about whether or not women proceed to the upper echelons of any power structure is still usually decided by men, and informally around the further suspicion that men are awful.

For instance: men are awful because they hire other men. This can happen subconsciously. Men who have advanced happily up the career ladder tend to assume – perfectly understandably, I suppose – that the things that made them successful are the things that will make others successful too. So if working sixteen-hour days or having a top-down management style has got them to the top, chances are they will count these traits as important for success, discounting other traits as less important.

When Terrance Fitzsimmons interviewed dozens of Australian CEOs and company directors for his 2011 doctoral thesis on gender differences in leadership, he asked them what they looked for when recruiting leaders. Fitzsimmons had read all the reams of corporate bumf about numbers of men and women and seniority and salary gaps and diversity programmes and so on, but he was more interested in the human story: how senior executives are actually chosen, and why. Here's the assessment of one board chair, whom Fitzsimmons asked to describe an ideal chief executive:

In all our chief executives, we tend to look for supermen, and no wonder we want some guy who wears his underpants on the outside, because he's got to be in charge of operational detail, he's got to be a good operations man who delivers on time and on budget, but equally we want people with a strategic vision, we want people to have an idea about where the business is going and we want people who, if they aren't charismatic leaders, then at least are deeply respected leaders so that people follow them.[13]

Now, that board chair might very well, if asked, have claimed to head an organisation that was 'passionate about gender equality' and about 'helping every employee to make a full and satisfying contribution'. But if, when you picture a CEO, that CEO is a 'good operations man', then chances are your CEO is also going to be a man, full stop.

Fitzsimmons' thesis is full of truly fascinating insights into the women who become CEOs, compared to the men who do. He found a considerable difference in the kinds of childhoods female and male CEOs had had. Almost all of the male leaders, for instance, had had stay-at-home mothers, comfortable and affluent childhoods, and every single one of them had played football. All but two had captained their teams. The 31 female CEOs, however, had had very different paths to success. Half of them had had working mothers. Many had experienced childhood disruptions – divorce, parental death or illness, repeated uprooting or other circumstances that obliged them to take on adult responsibilities earlier than might otherwise have been the case.

Of special interest to Fitzsimmons was the exact process by which corporate leaders actually achieved advancement. 'Track record' – experience – was extremely important, he found. But the standards for assessing 'track record', or taking a leap of judgement on a candidate who could go either way, are not always clear. Senior executive vacancies are not compulsorily advertised in a way that would invite a full range of applicants.

Fitzsimmons observed that 'when no formal process exists, people fall back on stereotypes and personal biases in decision-making, which often results in homo-social reproduction'. Homo-social reproduction sounds like something of which Cory Bernadi would instinctively disapprove, but turns out to mean people promoting people who remind them of themselves.

If a group of people go through their careers meeting only board members who are male, then at some deep and automatic level they will think of board members as male. In this environment, board members who are women are an exception. Meredith Hellicar, a long-standing Australian senior executive and board regular, recalls: 'Another woman and I were on a board together for a number of years. We looked nothing alike; she was short, and I'm tall. She had an elfin face and dark hair. I was blonde. And yet several of the male directors quite often mixed us up. Was it that we were just "the women" in their minds?'

It is perfectly possible for a man to behave this way while feeling genuinely supportive of the idea that women are equal, and believing absolutely that he is making appointments on merit. It is not impossible to see a man who generally promotes men appear smilingly on the flyleaf of the company's Gender Equality Report. Not impossible at all, because the human brain is not famously good at self-awareness. Even when we think we are being scrupulously fair, our assumptions have a way of seeping into the decisions that we make.

Sex Discrimination Commissioner Elizabeth Broderick – as part of her Male Champions of Change campaign – has worked with dozens of Australia's most senior CEOs, chairmen and bureaucrats to help them recognise the subterranean assumptions within their own organisations. Many of them were stunned – after learning about unconscious bias – to discover the implicit attitudes they never knew they had.

'It's so interesting to see how their conversation and action has evolved over the last three years,' says Broderick. 'They now call out each other's biases when they hear them, and when they get a glimpse of their own it pulls them up and helps them understand that even well intentioned individuals make invalid assumptions about women and work.'

In a famous 1991 experiment, Monica Biernat – a researcher at the University of Kansas – showed college students photographs of men and women and asked them to estimate their height in feet and inches. Obviously, this is a fiendishly difficult thing to assess from a photograph, so to assist the students, the subjects were photographed next to door-frames or desks, which provided some context. Some of the photographs were of men and women of exactly the same height, photographed next to exactly the same items. Nevertheless, the students consistently overestimated the height of the men, and underestimated that of the women. They were affected – even on this most basic and objective assessment – by their knowledge that men are on average taller than women.[14] Those ingrained assumptions were so strong, in fact, that they actually overrode the hard evidence reported by the optic nerve; the participants literally did not believe their eyes.

So what happens when this lamentably fallible collection of electric impulses and cells we call the human brain is entrusted with a decision on something far more complicated and far more subjective, like deciding which person is likely to be better for a job?

What happens is that selection panels – even those who are fully in agreement that any decision they make should be absolutely free of bias – tend to manipulate their assessments of a person's likely competence based on assumptions they have already made about that person, often because of their gender.

Two Yale researchers – Eric Uhlmann and Geoffrey Cohen – in 2005 asked seventy-three male and female undergraduates to review the files of two fictitious candidates for the position of 'police chief'.[15] One candidate was poorly educated and lacked administrative skills but was 'streetwise', in good shape physically, and popular with other officers. This candidate lived alone. The second applicant was well-educated, good at administrative stuff and a capable media performer, but lacked rapport with other officers, and didn't have much street experience. This candidate was married with a child.

The researchers mixed up the genders; sometimes the streetwise applicant was a man and the educated one a woman; sometimes the other way round. Participants were asked to rate the applicants for their suitability as a police chief, and to rate the importance of the individual job criteria. They were also asked to assess their own degree of gender bias.

Uhlmann and Cohen discovered that when participants were asked to choose between a tough, streetwise woman and a bookish man, they tended to inflate the importance of education. When the tough one was male and the bookish one female, they elevated the importance of street smarts over book-learning. Even the vaguely 'female' trait of parenthood didn't get the female candidate anywhere; participants rated 'family values' as more important when it was the male candidate who had the family, and less important when it was the female one. Either way, the male candidate consistently benefited. And the weirdest thing is this: the participants who were the most certain they were not biased tended to be the ones who showed the greatest degree of bias.

Why is this stuff part of the case for men being awful? It shouldn't be, really; in most of these and similar experiments, the participants included men and women, both of whom exhibited the same kind of unconscious bias.

Awfulness may well be an equal-opportunity character flaw. But because men are already over-represented among the hirers and firers, they wear the opprobrium for the behaviour.

Why else are men awful? Well, let's go through the file. They're awful because they overrate themselves. Research into the comparative intelligence of men and women hasn't offered much by way of plausible difference, but what has been established is that if you ask people to estimate their own IQ, men are likely to overshoot the mark, and women to undershoot it. Halla Beloff, a social psychologist at the University of Edinburgh, asked her students to estimate their own IQ and found that the male students put themselves an average six points ahead of their female colleagues. Professor Adrian Furnham, of the University College London, performed a review of the literature fifteen years later and found that Beloff's thesis held up globally.[16]

Men are also less likely to see bias in their own organisations. In 2012, the Financial Services Institute of Australasia (FINSIA) surveyed its members about gender balance in their industry. Financial services has one of the biggest gender pay gaps around: men are paid 31.3 per cent more than women, and women are under-represented in senior management roles. This is not especially unusual, but still – it's significant. When about 800 employees filled out the FINSIA survey, however, what emerged was two almost hilariously inconsistent impressions of the industry. 'Are women well represented at senior levels in your organisation?' the survey asked. 'Yes!' said 64 per cent of men. 'No!' said 62 per cent of women. 'Is your organisation transparent about remuneration and parity of pay?' 'Yes,' said 50 per cent of men. 'No,' insisted 72 per cent of women.

When FINSIA asked whether action was necessary to address the lack of women at executive level, 73 per cent of women thought it was. But 68 per cent of men thought it wasn't.[17]

All this stuff wouldn't be so bad, of course, were it not for the fact that 'women are hopeless'. Women's hopelessness, in all its forms, is the second popular analytical theme for explanations of why ladies get the rubber end of the plunger at work. There is a rich vein of material here; the most current is the theory popularised by Facebook's chief operating officer Sheryl Sandberg, which is that women are hopeless because they don't 'lean in' to their careers.[18] Faced with average workplace situations, Sandberg argues, women are more likely to take a back seat rather than forcing themselves up the front to where the action is. They don't take on big jobs if they think there's a chance they'll be having a baby soon. When a job or promotion is advertised for which they satisfy eight of the ten published criteria, they'll dither in a fug of anxiety about the other two for a bit, then get flattened by a galumphing herd of male applicants boasting four out of the ten criteria and a bullet-proof degree of confidence that they can scam the rest.

The computer giant Hewlett-Packard dug through its personnel files several years ago to investigate why it was that women weren't getting to senior roles as frequently as men were. They established that female internal candidates for promotion didn't put themselves forward until they believed they satisfied 100 per cent of the criteria given. Male candidates, on the other hand, tended to apply once they felt they had 60 per cent of the qualifications required.[19]

Hillary Clinton, who has hired many young men and young women over her career, noted the difference at a 2014 appearance at New York University with her daughter, Chelsea, and philanthropist Melinda Gates. 'Offering a promotion or expanded responsibilities to a young woman almost always provokes a response something like "Oh, I don't know if I can do that", or "Are you sure I could do that?" or "I'm not positive I could take that on,"' Clinton said. 'I have never heard that from a young man.'[20]

Another thing that hopeless women don't do is ask for a better deal when they are starting out in a job.

Linda Babcock, an economics professor at Carnegie Mellon University, was curious about how the gender pay gap developed, and ran a little investigation into graduates from her own institution. After stalking a whole class of Masters graduates and working out which jobs each got on graduation and what they were paid, she established that the starting salaries for male graduates were 7.6 per cent higher than those of the women. Digging deeper, Babcock asked the graduates whether they had simply accepted the first salary offered, or if they had haggled for more. It turned out that only 7 per cent of the women had asked for more money, while 57 per cent of the men had. And the men who asked for more money tended to be successful – they were paid about 7 per cent more as a result.[21]

Babcock was so struck by this that she went on to co-write a book on the phenomenon, called *Women Don't*

Ask. If this disinclination of women to ask for more money at the beginning of their careers is so pronounced, imagine how much more they miss out on over the rest of their working lives. Every time a woman decides not to ask for a pay rise, or not to negotiate over salary, it's not just a sacrifice she makes in the short term; it's a sacrifice that compounds over the course of her career and can cost – in the long term – an awful lot of money.

But women are rubbish at all sorts of other things too. The 'women are hopeless' genre has some compellingly gruesome extremes; *New York Times* bestsellers with invigorating titles along the lines of *Play Like a Woman, Lead Like a Man*, or *Discovering Your Inner Bitch*, which are all about the mistakes women make that mean they will never succeed.

Dipping into this literature can be a confronting experience. I needed a bit of a lie down after reading *Nice Girls Don't Get the Corner Office: 101 Unconscious Mistakes Women Make That Sabotage Their Careers*, for example, by the imperiously named Lois P. Frankel, PhD.[22] That PhD somehow renders the rest of the book's title Gothically complete; I picture Dr Frankel with a pinched accent, a mercilessly cut suit, and horn-rimmed glasses perched high on her powerful nose. These idle conjectures derive a certain corroborative force from the book's hardline stance on Mistake #80 (Dressing Inappropriately) and #84 (Wearing Your Reading Glasses Around Your Neck).

Of the 101 mistakes she lists, I could personally recall making sixty-three. Some of them elicited a hot flush of shame and recognition. 'Unless you're Betty Crocker, there shouldn't be home-baked cookies, M&M's, jelly beans, or other food on your desk,' barks Dr Frankel in her prologue to Mistake #27: Feeding Others. 'Hillary Rodham Clinton may have been lambasted for her comment about not staying home and baking cookies, but her point was well taken. We don't ascribe a sense of impact or import to people who feed others. It may seem like a small or inconsequential thing, but the fact is, you rarely see food on men's desks.'

It's not the doctor's last word on office décor, by the way; in Mistake #26: Decorating Your Office Like Your Living Room, she advises women to ditch the family photographs and throw rugs, noting acidly: 'By emphasizing your femininity, you diminish your credibility.'

This line of inquiry makes for compelling – if unnerving – reading, and over the course of the book I became increasingly convinced that I would now be running the ABC if I hadn't spent the early part of my career Avoiding Office Politics (#9), Polling Before Making A Decision (#15), Letting People Waste My Time (#39), and Leaving Trailing Voice Mails (#71).

By page 264 I was prepared to do anything that Dr Frankel told me (while simultaneously despising myself for my own suggestibility and my implied non-compliance with her express instructions on point #33: Obediently Following Instructions, and #25: Acquiescing To Bullies).

Women are hopeless for all sorts of other reasons. They step off onto the 'Mummy Track'. They think the workplace is a meritocracy. They develop something called Tiara Syndrome, where they work hard and don't cause trouble and follow the rules and believe that if they keep doing everything right, someone will eventually make them into a princess.[23] They put their own needs last, and will rather pack it in and leave a job than demand that it be changed to suit them.

A good deal of time, worry and expense has gone into the construction of all these theories, and many of them are sufficiently authoritative to convince the dabbler that some men are truly awful, and some women indeed hopeless.

Who hasn't met one of those male bosses who is clearly so much more comfortable with other men that he gives them work and attention without thinking? Or men who only address other men? I couldn't even count how many tales I've heard from amused female MPs or ministers about male lobbyists, colleagues or stakeholders who have shown up for a meeting only to address most of their remarks to her male chief of staff – or, even more hilariously, her male junior adviser. (Chaps: when you do this, ladies notice. And then they talk about it to each other. Quite often, they cackle about it. About *you*, I mean. Just so you know.)

When the efforts of awful men and hopeless women combine, the win–loss ratio between men and women at work becomes clear: women are more likely to lose, and men are more likely to win. Poor old women. Lucky old men.

But I have a couple of problems with this whole scenario. First – it can't be that simple. Some men are jerks, fine – but nowhere near all of them. And while I'm sure it is in many ways career-limiting for a woman to wear her glasses on a chain around her neck, or bring biscuits to work, or in other small but unmistakeable ways signal that she is a fluffhead who probably ought not to be made CEO, surely there must be more to this story.

The tale of what happens to women at work cannot possibly be told, and much less understood, until we pan back and understand what's going on with women outside the four walls of the workplace. Until you put work in context, and understand what other factors might influence women's capacity to compete equally, all the awful men and hopeless women in the world will never quite explain why things continue to turn out the way they do.

Cultural tendencies and discrimination are one thing. But brute structural differences are another. And how can we even begin to combat the minutiae of management oddities and human failing and so forth without dealing with the reality that men and women are unequal at work before they even show up?

We are so used to not counting domestic work as part of our economy that we don't accord it much relevance when running a diagnostic over the modern workplace. But the tentacles of home are everywhere at work, and not just in the illicit family photographs with which Dr Frankel recommends one should not clutter one's desk.

They are there when a person arrives at work. Has that person left home and proceeded to work in a stately and reflective fashion? Or has that person risen at the crack, fought and cursed their way through a mound of wet washing; wrestled several children into clothes, shoes, a semblance of oral hygiene and some sort of conveyance; transferred them to school or comically overpriced childcare facility, then sobbingly fallen through the door of their place of employ?

During the work day, will that person work calmly and absorbedly on the business at hand, perhaps taking a sensible break at lunch in order to get some air and try that new noodle place down the road? Or will that person punch through the workload with the demonic fervour of the chronically short-of-time, utilising any temporal air-pocket not for quiet reflection, or mutually productive conversation with colleagues, but for urgent, obsessive mental scrolling through the checklist of things that could possibly go wrong. (*What's for dinner? Do we have milk? Who's picking the kids up from school? Is it recorder day? Worse – is it Harmony Day?*)

And at the end of the work day, what will that person do then? Stick around until every last available scrap of work has been done, and walk out the door, turning out the lights with an approving supervisor who slaps them on the back and says, laughing: 'You work too hard!'? Go for a beer with a few colleagues, and get into a funny argument that ends up in an actually half-decent idea about a new product line they could make together, or a conference they could go to, or a new way of doing something that they already do that would make it better?

Or will that person belt out of there at half past five feeling like every eye in the place is on them, their horror at being thought a slacker in ironic counterpoint to the rival horror of arriving five minutes late to above-mentioned childcare facility and meeting a whole new set of critical eyes? And then get home to find themselves in the frame for a whole new set of crises, deadlines, and tactical debacles?

Surely, all this makes a difference to who prospers in the end, and who doesn't. And while people are people, and not statistics, surely the statistics give us fairly clear pointers about which of these scenarios are typically female and which are typically male, and consequently about which gender stands a greater chance of advancement – right?

I feel a bit lame and obvious pointing this out. But I'm doing it because I don't think it gets done enough.

'Leaders in a Global Economy', a study resulting in a high-level collaboration between giant international firms, including Deloitte, Eli Lilly, Goldman Sachs, IBM and a bunch of others, asked more than a thousand very senior executives a series of searching questions that covered not only the usual heavily trodden terrain of such surveys – workplace experience, satisfaction, ambition and so on – but deeper, broader questions about how things went down in other areas of their lives.[24] It came up with a shatteringly clear account of the differences between the lives of men at the top and those of their female competitors.

Of the 1192 executives surveyed, half were men and half were women. Three-quarters of the men had a wife or spouse who did not work. But that experience was exactly the opposite of the female executives. Three-quarters of them had a husband who – like them – worked full-time. The men got wives, in other words. And the women didn't.

In some very senior jobs, the existence of a cooperative spouse is simply assumed. 'Let's say you are required to go to Melbourne, or to Singapore, straight away,' offers Meredith Hellicar. 'The assumption is firstly that you can just go. Often, the assumption is that there is someone who can bring your stuff in so you don't have to waste time going home to pack.'

When the global executives in the survey who had children were asked the fundamental question: 'Who takes more responsibility for making childcare arrangements?' the division was immediately and resoundingly apparent. Fifty-seven per cent of the female senior business leaders answered: 'I do.' Among the male executives, only 1 per cent gave that answer. One per cent.

How can this disparity not be flagged loudly in every single glossy report published along the theme – and there are countless such reports – of female under-representation at senior leadership levels? How can the staggering asymmetry in domestic workload carried by men and women hoping to succeed continue to be something of a sleeper issue?

Perhaps, you might think, the figures in that study are a phenomenon driven by experience in other countries. Perhaps that imbalance is an oddity experienced at the very top of the executive tree, where men earn squillions and their wives don't need to work.

Actually, the vital statistics of those executives aren't terribly different from what happens in the lives of average Australian working families.

Let's imagine that you hold a party and invite 100 'average dads' – full-time working men who have children and a female wife or partner. If you went around the room and asked each of them what their wife does, only twenty-four of them would reply that she has a full-time job. The other seventy-six would tell you that their wife works part-time, or not at all.[25] If you were feeling especially nosy and you followed up by asking who was primarily responsible for child care and housework in their home, you would find that an overwhelming majority of them would say: 'She is.'

However, if you went to a party of full-time working mothers, you would get almost an opposite result – eighty-six of them would tell you that their husbands also worked full-time. Not that they would probably make it to the party anyway.

For all that we hear about the modernisation of Australian families, and as much as we enjoy the show *House Husbands*, the truth is that Australia remains unusually adherent to the male-breadwinner model. What proportion of nuclear families has a dad who works full-time, and a mum who doesn't? Sixty per cent. What proportion has a mum who works full-time, with a male 'wife'? Three per cent.

When they get their first jobs, young men and women *are* on an equal footing, or as close to it as they'll ever be; single, unencumbered, competitive. This equality of circumstance persists into the early years of employment. And indeed, the gender pay gap is barely observable at all if you look at Generation Y women only.[26]

But the point at which people start having babies is when the wife drought really hits, and where the Stupid Curve begins. Women who have taken a career break to look after children, in many cases acting rationally because they earn less than their husbands, earn even less when they return to work on a part-time basis or in a lower-status job with more flexibility. They are less competitive in the workplace. Their husbands, however, fuelled by the invisible power-pellet that is a wife, become more competitive.

These patterns in turn generate more patterns. Having a stay-at-home wife makes life easier for a male executive or leader – obviously. It makes his success more likely, in my view. But having a traditional domestic arrangement may also subtly influence the decisions he makes within his organisation.

American researchers in 2012 conducted a study of 232 male managers.[27] All of them worked in universities, and all of them were married; some with 'traditional' domestic arrangements (read: a 'wife'), and some with 'modern' arrangements. The participants were asked to assume the identity of an executive called Drew Anderson, chief financial officer of a software company called Infomitex. An opportunity had come up at the company's prestigious MBA programme, and the CEO was on the hunt for internal candidates. Could Drew take a look at this CV and give an opinion? If Drew recommended a candidate who turned out to be terrific, it would mean significant brownie points, participants were told. They were then handed a CV belonging to a promising-looking candidate. For half the participants, that candidate was called Diane Blake. For the other half, he was called David Blake, but in each case the qualifications and work history were exactly the same. The researchers found that men in 'traditional' marriages gave 'significantly poorer' evaluations of the female candidate compared to the male candidate.

Does this demonstrate that men are awful? Well, I guess in the traditional framework for the workplace gender debate – yes, it does. But I think what it probably demonstrates is that people are terminally, irrevocably, unavoidably changed and moulded by the way they live, the way they were brought up, and what they see as the normal or preferable way of doing things.

Lots of things change the way men think, even when they are otherwise embedded in fairly conservative ideas about how things work. Kate Morgan, a Sydney barrister who is one of only three women in her chambers, told me that she was often shocked to find the most conservative views on women and work among male colleagues of her own generation, the majority of whom had stay-at-home wives.

Morgan and her husband, fellow barrister Richard McHugh, both come from families in which mothers had both children and big jobs. His mother is Jeannette McHugh, the first New South Wales woman elected to federal Parliament. Kate's mother was the late Dr Philomena McGrath, a leading Australian anatomy expert and mother of eight. For Morgan – who navigates the demands of family through the famously demanding environment of life as a barrister – reactions from male colleagues tend to vary with their age.

'Junior male colleagues without children, and with partners or wives in a similar position to them – lawyers, say, or doctors – tend to be very supportive, and are routinely shocked by structural discrimination within the law, or at the Bar,' she says.

'But the generation above them – men my age – are very likely to have a family dynamic where their wives have "elected" to take a back seat. When you're a barrister, your income corresponds directly to the number of hours you work, so even if the wife's a doctor or lawyer, it makes more sense for her to be at home.

'But when these guys go to work, they run into women who are exactly like their wives – intelligent, well-educated – but who are still working. And it's amazing how often they'll make assumptions about their female colleagues based on what their own wives have done. When choosing junior counsel in a large or very urgent case that's going to involve long hours or weekend work, they'll never choose or recommend a mother because – of course – she would rather be with her children and do more "manageable" (read: less prestigious and less well-paid) work. Or when voting for a new barrister to join the floor, and a mother is up for consideration, they might make comments like "What if she wants to work part-time?" Which means, "Of course, she would prefer to be with her children, as our wives do."'

Older men, however, have often moderated their views, says Morgan.

'The last generation has grown up and is not threatened by the comparison between their family's own choices and instead is viewing the workplace from the perspective of their grown daughters. Those daughters, with potentially thirteen years of private school and up to six years of university, should have the world at their feet. Instead, this generation sees and hears the complaints of the current generation of working mothers and recognises that their intelligent, well-educated daughter will also be faced with a workplace that still places limits on their capacity and their advancement.'

This phenomenon is not Kate's imagination. The birth of daughters makes male executives more generous towards female employees, found another American study in 2012.[28] And the Yale economist Ebonya Washington, in a rather epic 2008 analysis of the US House of Representatives, found that every daughter born to a US Congressman made him 25 per cent more likely to vote progressively on women's issues.[29]

This clears the way for some fairly blue-sky thinking about how you might improve the legislative environment for women by means of a strategic air-drop of female infants around Canberra. But, mainly, it reinforces my view that our discussion of what happens to women at work can never really make sense until it stretches well beyond work and encompasses what the woman is doing when she gets home from work, and – conversely – what attitudes might subtly be reinforced in a man who has the luxury of a wife.

The wife drought both underpins and perpetuates all the other elements that influence women's experience in the workplace. There are plenty of exceptions – redemptive male bosses, women who succeed – but the tendency of women to take on responsibility for domestic work, and the tendency of men not to, is the great rhythm of the Australian workplace that escapes the naked eye. Men get wives, and women don't.

2

LOOKING AT THINGS
THE WRONG WAY UP

Now, this whole state of affairs is annoying, mostly if you're a woman. I mean, if you're interested in having a career, it would be nice to think you had the same chances of success and fulfilment as the person next to you, regardless of their possession or otherwise of certain primary sexual characteristics. But that's not how it works.

Feeling bad, or sad, or even angry about women getting a rough trot in the workplace seems a natural sort of response; it's what feminists have been trained for. And the remedy for decades now has been to suggest all sorts of devices to help women prosper in the workplace. Quotas. Mentoring systems. Book clubs. Ladies-only poker nights. Networking sessions. Interesting speakers.

To some extent, this has been a success. More women are now in work than were working fifty years ago. We've had a female prime minister, a female governor-general, and a handful of female CEOs in the ASX200.

On the other hand, it's also bred a generation of half-crazed 'superwomen', for whom real incursions into the 'male' world of work have not included – to any commensurate degree – a corresponding retreat from the 'female' world of work in the home; they just do both.

For many modern mothers, progress at work means the privilege of working herself into the ground in two places rather than one. According to the Australian Work and Life Index, a growing majority of working women with children now report that they 'often or always' feel stressed and pushed for time.[1]

It might seem convenient to try and jam this situation into the customary frame of gender debate. Awful men, reaping the benefits of having hard-working wives, shamelessly enjoying an economic leg-up over the rest of us. Hopeless women dashing about trying to make things work in a system that is spring-loaded to drive them slowly berserk, bashing their heads against the glass ceiling in a daze of guilt and anxiety, and still ending up with crappy superannuation.

But what if we are looking at things the wrong way up? What if the structural problem here is not just how to get women into the workplace, but how to get men out of it? All this time, we've been trying to win equality by eliminating the disadvantages women incur when they take time out to have children. But what if we just accepted that people might well be disadvantaged when they take time out of work, and concentrated instead on spreading the responsibility around?

We pay so much attention to the barriers that face women trying to break in to the workplace, and the glass ceiling that prevents them from climbing to the top.

But what about the barriers that make it hard for men to get out of the workplace? What about the glass fire escapes?

Forget everything for a minute; forget the history, forget the politics, forget the ancient resentments and hurts and the millions of women who have ever started on a career and felt it didn't go where they thought it could have. Forget the money. Forget that long, plaque-like accumulation of disadvantage. Forget – and this is a big ask, in any workplace, for anyone – the dreadful canker of resentment that grows among any class of people who look at another class of people and suspect that those people get an easier ride. Just for a minute, forget all that.

And look at it the other way up, instead.

Getting together and having babies is still something that a large proportion of working Australians do. And when that happens, 76 per cent of working mothers will take the opportunity to change their working lives in some way: to work part-time, to negotiate flexible work hours, to work at home, or undertake shift work of some kind. That's three-quarters of working mothers with children aged eleven and younger, according to the Australian Bureau of Statistics.[2]

But for most fathers, it doesn't function that way at all. Our system encourages them to keep on working as though nothing has changed. Of working fathers with a child aged eleven or under, only one in three change their working pattern in any way at all, and the vast majority of those are talking about flexi-time, not about working part-time or making significant adjustments of the kind women routinely make. In fact, fathers – on average – will slightly increase their working hours by four hours a week with the birth of a first child.[3]

Why is this? Isn't it a bit outrageous? Why should we so readily agree for men to be painted out of the picture? Having a child is a life-changing experience, or so a convincing majority of parenting blogs consistently maintain. So why does our system pretend that parenthood only changes women's lives?

In the great and ongoing wing-ding about gender and work, why do we spend so much time arguing about what women lose at work, and hardly ever about what men lose at home? Is it because what men lose at home is so banal that we don't assign it a value? And if so, isn't that rather an insult to the great work of raising children?

If we value work at home then we should value it properly, and that means not just lamenting that women don't get paid for it, but also that our system doesn't really encourage men to do it.

Men miss out on the vertiginous thrill of losing a significant per cent of your income, and of spending a few years when people at barbecues look blankly at you after you answer the 'And what do *you* do?' question. And maybe that doesn't smart too much, all things considered.

But there is a whole lot of stuff they do miss out on which is pretty cool. Hanging out with their children, for instance. Viewed as an economic equation, stepping back from work to have a family is an unambiguously terrible option. There really isn't a faster way to earn permanent devaluation in the workplace than sloping off for a few years to spend time with the under-threes.

Viewed the other way up, though – the way that assumes that there's more to life than work, and that having a good relationship with your children is valuable – it's not a bad investment. Yet we live in a system that consistently, in one way or other, discourages men from even attempting to make that investment.

Men miss out – in disproportionate numbers – on the opportunity to work flexibly, and to bend the way they work in order to accommodate the other things going on in their lives. Now, I'm not arguing that mothers always get the right to work flexibly, or even that it works out to be all sunbeams and fairy dust when they do. But the expectation that a woman will probably be looking to work a bit differently after she has a kid is sort of scorched into our national employment model – it's why women of a certain age get funny looks at promotion time. But we don't expect men to work differently after they have kids. And even though there is legislation enshrining the right to ask for flexibility, far fewer men use it; they don't expect that they will change their work patterns, and often neither do their families. And they know their employers don't really expect them to either.

Graeme Russell is a fathering expert. He's one of Australia's best-known fathering experts, in fact, and something of an international authority, and if you haven't heard of him, it's not because of any shortfall of expertise on his part but because, in this country, fathering experts don't tend to get their own TV shows.

Russell wasn't originally trained as a fathering expert, either; he made the career change after becoming a hands-on parent, quite by accident, in the 1970s. 'My first degree was in pure mathematics,' he says. 'It had nothing to do with families.' But Russell then started a PhD in experimental psychology, and was – by chance – spending a lot of time at home writing when he and his wife, Susan, had their first child. 'Did I want to be a dad? Yeah, I suppose, in that "I'll definitely do that at some point" way,' he says. 'But what happened to me was I had that experience, of my first child coming home from hospital, and being around, and being actively involved.' He laughs. 'We were both sort of struggling with it all and I thought, shit, I sort of thought Susan would know a bit more about all of this. But she didn't know anything more than I did. So we did it together. And being around, and developing those habits is important . . . I found that as I got involved, I could see the value of it, and I enjoyed it.'

Russell's opportunity to be involved with his baby straight-up, rather than spending the days away at an office, didn't just make him a more involved father – it made him change his line of work. 'Taking time out of the workforce and being involved in something else can have an enormous positive impact,' he observes.

Leaving work can be quite a useful thing to do. If you're in a job that's annoying you, human nature dictates that the most normal response is to keep doing the job, while whingeing about the stuff you don't like. Maybe you don't dislike that job enough to actually quit it, and lose the income and job security. In that case, whining in private seems a satisfying and low-cost alternative.

It's hard to be completely objective about a job when you are still turning up to it every day. When you have a break from it – especially one occasioned by independently occurring circumstances, like parental leave or long-service leave (that increasingly antiquated phenomenon) – you have an opportunity to ask yourself whether you really want to stick around.

Blessed with the clarifying distance of temporary absence, some women find that they want to do something else. Not all of them, by any means – enough of them want to come back, and find it difficult for other reasons, for me not to insult them here by pretending they opted out – but some of them do. They might decide they want to be with the kids full-time. Or that they want to go back to study. Or that they want an entirely different career, or a slightly different one, or to invent a revolutionary storage bag for LEGO pieces.

Family circumstances might make one job unworkable, but lead you to another job you love. I left newspapers in 2009 when – pregnant with my second child – I realised I wasn't going to be able to pull off certain aspects of the job I had been doing. I'd been commuting from Sydney to Canberra during parliamentary sitting weeks to write political sketches for the *Sydney Morning Herald*, often driving there for the week and taking my small daughter along. We had an au pair at the time who was happy to explore Canberra during the day with her, and it worked pretty well, but things were probably going to tip over into unfeasibility once there was a second squealer involved. Moving to Canberra wasn't an option because of my partner's job. My employer had been very generous and flexible, agreeing – for instance – that I could stay in a flat rather than a hotel room when I went to Canberra, but whichever way I looked at the situation, the prospect of keeping it up with two small children made me feel sort of faint.

The other problem I discovered about newspapers is that they actually are quite a bit like children. They need constant attention towards the end of the day. They aren't always rational. They send you on wild goose chases some days. And – worst of all – they go to bed at the same time as children, with a comparable incidence of tantrums, last-minute projects that urgently need doing, and repeat re-emergences on spurious business right when you think it's finally all over.

Amanda Wilson, the first woman to edit the *Sydney Morning Herald*, told the story – in a 2011 speech – about the time her son, then eight years old, was asked if he would like to be a journalist. 'No,' he replied, with feeling. 'They never see their children.'

'It's things like that which see many talented women in my profession hit the wall,' Wilson said. 'It's often not a glass ceiling but a pair of pleading eyes.' While it's common for male newspaper editors to combine their demanding jobs with raising young families – usually thanks to resourceful spouses – women who become editors tend either not to have children at all, or to wait until their kids are older.

'At one point my boss wanted me to be night editor, a fabulous leadership opportunity,' recalled Wilson, a single parent. 'I politely declined on the grounds I would be starting work as my son's school day ended, and getting home about five hours before he woke up. The only people who'd see him would be his teacher and his child-minder. My boss couldn't hide his irritation: "When is this child problem going to end?" he asked.'

Even in my own far less senior job at the *Herald*, the daily non-sitting-week routine in Sydney was pretty brisk – drive to the childcare centre, find a park, drop off my daughter, get back in the car, drive to work, find a park, work all day, leave at 5 pm when the paper was just getting busy, get to the childcare centre, find a park, pick up my daughter, drive home, cook dinner while rewriting copy or negotiating with subs or monitoring news services to ensure that the prime minister hadn't quit – GAH, it was ridiculous. Throw another kid in there and I was looking at some kind of breakdown.

There is a point at which the appeal even of a job you fiercely love can be eaten away to nothing by the layers of debacle and expense that must be undergone simply in order to get there every day.

As it happened, I was – entirely independently of this impending two-kid-tastrophe – also getting really interested in the new ways the Internet offered of covering politics. When in 2009 the parliamentary rules changed to allow reporters to bring (appropriately silenced) electronic devices into the gallery during Question Time, a whole new world opened up; using Twitter, you could report what was happening in real time. I felt as if we were all on the verge of something exciting, but Fairfax was in the middle of a customary round of board-level skirmish and no one could even agree on who should run the website. Even some of the online people were lukewarm on social media. 'Twitter's a fad,' I remember one of them telling me pityingly at a meeting, as I argued that we should find a way of incorporating Twitter streams directly into our website. 'And you only have 3000 followers anyway.' As I write, Twitter is laced through most newspaper websites, and I have as many followers as the *Herald* sells weekday copies.

Having another baby was going to force me to change the way I worked. But there were things about the place where I worked that were irking me anyway. When Mark Scott, the ABC's managing director, suggested that I should come and work for the ABC as an online writer, the idea looked like an obvious circuit-breaker. In the online world, I would be released from the evening deadline. I could still write about politics, but I could do it at any hour of the day or night – as the news happened, not as the trucks warmed up to deliver papers all over the state. Plus, the ABC offered the chance of on-site child care. And all the social media widgets I could handle. It was like winning the lottery.

So while my initial dilemma was triggered by children, the solution fixed a bunch of other stuff I was worried about too. Thinking about how I was going to manage my job with an extra child ended up forcing me to ask all sorts of questions I probably would otherwise have kept on avoiding: Is this job working out for me? Am I on the same page as my employer? Am I as useful as I could be?

Here we arrive at the sticky business of accounting for women's decisions. Proponents of the 'Mummy Track' theory would claim me as evidence of the notion that women tend to 'opt out' of the workforce, to take the exit ramp from their jobs when they have children. But looking back on it, I don't see it that way at all. I changed some things about the way I work so that I could raise children without going out of my brain with stress, but essentially I changed jobs because I wanted to.

Awful things can happen to women who take maternity leave; I'm not for a moment suggesting otherwise. There are plenty of cases in which workers returning from parental leave find that they've coincidentally been made redundant, or put in charge of pencil-sharpening.

Even statutory provisions dictating fair treatment for returning parents can disappear into a perilous grey zone of enforcement. I once sat, with a close friend, through the meetings she had with her employer trying to negotiate the part-time work they were legally obliged to make available to her after her first child. They couldn't find anyone for a job-share. They didn't think the days she could work were convenient. In the end, the ultimatum was effectively: work full-time, or don't work at all. Stricken, my friend left. She lost a job she loved, and the company lost an experienced worker.

The Sex Discrimination Commissioner's 2014 inquiry into the experience of people taking parental leave found countless such stories, with about a third of women reporting some kind of discrimination or ill-treatment at work.[4] But for many women, maternity leave is an extremely happy time, both for the opportunity to be with their children, and the chance for some clarifying distance from work.

And what comparable breaks from work do men have? What enforced opportunities do they have to stop doing what they're doing for a bit, and consider seriously whether they want to start again?

Well – let's be honest. In the past century, apart from sudden death or incapacity, the only two mass factors that have interfered with men's working lives in any statistically significant way have been conscription and redundancy.

Conscription stopped being an issue in 1972, and the incidence of redundancy is dictated by macroeconomic elements entirely unrelated to the specific needs of people having children. And yet, redundancy – if you trawl the daddy blogs – is the circumstance that crops up again and again as the initiating event in many a successful stay-at-home dad story.

Redundancy has a few things in common with maternity leave. There's the dislocation, and the utter shock of one's new circumstances. There's the exultant thrill of not knowing or caring what exact time it is, and the creeping new acceptability of tracksuit pants. And the veterans of redundancy are just as apt as childbirth's adult survivors to emerge, after twenty-two months of whey-faced misery, and declare that 'it was the best thing that ever happened to me'.

For men, this is a rather brutal set of circumstances. Having children, and enjoying their company, should – ideally – be a happy thing. Mothers change their work patterns to be with their children and it is viewed as a perfectly normal and organic development. Men have to be ripped from their jobs, or – like Graeme Russell – accidentally find themselves on the scene with some spare time for nappy-changing before they experience the epiphany that is any mother's for the asking. This does not seem like a fair arrangement.

The United States gives us all the evidence we need that changes in the behaviour of fathers are driven more by mass economic events than organic human factors. The percentage of American families with a stay-at-home dad has shot to 3.5 per cent in the last decade, according to Pew Research, in a bulletin entitled 'More Men on the "Daddy Track"'.[5]

The financial crisis of 2008 is immediately apprehended as the prime culprit for this viral new outbreak of Daddism. And, like many catastrophic economic events, it is additionally responsible for a series of related aftershocks, like the noticeable uptick in opinion articles written by stay-at-home dads in the *Atlantic Monthly*. In fact, the general interest in parenting escalated appreciably in the United States right about the same time as so many recently retrenched men allegedly started doing it. Here's some evidence, from the *New Yorker* blog, which announced on 24 March 2014:

A recent study has shown that if American parents read one more long-form think piece about parenting they will go fucking ape-shit. The study was conducted by Susan Waterson, a professor at the University of Massachusetts and the author of zero books, because, Waterson says, 'another book at this point would just be cruel'. In the course of seven weeks, Waterson interviewed a hundred and twenty-seven families about their reaction to articles that begin with a wryly affectionate parenting anecdote, segue into a dry cataloguing of sociological research enlivened with alternately sarcastic and tender asides, and end with another wryly affectionate anecdote that aims to add a touch of irony or, failing at that, sentimentality.[6]

Let's keep this in perspective. The boom in American house husbands, according to Pew Research, amounts to a shift since 1979 from 2 per cent of families where the father stays at home, to a current level of 3.5 per cent.[7] In an Australian political opinion poll, this would be a change viewed as statistically insignificant. But change it nonetheless is, and it has been duly celebrated, with plenteous magazine covers agape at the Daddy Syndrome, and a timely new NBC comedy series written by Jimmy Fallon, the coolest guy in America, called *Guys with Kids*.

The funny thing is, though, that the real Guys with Kids aren't necessarily out-and-proud, Baby-Björn-wearing home dads who are in it for the thrill of parenting. When stay-at-home dads in the US are asked why they are out of the workforce, only one in five says that it's to look after his kids. The rest cite illness, difficulty finding work, or disability as the main reason. They might be at home looking after kids, but they were driven there by other circumstances; they needed an additional push. Stay-at-home moms, however, are completely different: 90 per cent of them, when asked, say that they are out of the workforce because they are raising their children.[8]

In Australia, exactly the same patterns emerge. There aren't so many stay-at-home dads, as we know, but only one in five of them – when asked – ticked the box saying he was home by preference to look after children. Mothers, again, saw things differently: four out of five declared that they were at home because of the kids.[9]

This tells us something rather profound about the barriers that stand between men and their children. Hardly any men take up the job of primary caregiver in the home anyway, and of the small band who do, four out of five had another formal reason for being there. Children alone, in other words, are not a sufficient driver to get men out of the workplace; you need something else, be it redundancy or misadventure, to actually yank them out the door.

Like all forms of human behaviour, this one is a sinewy knot of many factors.

But men do want more flexibility at work than they are presently getting. Some research done in 2012 by the Diversity Council established that 79 per cent of young fathers, for instance, would like to try a compressed work week. But only 24 per cent of them actually did. As we know, new fathers increase their work hours by four hours a week, rather than reducing them. Fifty-six per cent of young fathers, meanwhile, said they would like to work part of their regular hours at home, but only 13 per cent of them actually did.[10]

Even those for whom statistics are a confounding language could spot quite a gap there between the number of men who want to change the way they work, and the number of men who change the way they work. This creates four possibilities.

Possibility One is that they are not telling the truth, and are worried that their wives are listening in when the wonk from the Diversity Council calls them at home after dinner. 'Hello? Yes, I would VERY MUCH LIKE to spend more time with my children. I am UNHAPPY leaving them every morning for my nice quiet office. I would very much like to WORK FROM HOME, where I can be closer to their petty disagreements and irritating honky toy things. THANK YOU FOR YOUR TIME!'

Possibility Two is that men have an unfounded fear that asking for flexibility might cause them to be thought less ambitious, successful or suitable for promotion. Possibility Three – closely related to Possibility Two – is that men have a well-founded fear that asking for flexibility might cause them to be thought less ambitious, successful or suitable for promotion.

Possibility Four is that they genuinely want to work more flexibly, and would be prepared to wear the opprobrium at work should any arise, but cannot afford to take the financial hit. This is the point at which the wife drought's vicious circle completes itself. Women earn less over their lifetimes because they either leave the workforce to look after children, or are silently marked down on the expectation that they will do so. Fathers are paid more, partly because they are thought less likely to leave the workforce. As a result of being paid more, they are indeed less likely to leave the workforce, and thus continue to be paid more than their wives, who are paid less because they are thought more likely to leave the workforce, and – seeing as they're being paid less already – frequently do just that.

Let's look at Possibility One first. As we know from earlier chapters, human beings are fabulously complex creatures and it is quite easy for us to be passionately convinced that we believe one thing, even when everything we do and say suggests the opposite. And there is quite a bit of pressure on men to take an interest in their children; it's not just mothers who have had their KPIs remorselessly jacked up by the Intensive Parenting movement, after all. There are all sorts of reasons, in other words, why a man might declare an aspiration to spend more time with his beloved progeny, while secretly thanking God that circumstances do not technically require him to.

'A house with a newborn in it is a hellish place to be,' remarks the writer John Birmingham, who – having worked from home for much of his career, has found himself unavoidably on-scene for all the seamier aspects of his two children's early lives. 'If you can go to your office, where everything runs smoothly and everything is quiet and you might even be able to have a sleep – why wouldn't you?

'It's such a shameful thing to admit, so actually finding people to 'fess up to it is probably pretty hard work.'

Let's give men the benefit of the doubt, though, and work with possibilities Two through Four, which assume that when they say they would like to be able to change their work hours, they mean it. Why don't they ask? After all, every available piece of workplace-related behavioural psychology research indicates that men have less trouble than women in asking for promotions, pay rises, corner offices, special titles; why should it be any different for parental leave?

The difference is that all those things are about asking for more: more money, more status, more responsibility. Asking for less is a completely different matter, and it's completely out of whack with what we expect of men at work. Facebook chief operating officer Sheryl Sandberg compared the modern career to a marathon, in which spectators urge male runners to press on (*'Lookin' strong! On your way!'*) but shout encouragement of a different kind to women (*'You know you don't have to do this! Good start – but you probably won't want to finish!'*).[11]

The truth is that people find it easier to ask for things that they are expected to ask for. We expect that women will ask for flexible work hours, or to come back to work part-time after having a baby. We expect that, because most of the time that's what happens. We don't expect men to ask. And sure enough, they don't. Sandberg's point is that women aren't encouraged to stay in the race. But the problem for men is that nobody teaches them how to stop.

The fact that we don't expect men to ask for less work is telegraphed both explicitly and implicitly at every level of public and private life. Prime Minister Tony Abbott's avowal, when he took office, of his determination to help 'women struggling to combine career and family', had a headline message: helping women. But the underlying message – unintentional, almost certainly – pulsed out like a beacon: this is a problem that women face. It's not a problem that men face. And for men paddling against the tide of this great and largely unspoken national expectation, that might have proved a dispiriting moment.

Flexible work schemes are the sexual harassment policies of the twenty-first century – it seems every large company is scrambling to get one. There are a couple of reasons for the craze. One is that ever since companies started calculating what it was costing them to train women to a certain level and then make it impossible for them to come back to work after having children, there's been a lot more enthusiasm for finding ways to keep those women on. Another is that saving money on expensive work space, and having an employee use their own office or kitchen table at home instead, is what we in the human resource management field call a no-brainer.

Moreover, there is strong evidence that if you allow employees to work flexibly, you can squeeze a good deal more work out of them, while also making them feel like you might be doing them a favour by allowing them to work in their jarmies every now and again, which does – admit it! – carry with it a slight, Hefneresque thrill of privilege.

In 2010, a group of researchers conducted a study of nearly 25,000 IBM employees from seventy-five different countries. Looking at the hours that people worked and the other responsibilities in their lives, the researchers established what they called their 'break point', which they defined as the number of work hours at which 'work/life interference' began having a negative impact on an employee's effectiveness. (I would identify 'break point' as the point at which the employee communicates with his or her family exclusively in shrieks, and can only work while drunk, but let's go with the eggheads here.)

Anyway, it turned out that when men were given the opportunity both to work from home and to choose their own hours, their 'break point' rose by twenty hours. That is to say, they could perform an additional twenty hours every week before losing their minds. And for men with children under five, the 'break point' rose by a staggering thirty hours when they were allowed to work flexibly.[12]

And yet, flexible work for parents is still deeply associated with women. More particularly, it's associated with mothers. Where will you find the flexible work scheme in the annual report? Right there in the 'Workplace Diversity' section, in all likelihood. ('Workplace Diversity', in case you are unfamiliar with corporate-speak, commonly means 'Women', because for some reason, even in 2014, just having women around is sufficient to qualify one as 'diverse'.)

Graeme Russell says that workplace flexibility is almost exclusively viewed as an initiative for women. 'Of the organisations that I've worked with, I can't say any of them are really serious about extending this to men as well as women,' he says. 'If it's extended at all, it's from women with children to women with other caring responsibilities.'

According to Daniel Petre, whose book *Father Time* was written about his active decision – as a senior Microsoft executive – to change the way he worked and put his family and children first, there is a certain degree of coded messaging going on in workplaces.

'If you want to point the finger, it's the board who appoints the CEO, and the CEO who says, "Yep, work–life balance, fantastic," but he's at his desk by six and others know that means they've got to be there by seven,' Petre says. 'If you offer people flexibility of choice in an environment where it's clear that promotions are a function of time spent and hours worked, what are they going to choose?

'I do a lot of advisory work. I see a lot of CEOs, of senior executives. They're all the same – mainly made up of older men who are obsessed by work. Who make token gestures both in terms of their own families, and the women who work for them.

'It's very difficult for men who are serious about being fathers, in that culture, to be promoted and seen.

'The men who really do want to do it – they lie. They pretend that they're off to root canal surgery when really it's their daughter's swimming carnival.

'Why don't fathers take paternity leave? Because in many environments it's seen as the wrong thing to do. What should happen? The CEO should take it. That would make a difference. If you really believe work–life balance is important, say "No one has to be here before nine. No meetings will occur after five."'

Both men and women commonly feel overworked. We know this because the Centre for Work and Life at the University of South Australia asked nearly 3000 Australians exactly this question, and full-time workers of both sexes said they would ideally like to work about half a day less every week. But women were more likely to act on this desire by requesting flexible work arrangements for family reasons than men were. Men were more likely to ask for flexibility so that they could study, or take on a different and more challenging role. And men, in the cases where they asked for flexibility, were twice as likely as women to have their requests declined.[13]

The ability to work when it suits you, and to do it from home if that's what steams your beans, has potential for all sorts of people, not just parents. In all the excitement of the argument about how people organise themselves after having children, it should always be remembered that it's good for all people to do things differently every now and again.

Many people do not have children. But that doesn't stop them from needing flexibility in their lives, whether it's to make room for interests, self-improvement, or looking after another family member.

But there is one kind of leave that really is designed only to be used by people who have just taken delivery of a squealing infant, and that's parental leave. In Australia, we didn't have a national paid parental leave system for an extremely long time, but in 2009 Kevin Rudd introduced one scheme, only for a subsequent election to be won by Tony Abbott, promising another. In this way, prospective parents have had something approaching the experience of waiting for a bus in Adelaide: nothing for 109 years, and then suddenly two turn up at once.

The Rudd scheme plumped for eighteen weeks' leave at the minimum wage. Paid out by the state under the prudently neutral contemporary banner of 'parental leave', it was claimable by either Mum or Dad, though very few of the recipients had any trouble working out who was really supposed to be getting it. In the first two and a half years of the scheme, bureaucrats told a Senate estimates hearing in 2013, paid parental leave was taken by 10,000 women a month, and just a shade under twenty men. Yes: that is about a 500 to one ratio.[14]

Men, possibly because they are specifically mentioned in the title, proved to be a bit more interested in the adjunct policy called 'Dad and Partner Pay', which offered an additional two weeks' leave, also paid at the minimum wage. An acceptably brief period of leave, with a blokey name to boot, Dad and Partner Pay walked off the shelves like it came with a free slab: 20,000 claimants in its first three months of operation.

Tony Abbott's proposal for a paid parental leave scheme is much more controversial, and not just because of his memorable 2002 request to the gods of the Liberal Party to render him a eunuch forthwith should he ever be foolish enough to contemplate such a thing. Or words to that general effect.[15]

The scheme Tony Abbott took to the 2013 election, part-funded by a levy on big business, plans to pay mothers for twenty-six weeks at their actual wage, up to a cap of $75,000 (since moderated to $50,000 in the Coalition's first budget). Fathers can choose to take the leave instead, but in those circumstances would have to settle for their wife's wage, if she has one, or the minimum wage, if she doesn't. To economists, this looks like a sensible precaution. It precludes the Palmer family, for instance – who would be eligible for paid parental leave under the Abbott scheme – from claiming six months at Clive's salary, which would sink the federal budget faster than another six months of the Rudd administration. To ordinary eyes, however, it carries another subtle yet unmistakeable coded message: chaps, if you're thinking of becoming the primary caregiver, you might as well put on a frilly apron while you're doing it. (At the time of writing, Mr Abbott's paid parental leave scheme was caught up in a murderous snarl of opposition from Senate cross-benchers and his own colleagues; its survival in any form is far from assured.)

But even men who took the existing Dad and Partner Pay leave – and the vast majority of them took fewer than four weeks – found that the decision was not without controversy at work.

When Sex Discrimination Commissioner Liz Broderick staged her inquiry into pregnancy and return to work, she surveyed 1000 fathers who had taken Dad and Partner Pay, and found that 27 per cent of these dads said they had experienced blowback from their bosses and colleagues over taking leave.[16]

Half of the respondents thus afflicted said they had fielded negative attitudes and comments. Half said they had suffered adverse treatment on pay decisions, and decisions about conditions and duties. A quarter of them looked for other work as a result, and one in ten actually resigned.

Now, to take a cautious view, it must be remembered that the survey canvassed only the recollections of those men, and not the balancing views of their employers, about what exactly was said and why. These statistics cannot be taken as an authoritative estimate of actual discrimination. But perception is what this game is all about. If the fear of adverse consequences plays any role at all in the disinclination of men more broadly to change the way they work when they have children, then the experience of these men – amplified by the fact that for each man thus affected, there are untold numbers of colleagues watching what happened and learning deeply from the spectacle – must surely be instructive.

Our first child was born when we lived in London – me working as a correspondent, Jeremy slaving long hours in a large City law firm with an extensive avant-garde art collection and smoking rooms on every floor. When Audrey was born, I was at home with her for six lovely months. Then I was offered a job in Sydney, as political sketchwriter for the *Herald*. We had always taken turns, and we decided that we would move back to Australia – me to start my new job, Jeremy to take six months at home with our baby. He had a standing offer from his old Australian firm to go back to his former job. But how would we explain to them why he wasn't available to start right away, even though he was in Sydney?

Half-jokingly, we canvassed a range of more acceptable alibis. Perhaps we could tell them that Jeremy had developed a serious prescription drug addiction? Or that he was conducting a six-month surfing tour of remote Australian beaches? It was only half a joke, because for all the sincerity of Jeremy's belief that raising a child should be a genuinely cooperative affair, he retained a reasonable apprehension about how such an approach would be viewed, professionally speaking. In the end, he took the time at home, and they coped. The births of our second and third children were celebrated by far more routine paternal circumstance: two weeks' paternity leave each, involving about thirty trips to the chemist and at least one week spent abortively trying to assemble a flat-pack garden shed. An entirely uncontroversial affair.

Everyone has a story about what happened when they had a baby. An entire online biosphere draws its lifeblood from such experiences. And when I asked men on Twitter to tell me their stories, a babel of experience presented itself almost immediately. Some had glorious tales to tell: sympathetic bosses, colleagues who encouraged them all the way. (Mainly, they worked in the public sector or in the arts.) Some had horror stories. The two I reproduce here are interesting because they signify, for me, the possibilities of what men can do if they persist.

Let's take the case of Charlie first. He works in a call centre for a major utility company. 'Call centres are an odd beast,' Charlie reports. 'They are the blue-collar end of white-collar. As such, they are more genteel than retail or hospitality but without the clinical, politically correct dynamic of the public service or high-end private sector work. There is a robust group dynamic where ribald discussion is still permitted (to a degree) without fear of reprimand; the line that keeps it civil and respectful is almost solely determined by the attitude of management. As such, people can still say what they think without feeling like they are being muzzled. It's not a garage, but it's not a boardroom.'

Charlie is married. He and his wife decided they were ready to have a baby, and it more or less happened overnight. Charlie had no qualms about asking for a compressed roster – four days of ten hours, rather than five of eight hours – so that he could go to doctors' appointments, shop for baby gear and otherwise be a part of what was about to be a large change in his life. Compressed rosters are a bit of a treat, as they make life harder for managers trying to ensure all shifts are reliably covered.

'I am not career focused but I am diligent towards my job, and am afforded more flexibility than some other employees as I am consistent and deliver good results,' Charlie says. 'I am often confident in approaching my employer about asking for "favours" as I am never reprimanded or counselled about my performance.'

Charlie's request was approved.

'I was often gently chided by male workmates about "doing women's chores" when I told them how I spent my days, but I didn't care. The happiness of my wife and me was more important than trying to exude an alpha dynamic at work.'

Charlie found out about the Dad and Partner Pay entitlement, and approached his supervisor to apply for it: 'Her face dropped, like she had been shot in the stomach.'

Charlie provides some context. 'Management are graded by KPIs around effective leadership of staff. High levels of "unplanned" leave or unpaid leave is therefore a black mark against them; it indicates that they are not engaging with their charges effectively. So I had just barrelled up and asked for a very large hole to be punched in the numbers her yearly bonus was to be calculated on! To her credit, she diplomatically suggested she could look into it.' As it turned out, the supervisor's fears were unfounded. This was a new category of leave, with a different classification, and wouldn't affect her targets. She brightened considerably, thanked Charlie, and all was well. When the baby was born, the supervisor was one of the first people Charlie called. 'I felt very, very supported by her and wanted to let her know first,' he says.

The call centre was closed, and Charlie made redundant, about halfway through his wife's maternity leave, but he found another job, without losing a day's pay, in another centre which also took a number of his colleagues, and agreed to give Charlie the Dad and Partner leave he hadn't had the chance to take from his first employer. They also agreed to a compressed roster for him.

Charlie's story is a success story, but it required persistence, both to identify and pursue the flexibility available to him, and to ignore the gentle resistance from colleagues. 'In a social context, the men chattered the most,' he says. 'None was overtly malicious, but it seemed like it was an opportunity for alpha males to assert their dominance, loudly, and to announce to the workplace at large how much more committed they were to their jobs. Management would recognise their behaviour for what it was, but a male who was bent on advancement may have thought twice about approaching it as I had, if they were very career focused.'

Sometimes, though, it can all come down to who your boss is.

Brendan, who is a contract administrative officer in the resources industry, negotiated a deal when he started his job that he would take one morning off a week, and make up the hours elsewhere.

'My American boss was happy with that situation, and all the other managers were afraid of him, so I had no problems for a year or so,' he says. 'I got to spend a lot of time with my eldest daughter (she is now seven) when she was an adorable small child. I will treasure that time my whole life.'

But then Brendan's boss got the boot. 'Suddenly I had a new boss, and I got the talk about my hours and how increasing responsibility and what-not meant greater commitment to the workplace was required. I conceded that a whole morning off was less than ideal if I wanted to climb the ladder in order to be able to better provide for my family, but argued strongly for an hour and a half or so away from work once a week to drop the piglets off at school and be part of that daily experience of their lives. My workplace has official policies on all of these things, including work–life balance. Despite this, I was pressured quite strongly by my direct boss to confirm to 8 am to 5 pm, Monday to Friday (I only get paid for thirty-eight of these forty hours), unless, of course, they needed me longer. When I argued that the company had a purported commit-ment to work–life balance and I wanted to spend precious time outside work hours with my kids, my boss simply said "We all have families. What makes yours special?"

'Worse than that, however, was the CFO, a dapper-suited, neat-haired new age carapace containing an uninhibited misogynistic bogan, whose actual words to me, in concert with my boss in the same room, were: "To be successful you have to accept that weekends are for families."'

Brendan opted for a discreet partial retreat. He stopped taking the whole morning off, but insisted on his right to do the school run once a week. And that's how he's proceeded ever since. Every now and again, his boss corners him and asks him when he's going to cut out the school drop-off. The exchange always goes the same way, Brendan asking 'Do you believe I'm neglecting to put in the hours?' and his boss agreeing that he works longer hours than required; Brendan asking if there are any concerns about the quality of his work and his boss replying that he was satisfied with the work. The problem, says his boss when pressed, is that it's better for everybody to work the same hours.

On the whole, the palaver involved in seizing a whiff of flexibility, one morning a week, has left Brendan feeling wrung out. 'Despite the year, and the new touchy-feely edge to corporate business and all the right words about work–life balance and looking after oneself and the family – my experience is that it remains lip-service when it comes down to it,' he says. 'I actually think it's worse for men, because the expectation on us is to conform to the stereotype of male success – you'll be at the office early and leave late. Weekends are for families. The ladies in the office don't seem to get as much grief because, after all, women are the caregivers and that's just expected, isn't it?

In these people's world view? And these people, sadly, in oil and gas, anyway, are still older white males. I just keep doing my thing. I take my girls to school at least once a week, and stay with them in the classroom until the bell goes, and then make my way into work by 9.30. And I make up the hours easily by staying back until six, once or twice a week, and starting at seven every other day. But I know that it's a pebble in the management's shoe that I won't conform, and if it comes down to it, in these uncertain times for resources, it'll be one of the marks against my name.'

Low-level hassling is a common enough story for men who take time out of work to tend to their families, even if they make the time up elsewhere. And Brendan's impression that it's harder for men has some scholarly support. A 2013 study of middle-class workers in Canada found that 'caregiving' fathers were subjected to more mistreatment at work than traditional fathers, and in some workplaces more than twice as much mistreatment as 'caregiving' mothers.[17] Of the women studied, in fact, those without children were hassled more than mothers. In fact, patterns of mistreatment – the researchers found – was much more to do with how closely workers conformed to traditional expectations of them, much more than it was to do with gender. The least mistreated people tended to be men who had children but did not take anything beyond customary responsibility for them, and women who had children and did. Those in line for a tougher time were women without children, who were thought cold or indifferent, and men looking after their children, who were thought soft.

Employees measure how they're going at work in all

sorts of ways. There are the obvious, structural elements: Have I been fired? Have I been given a pay rise recently? Am I on my final formal warning? In some workplaces there are other measurements; the brain-constricting horror of the formal performance appraisal process, for instance, in which two people who deeply do not want to be there talk awkwardly about dot points. These processes are the revenge that human resources professionals take upon the world, and it is a cruel revenge. (My favourite ever performance review was with my political editor Michael Gordon in Canberra at the *Age*. Michael, a great journalist, a lovely person, and a reluctant manager, sat down and we were silent for about two minutes. 'Happy?' he eventually asked. 'Yep!' I responded. Relieved, we wrapped things up.)

But the most immediate feedback an employee gets at work is much more low-level, and much more constant; it's how they're treated every day, both by their employers and by colleagues. Does she get invited along for planning sessions? If a bunch of people are going out for a sandwich, is he invited along or not? Do people interrupt her when she's speaking, and do others think that's okay? Does he get teased? Does the boss smile and joke with her? These are the status indicators that can let you know – at work – how you're going.

People are quite sophisticated gadgets, really. If it becomes clear that a certain course of behaviour results in mistreatment, then most people will avoid that course of behaviour if feasible to do so. Thus, the low-level responses you get at work to things like leaving early to pick up a child may be quite influential on subsequent decisions.

Sometimes, of course, you can navigate your way through it. My boss at the ABC, Kate Torney, has three children and, back when she worked as a producer in Melbourne, used to come in at 7 am and work until 3 pm, so that she could collect her children from school. Every afternoon, one of her colleagues, a bloke we'll call Geoff, made – without fail – a remark. 'That's it for the day, is it, Kate?' he'd call out as she departed. 'Nice to have an early mark?'

One day, as Kate was buckling herself in for the dawn drive to work, she placed a call to Geoff's mobile. It rang out. 'Morning, Geoff! It's ten to seven. Just letting you know I'm on my way in to the office,' she trilled, in a message to his voicemail. 'Maybe see you there later on!' Geoff never mentioned the matter again.

All of these patterns are changeable. What it takes is for people to have the determination to do it: Charlie, ignoring the teasing from his colleagues, or Brendan, staring down his boss. Kate, defusing a low-level situation with a deft comeback. But humans are humans. We usually find it easier not to change. And that's why, for all the changes that the last five decades have held for women, the changes for men have been scandalously narrow. Men continue to be over-represented at work, and under-represented at home. Viewed one way, this is an unforgivable and continuing annexation of money, power and influence. Viewed the other way up, it's a continuing tragedy for children and for men, bound tight into a web of expectations no one even asked them if they wanted.

3

WITH THIS RING, I THEE MAKE REDUNDANT

Marriage is an ancient and continuing tradition, with a ready knack of providing fodder for human controversy. As a species, we are capable of worrying simultaneously that not enough people want to be married (spiralling divorce rates) and that too many people want to be married (same-sex unions). The fact that marriage is a life-changing experience is a widely made point. It renders one statistically more likely to own platters. And four-wheel-drives. Research is thin on this point, but I bet it would support my suspicion that marriage makes romantic comedy somehow more palatable. Fifty years ago, however, marriage did even more profound things for women than causing them furtively to enjoy reruns of *Love, Actually*. For many, marriage meant an abrupt and compulsory end to their careers.

Even the most articulate, reasonable and well-informed modern lady-whinger about inequities in the contemporary workplace would draw breath at the terms of the old Commonwealth Public Service Act, section 49, part (2), which decreed that 'Every female officer shall be deemed to have retired from the Commonwealth service upon her marriage.'[1]

That's correct: women were obliged to resign once they got married. A lady whose yearning for a suitable husband had temporarily been sidelined for a career in the public service would thus be required – upon the magical appearance of the longed-for squire – to gather her things and head home for a new life of domesticity. This law was known as the 'marriage bar', although, as it only applied to women and not to men, it might more accurately have been called the 'wife bar'.

There were exceptions: typists, for instance, were deemed to do work that was unsuitable for men, and were thus permitted to stay at work, albeit on a temporary basis, with neither entitlements nor superannuation.

Teachers, too, had slightly different terms. They were employed by state governments, which in the main had similar laws to the federal one. But teaching was awkwardly dependent on the work of women, and the prospect of fragrant mass desertion in a flurry of confetti was not one the nation's education systems could necessarily countenance. So, in many states, female teachers who got married were merely obliged to resign their permanent positions and be re-employed in a 'supply' position.

This meant renouncing long service leave, any seniority or promotion they might hitherto have earned, any prospect of further advancement, and any expectation to be paid during school holidays. Disclosure of any matrimonial tendency was mandatory; as Regulation 14 of the Western Australian Education Department barked in 1898: 'Female teachers intending to marry must notify the Minister of such intention and will only be allowed to retain their position by special consent.'[2]

The marriage bar was in place from Federation. Its spirit was inherited, along with much of the shape of Australia's federal legislative framework, from Westminster, which had enacted a similar provision for women in the British civil service. But in 1922, the ban was spelled out in greater detail in a new amendment passed by the government of Billy Hughes.

The measure had a number of purposes. Such as protecting the children of Australia who otherwise were in grave danger of cold dinners. And ensuring that married women, who by definition already had someone to earn the money, didn't swipe good jobs either from men, who were supposed to be the providers, or from spinsters, who presumably needed the money for cat food and insulation against the gnawing despair of their unmarried state.

It is worth revisiting the genteel back-and-forth in the House of Representatives that preceded the passage of the 1922 legislation. At that time, Reps debate was still a gentlemanly affair. Enid Lyons, the first woman elected to that stately place, was still twenty-one years away. (She was still in Tasmania, not even halfway through her spectacular maternal innings of twelve live births.)

Section 49 of the Commonwealth Public Service Act was squired through the Parliament by Attorney-General Littleton Groom, Nationalist MP for the seat of Darling Downs. In one of the more compelling sequences of the debate, he was cross-examined as to the section's purpose by Austin Chapman MP, a fellow Nationalist and the Member for Eden-Monaro. Chapman – an independent type – had already made a name for himself by lobbying strongly for the location of the new parliament in Canberra, and having designed a light-weight wheat bag known as the 'Chapman Sack'. Thanks to a stroke, he had the use of only one arm, but his brain was all right.

The exchange is remarkable for several reasons, not least the sheer exoticism of seeing a minister challenged lucidly and publicly by a member of his own political party; not something that would ever happen today. Keep an eye out for contributions from two other Nationalists – Frederick Francis, the Member for Henty, and George Maxwell, who was born in Scotland, was blind in one eye, and represented the Victorian seat of Fawkner. Also Labor's James Fenton, the Member for Maribyrnong.

Mr Chapman: Why should a female officer be deemed to have retired from the Service upon her marriage?

Attorney-General: Because it would be difficult for a woman to attend to her household as well as her departmental duties. There would be a conflict of duty. This clause is in accordance with the practice of all Public Servants.

Mr Francis: But supposing a woman has an invalid husband?

Attorney-General: The Board may take into account 'special circumstances'. A married woman may in certain circumstances be given temporary employment in the Service, and as a matter of fact, many widows are in many cases temporarily employed as office-cleaners. In this clause, however, we are dealing with the permanent Service, entrance to which is to be secured only by passing the prescribed examination. I do not think we could adopt any other course than that for which the clause provides.

Mr Chapman: Under this clause a female officer on her marriage will be discharged from the Service.

Attorney-General: That has always been the law.

Mr Chapman: Is there any reason we should perpetuate such an anomaly? Why should we not depart from some of these musty old precedents? I know of a lady in the Public Service who wants to get married, but is told that if she does so she must retire. She has a splendid record, has done good work in the Service, and does not wish to leave it. It is not fair that she should be called, upon her marriage, to retire.

Mr Maxwell: Is it not in the public interest that a female officer on her marriage should retire from the Service?

Mr Chapman: Why?

Mr Maxwell: Because if she remained in the Service she would have to neglect her home duties.

Mr Chapman: If the Government is charged with the responsibility of seeing that every woman attends to her home duties, that is another matter. Women in the Service are paid to attend – not to home, but to public duties. What would the single members of this Committee say if a Bill were introduced providing that on their marriage they should automatically cease to be members of this Parliament? In this clause the Government are merely seeking to perpetuate a silly tradition. Escape from such a provision will be possible only by the use of political influence. All that a woman in the Service should be asked when she is about to marry is: 'Can you carry on your duties satisfactorily after your marriage?' If she says that she can, why should she be called upon to leave the Service?

Mr Fenton (Maribyrnong): I cannot agree with all that has been said by the Honorable Member for Eden-Monaro. Surely he would not contend that a female officer who marries a man with an income of £1000 a year should be allowed to remain in the Service?

Mr Chapman: Why should she be discharged?

Mr Fenton: A woman who is maintained by her husband should not come into competition with single women or men desiring to enter the Service . . . In my view, there should be a preference to men, in order that they may qualify to marry and maintain the women.[3]

(Mr Fenton did, later in his address, soften insofar as to concede that 'in a thinly-populated district, the wife of a storekeeper could act as postmistress'. This gimlet-eyed pragmatism in respect of matters postal paid off ten years later, when Joe Lyons made him Postmaster General.)

Mr Chapman: I move that sub-clause be left out. The sub-clause that I wish to omit provides that every female officer shall be deemed to have retired from the Service upon her marriage . . . There is no need for a provision such as this, and the only reason the Minister gave for its appearance in the clause is that it has been the custom for women in the past to retire on their marriage. Why should women be penalised? Why should they not be paid as much for their services as is paid to men? Equal pay for equal work.

They are admitted to the legal and medical professions on equal terms with men, and I fail to see why they should be penalised if they enter the Public Service. I refuse to accept the Minister's assurance that the Board will have the power to consider 'special circumstances'. Those who are humble and poor, and cannot pull strings, will be differently treated from those who can use influence. If the Minister wishes to retain the sub-clause, he should give us good reasons for its retention. A woman who is giving good service should not be dismissed merely because she is married.

Mr Pratten: It is placing a premium on spinsterhood!

Attorney-General: The honorable Member for Eden-Monaro proposes that women in the Service who marry shall be allowed to remain, but I do not think that at all desirable. Indeed, experience has proven it to be quite undesirable. The provision to which he takes exception is one which applies generally to the Public Services.

Chapman: Why not sack a man when he gets married?[4]

And with that quixotic final volley from the Member for Eden-Monaro, the matter was put to a vote, and Chapman's amendment went down in a screaming heap, thirty-five votes to six. The marriage bar was passed.

It is at this point in the Hansard that I consider finding out where Mr Chapman is buried, and taking a large bunch of flowers to plonk on him, the dear old chap. His independence of thought does not seem to have hampered his progression; Chapman was made Minister for Trade and Customs in 1923, but his time there was both brief and unhappy. He resigned due to ill-health in 1924 and was dead by 1926, God rest his soul.

In this and similar debates at the time, it was not uncommon for the question of equal pay for women to crop up. Though, it must be said, support for equal pay was based not so much on any sense that it was unfair to pay women less, and more on the fear that cheap female labour would fiendishly undercut male wages.

The marriage bar persisted for another forty-four years. The United States and Canada repealed their equivalent legislation, as did the UK in 1946, but still Australian wives, through the 1940s and the 1950s, were obliged to choose between work in the public service and marriage. Most women copped it sweet and left without a fuss. But for some, the laws represented a challenge to their personal ingenuity.

Merle Thornton, now in her eighties, got a job in the federal Department of Social Services in 1952. She had a degree in English Literature from the University of Sydney. 'I was very unhappy there, because it was very routinised work,' she recalls. 'I had been appointed as a graduate clerk, and they really felt I ought to get my comeuppance, so they sat me down with a typed list, and a pile of envelopes to address.'

Such repetitive work obviously left Merle vulnerable to other fascinations and quite soon, in her spare time, she had fallen in love with a man called Neil, whom she swiftly decided to marry. The extent to which this happy event would mess with her career was something Merle only realised when the woman who sat next to her – ostensibly a single lass – was summarily sacked one day. A caller to the switchboard had asked for her by her married name. Merle was appalled. 'I thought – Oh! Okay, I'll call the

union. Only to find that the unions were the major supporters of the bar,' she recalls.

So Merle became one of many white-veil criminals; she
got married in secret. 'I just didn't tell anyone. I thought,
Whatever am I doing? What does this train me for? Being
a spy? It was difficult. The punishment for living in sin at
the time was horrendous – full-face disapprobation and
discrimination, not only in society but at work, or when
looking for accommodation.'

Merle eventually applied successfully for a transfer –
'I explained that I was occupationally maladjusted' – and
landed in the ABC managing director Charles Moses' office
as his personal assistant and correspondence officer. It was
a job she loved. But her first child – a son – was already
on his way, a fact which even strategic wardrobe choices
could disguise for only so long; in the end, it was almost a
relief to abandon the pretence and resign.

The taste for civil disobedience, once acquired, is hard
to repress. In 1965, Merle became an international sensa-
tion when – having moved to Queensland – she chained
herself, with a friend, to the public bar of Brisbane's
Regatta Hotel (a bar from which, like all public bars,
she and her friend, like all women, were still banned).
With the resultant notoriety and publicity, she helped
form the Equal Opportunities for Women Association,
which lobbied the Menzies Government hard to repeal
the marriage bar.

The group collected stories from women all around
Australia, demonstrating the hardship and idiocy occasioned by the law. They make plaintive reading.

My name is Rita Grey. I was employed as a physicist by the State Public Service in Western Australia. When I met the man of whom I became very fond I realised that by marrying him, I would have to give up my career. I knew that if I did this I would be absolutely frustrated and was realistic enough to predict that our marriage would suffer as a result. So I decided to 'live in sin' as an alternative. I did this quite openly and continued to work for the Public Service for eight years. During this time I reared three children and the Public Service officials were cooperative in enabling me to take my annual leave to correspond with confinement periods. Yet when for the sake of the children I decided to marry their father, I was asked to resign. One of the officials pointed out that it was not morally desirable for a married woman to work.[5]

Another woman, 'Joan F', married in secret, and lived in a state of professional paranoia as a result.

I found myself in a constant state of tension, frightened of a slip of the tongue which might mean the arbitrary end of my job. For obvious reasons I tended not to answer questions put in a friendly fashion by my friends. Then I became pregnant and as my husband and I were saving for him to have a period out of work to study for a higher degree, I continued to work until I became visibly pregnant. I would very much have liked to continue working up to and after the birth of my child. If necessary I would not have hesitated spending all my earnings on providing good care for my child so that I could continue with the work for which I was trained and which gave me satisfaction.[6]

That a piece of legislation designed to reinforce the holy union of marriage was indirectly encouraging some women to lie, cheat and fornicate does not seem to have occasioned much comment in the federal legislature. But in 1958, the Boyer Committee's inquiry into public service recruitment recommended that the ban be repealed.

The Minister for Labour and National Service, Billy McMahon, received a confidential memo from his departmental secretary, Harry Bland, urging him to back the recommendation, as doing so would 'enable us to hold up our own heads at ILO [International Labour Organisation] conferences'.

'I should have thought it has political value,' Bland scribbled by hand, adding slyly: 'Get rid of this and we may have a little more peace on equal pay.'[7]

But the office of Prime Minister Robert Menzies was underwhelmed. 'There is altogether a curious tangle here,' wrote Menzies' senior adviser Dr Ronald Mendelsohn to his boss in 1962. 'Were you to refer the question of employment of married women, or the somewhat related question of equal pay for equal work, to an appointed Committee nicely balanced pro and con, guineas to peanuts it would recommend the feminist view-point. Were you to take a popular vote the conservative view would have a much better run. The issue is far more likely to lose votes than to win votes, however it is played. Delay seems the best gambit . . .'[8]

It was – politically – a dicey call. Unemployment was on the rise, and the unions did not like the idea of inviting married women to join the work-seeking scrum. And the marriage bar itself was not – it must be said – unpopular.

As late as 1956, *Woman's Day* polled its readers and found that they were six-to-one against married women working, mainly because it was felt that the needs of young children should be put first. In 1960, a Gallup poll reported that 78 per cent of Australians opposed the mothers of young children entering the workforce.[9]

'The Cabinet expressed no enthusiasm,' records Cabinet Secretary John Bunting in a 1962 minute. 'It preferred the status quo, though so as not to provoke the feminists and others, decided to lie low for the time being rather than come out with a statement. The question is whether standing still is any longer an acceptable gambit.'[10]

The government indeed lay low for several more years, and it was not until October 1966 that the Holt government finally repealed the legislation, and married women were freed to work in the public sector. Merle Thornton later became an academic, designing Australia's first women's studies course. The Regatta Hotel named a room after her: The Thornton Room, where women go for refreshments. She writes plays, periodically including roles for her famous second-born child, Sigrid.

If I've recounted this particular episode at some length, it's only to reinforce how serious a matter of overt government policy it was, barely fifty years ago, to ensure that men should be provided with a reliable source of wives. Proper wives, that is; not some distracted working girl with half an eye on the office who would in all likelihood burn the chops.

Wives were a particular kind of national resource. They were no threat to men in an employment sense; far from it. Rather, they improved men's ability to work by supplying a stable home environment, various broadly understood comforts and adorable children, whose very existence would in turn contribute a powerful evolutionary impetus to work hard and prosper. The act of getting hitched made men into more valuable employees, and gave them a stronger moral position from which to ask for a promotion of more job security.

The phrase 'family man' still evokes a whole series of reassuring impressions concerning a potential employee's home life; something about the phrase connotes solidity, dependability, a home life filled with nourishing meals and games of Scrabble. Possibly, a labrador could be involved. Being married, as a man, meant you were contributing to the stability of the nation, and could probably be depended upon to continue doing so, starting with your job.

Getting married as a woman, though, had exactly the opposite effect. The very same factor – the acquisition of a home, and possibly children – was not expected to make women more reliable at work. It was thought to make them unreliable. Worse than that, a woman who sought to work after her marriage was considered to be a destabilising influence both at home and at work, where she thoughtlessly weakened the fabric of the nation by occupying a job that should have been a man's, thereby occasioning two households to go hungry, rather than just one.

Obviously, women are no longer compelled to quit their jobs upon getting married. The marriage rate is now lower, so it would be a less effective piece of policy anyway. And no one publicly prosecutes, any more, the idea that a woman with a family should not work. The marriage ban has the gently ridiculous feel of ancient history; tales of taking off your wedding ring to go to work sound as though they should rank with men riding to factories on penny-farthings.

But even when it seems ancient – or ridiculous – history shapes us, and leaves its unmistakeable crenellations upon our modern lives. Women are not now routinely fired as a result of getting married; we can file that one away with 'not allowed to vote' and 'being burned as a witch' as one of those funny old things that doesn't happen any more. But that is not to say that marriage and children don't – in the workplace – still do very different things for women compared with what they do for men.

Marriage, for men, means being paid more money. The phenomenon known as the 'marriage premium' is recorded in many countries, and in Australia married men earn on average about 15 per cent more than unmarried ones.[11]

Why is this? Well, you could assemble a group of sociologists and have a long and exciting argument on this question, but it all boils down to two basic theories, as far as I can tell.

The first is something called 'selection', which is the theory that the kinds of men who are successful at work are also the kinds of men who are more likely to find spouses easily. There is plenty of evidence that people who are good-looking and socially confident do better at work, and tend to get promoted, not to mention sent on all the good conferences. These are also characteristics that historically make a man a good catch, maritally speaking. Obviously, there are some natural limits to this theory, given that there are also some characteristics that simultaneously make a man a very good employee and a very annoying husband, like being at work until 11 pm, or wearing company merchandise to unrelated social occasions.

As ever, human relationships are confounding. Why do we do what we do? And when is a pattern a pattern? Is the marriage premium just about the same cohort of blokes monopolising all the good jobs *and* all the chicks, or is there something else going on?

In the late 1990s, two intrepid researchers at the Federal Reserve Bank of Atlanta conducted a study of men in 'shotgun marriages' to see if the pattern held.[12] The researchers reasoned that while women pursuing a rigorous recruitment process to find a husband might behave similarly to employers, unions that were mandated by an incautious bout of grappling in the back seat of a Pontiac might be a little more . . . uncluttered by the more orthodox mechanics of spousal choice.

They found that even in shotgun marriages, 90 per cent of the marriage premium remained. Married men get paid more, even when marriage was kind of accidental.

This suggests that there is something intrinsic about being lashed to a lady that makes a man – in the eyes of the world – a better bet.

The other theory for why married men are better paid is to do with 'specialisation'. That is the idea that when couples settle down to live together, they implicitly begin to divide life's labours between themselves. If one partner takes care of cooking, for instance, that not only relieves the other partner of that job; it actively creates time which he or she can spend on getting much better at doing something else. If one partner takes responsibility for earning enough to support the household, the other can run the household.

It is as true for small jobs as big ones. In my house, for instance, I am responsible for present-wrapping. This is partly because I am supremely good at it; for some reason, I was born with an ability to tie bows that look good, and when I wrap a present, I like to use a proper ribbon, and paper that jauntily offsets that ribbon. Also, I will usually make a card. For these reasons, and also because I care if someone gets a present or not, I have been the Gift Procurement Officer for many years now. So I keep getting better at it, while Jeremy's skills have eroded to the point where his parcels look like the hastily concealed murder weapons of a homicidal maniac.

Not that he's been idle, mind; the free hours each week in which Jeremy might – had things panned out differently – have spent gift-wrapping have instead been used productively to make him much better than me at some other stuff. Becoming the IT Help Desk, for instance. His command of software, hardware, and which-cords-go-where are so noticeably superior to mine that I have given up even trying to maintain basic competency, and am as helpless in the face of Apple TV as he is when confronted by an awkwardly shaped gift item.

This is specialisation, and in terms of human economy it's very effective. As a team, we are collectively excellent both at present-wrapping and information technology. If we were to split up, however, I could never watch movies and he would be an underwhelming birthday party guest. Such fracture of these domestic chore-allocation arrangements, which begin casually and over time become absolute, is part of the reason why divorce is so painful; added to the pain of lost love is the altogether more humiliating task of having to relearn incredibly basic stuff from the ground up.

But specialisation also applies to big stuff. Despite all the changes that have taken place in Australian society in the past few decades, there is a clear and change-resistant pattern in the way heterosexual couples – especially those with children – divide work between themselves. Men do more of the paid work, and women more of the unpaid. The theory is that this liberates husbands to excel in the workplace and collect all the benefits of a well-run home (good nutrition, clean clothes, a feeling of security and purpose, children, something uncontroversial to make small talk with the boss about during those awkward lift rides) without having to do all the grunt work themselves. Wives, meanwhile, spared by this arrangement from the necessity to do all the earning, are able to become very good at the unpaid jobs, such as raising children, knowing if the school concert is tonight or next week, and making sure there's milk.

I know this all sounds pretty hokey. No one buys that 1950s husband-and-wife stuff any more – right? Well, the fact is that we do still buy it. The most common arrangement among Australian families with children is for Dad to work full-time, and for Mum to work either part-time or not at all, while Mum will do about twice as much housework as Dad.

What does marriage do to a woman's job prospects? Not much at all, is the most likely answer; whereas Australian men can look forward to a 'marital bump' in earnings after the happy event, no such phenomenon has been recorded for women. For women, anyway, the big, life-changing difference doesn't come with marriage itself; it comes with children.

Children change things for both men and women. In Australia, an average 25-year-old man can expect to earn a lifetime total of $2 million over a forty-year working life, if he doesn't have children. If he does have children, however, this figure is bumped up to $2.5 million.[13]

For women, though, parenthood exerts the opposite effect. A childless woman can actually expect to earn just about as much as her childless male counterpart – $1.9 million over the course of her forty years at work. But if she has babies, that total dips to just $1.3 million. She will earn $600,000 less than a childless woman, and a full $1.2 million less than a father.

This is where the economics of the wife drought become rather brutal. *Having* a wife carries all sorts of economic advantages – like being able to work harder and for longer hours, and not having to drive a carload of yammering progeny to swimming lessons. *Being* a wife, however, carries all sorts of economic disadvantages. Like not being paid for any of the above-mentioned stuff.

One of the standout pieces of research in this area was conducted in 2007 at Stanford University.[14] Researchers called in a bunch of undergraduate participants and told them their assistance was being sought by a Californian startup communications company looking for a marketing officer to set up a new East Coast office.

Each participant was told that the successful candidate's salary range would be between $135,000 and $180,000. Each participant was given two candidates to consider: either two women or two men. In each case, the candidates had qualifications that had proven functionally identical in a pre-testing round; but one was a parent, and one wasn't, a fact made clear by the inclusion – in one CV – of a reference to the candidate being a 'Parent–Teacher Association Coordinator'.

So what happened?

When two women were up against each other, one clearly a parent and one from whose CV it could readily be inferred that she was childless, the mother lost out on just about every factor. She was considered slightly less competent. She was considered significantly less committed. She was considered suitable for hiring 47 per cent of the time, while her childless competitor was recommended for hire 84 per cent of the time. Her recommended starting salary averaged $137,000, compared to $148,000 for the non-mother. And she was thought to be potential management material by 69 per cent of respondents, compared to 84 per cent who fancied the long-term chances of her rival.

But when the two candidates were a father and a non-father, participants in the experiment had entirely different responses.

The father candidate was considered slightly more competent than the non-father. He was anticipated to be more committed to the work. His recommended starting salary averaged out at $150,000 – more than either of the female candidates, and more than the childless bloke whose qualifications were otherwise functionally identical, and who got the nod for a starting wage of $144,000. And as for his prospects: Dad was thought likely to be management material by a thumping 93.6 per cent of respondents.

His non-dad competitor was thought appropriate for advancement by 85 per cent.

So having a child made women less likely to be employed, and less likely to be trusted, promoted, and generally thought suitable. But for fathers, having a family actually gave them a competitive edge. Weirdly enough, the very same reservations that were aroused by the discreet existence of children in a woman's CV – potential lack of commitment, unworthiness for promotion, and so on – were actively abolished by the existence of children in a man's.

How can the very same factor – having children – cause such differing effects in men and women? When the starting assumptions are different. And starting assumptions about how women and men will behave – even in a regulated environment like the Australian workplace – continue to be different.

The assumption is that men and women will respond differently to becoming parents. And the cold, hard truth is that that assumption is a fair one. Men and women *do* respond differently to becoming parents. Men do not adjust their work patterns very much at all when they have their first child; in fact, if anything, as we've already seen, they increase their work hours.[15]

Women, however, are much more likely to work part-time after having a child. Of employed mothers of young children, 43 per cent work part-time, but only 5 per cent of corresponding fathers do.[16]

This is the shape of women's and men's lives in the Australian workplace. When children grow up and progress through school and university, girls outperform boys; and, of the children who grow up into young people who want to go to university, more women will graduate than men. They get jobs at roughly equal rates, and move into middle-management roles in about the same numbers.

But when they have children, the paths diverge. Men's careers rattle along uninterrupted, while women are far more apt to change the way they work to suit the other things going on in their lives. Men's jobs are disrupted by recessions; women's jobs are disrupted by family.

So whatever we have weeded out of our system in terms of actual restrictions on married women working in paid jobs, there remains a stubborn series of assumptions about what men and women will probably be good at, how they will behave, and what they will likely rate as their first priority. These assumptions, as I explained in Chapter 1, are not always even conscious. They distort the judgement of employers without those employers necessarily realising it.

They evolve like a muscle memory, and they are wordlessly reinforced by experience. This happens in big things just as it does in small. The better I get at wrapping presents, the more I do it, and the more settled and reasonable the proposition becomes that I am the present-wrapping type, while Jeremy is your go-to man if you want to series-link *Breaking Bad*.

I didn't really intend things to turn out this way, and neither did he. Present-wrapping is so girly, and the fact that I can't (I lapse here into antique terminology) programme a video recorder is substantially embarrassing to my feminist self. But that's where we are. It just happened. I might defensively add that he is better than me at laundry and tidying up. But I cannot deny the gendered quality of our most obviously diversified skills. If there is a button to be sewn on, I'm your first point of contact. Hard rubbish issues? See my husband.

In the workplace, this microbial pattern of behaviour translates into something much broader. Being a husband and father carries an undeniable cachet; there's the corroborative fact of having been chosen and valued by someone, of course, but also there's an additional, whispered assurance; chances are this person will be able to hang about till stumps without any fuss about having to get to child care. The assumption – so richly and overtly present in the parliamentary debates of 1922 – that a woman's first priority is the home is still a strong subterranean influence today.

Are attitudes changing? One would assume so; barely a day can go by without some new story about a male CEO who is 'taking on' gender imbalances in his company, or some flexible work initiative that is going to make all the difference. But the truth is that attitudes – at least on the question of who is expected to do what in an average family – aren't changing the way you might expect them to.

Have a look at the results when Australians are asked if they agree or disagree with the statement: 'It is better for the family if the husband is the principal breadwinner outside the home and the wife has primary responsibility for the home and children.'

In 1986, just over 55 per cent of men agreed with that proposition. That proportion swan-dived down to about 30 per cent by 2001, but by 2005, it had gone up again, to 41.4 per cent. Women subscribe to that view less enthusiastically than men on the whole, but they too have waxed and waned over the last 30 years. In 1986, 33 per cent of them thought it was better for men to work and women to keep house. By 2001, that had dipped to 19 per cent. But by 2005, it had bobbed back up to 36.4 per cent.[17]

What's happening? It's one thing to muse indulgently on the antiquated day of the wife ban, and its outdated assumptions about the role of men and women. It's another entirely to be executing some sort of national handbrake-turn and heading right on back there. My own suspicion is that while women's shift into work has been considerable, the lack of a corresponding shift the other way by men means that combining work and family, for women, is harder than it should be. It's hard, too, for men who want to be better fathers than their dads were. Is it any wonder that the old models might gently re-assert themselves as the easiest and least stressful solution?

Merle Thornton, reflecting on a life lived among the cordite whiff of the gender war's frontline, has this to say: 'The things that have changed have changed faster than anything in human history. But in the end, it comes down to personal relationships between men and women. And a lot of that still has a long way to go.'

The truth is that workplaces don't function in a vacuum, even though we often pretend that they do. And for all the combing of offices and workshops and factories and hospitals and schools and farms and shops for patterns to tell us how men and women work, they only make sense when we take a step closer, and check out what men and women do when they're at home.

4

MEANWHILE, ON THE HOME FRONT

The average Australian is a 37-year-old woman. She was born in Australia, of Australian parents, and has Anglo-Celtic ancestry. When at home with her husband and her two children – a boy and a girl aged nine and six – the Average Australian speaks only English. The house she lives in is located in a suburb of a capital city; it has three bedrooms, and a mortgage on which the Average Australian and her husband pay $1800 a month. They have lived in that house for more than five years, and every day the Average Australian drives in one of the family's two cars to her job as a sales assistant, a job in which she works thirty-two hours a week. She has a certificate in Business and Management, but the Average Australian finds the flexible hours in retail suit her perfectly well, because she needs to juggle things with the kids.

This portrait was issued by the Australian Bureau of Statistics after Census 2011.[1] The Average Australian is the proton-pellet of information excreted by the nation's premier statisticians after digesting the lives, habits, family structures, religious beliefs, income, education and lives of 22 million people, as they stood on the evening of 9 August 2011. To assemble this Identikit Australian, the ABS simply grafted the most common gender (female, since 1979) on to the most common occupation for that gender (sales assistant), and plonked her in the most common relationship, with the most common number of kids and so forth.

The Average Australian changes every Census, as the population grows, diversifies, and in other ways evolves into a pattern we could not have imagined a generation earlier; in 1911, for example, the Average Australian was a 24-year-old Anglican farmer. By 1961, he was a 29-year-old clerk.

But here's the funny thing about averages. It's not that they don't represent everyone; we all understand that. The fascinating thing is that, according to the Australian Bureau of Statistics, they don't actually represent *anyone*: 'While many people will share a number of characteristics in common with this "average" Australian, out of the nearly 20 million people counted in Australia on Census night . . . no single person met all these criteria,' announces the Bureau, with enviable bureaucratic poise, in its 2013 edition of Australian Social Trends.[2]

Ah, statistics. So useful, so fascinating, and yet so full of holes. Statistics give us the degree of likelihood that something will happen to us; the evanescent, predictive shape to our human endeavours. But the holes are our audacious expression of hope, our teensy-weensy human yelp of exceptionalism; our faith in our own autonomy, our originality, our capacity to be the pack-a-day smoker who doesn't get cancer, or to back the long-odds horse that comes home in a canter.

Right up close, we all look different; we all have a chance of bucking the system. To ourselves, we look utterly unique. It's only when viewed from space – or from a Canberra eyrie atop a tottering stack of Census papers – that the patterns become dully apparent.

So when we consider how things go down in the average home, and what happens when human organisms shack up together, we must thus remember, first of all, that to individuals and the people they love there is no such thing as average. The averageness is only apparent in hindsight, or in long-sight, or when a million such individuals are fed into vast, peristaltic information-munching machines, the results pooped out in a tidy string of statistical luncheon-meat.

We have looked at what happens at work when couples get together and have children. But what happens at home when men and women A) fall in love, B) move in together, C) get married, and D) have children? I have mentioned these events, ABS-style, in the chronological order that our modern age currently registers as the commonest, but of course some couples do things in a different way. Some of them do A first, then C, then D. Some do A, then B, then D. Some just leave it at A, or A then B, or A then C. It's even possible – although, if Woody Allen and Mia Farrow are anything to go by, not always entirely successful – to do A and D, and skip everything in between.

By hook or by crook, though, a vast number of Australians still wind up living in houses that have a dad, a mum, and a certain number of children. Who does what in those houses?

Let's take the visible-from-space view first, which delivers the least-surprising bulletin internationally available on this topic: women do more work in the home than men. This is true everywhere, although the phenomenon has different extremes in different countries. The country in which a randomly chosen female spouse has the best chance of a hand with the washing-up is Norway, where – according to the OECD – blokes put in three hours of domestic work a day, as opposed to their wives who rack up three and a half.[3] Norway, incidentally, has one of the world's most generous paternity leave schemes.

And then you get countries like Japan, where the average man does just an hour of chores, cleaning, child care and so on, but finds that home ticks along okay because his wife does five hours.

Australian women do an unusually high amount of housework and child care: five hours and eleven minutes a day, which is eleven minutes more than the Japanese lady we were feeling sorry for in the last paragraph. But on the bright side, Mrs Australia isn't married to Mr Japan: she's married to Mr Australia instead, and he does nearly three hours' work a day in the home – lots less than his wife, sure, but lots more than his brothers in Mexico, Korea or Italy.

One of the reasons that Australian men and women do more work in the home than their international counterparts is that we do not have a culture of low-paid domestic service. In the United States, for instance, both men and women do less housework than we do, but they are also much more likely to have a representative of a social underclass helping out. Domestic workers in the US are 94 per cent women anyway, so it doesn't mess with the gender statistics too much, but outsourcing housework brings in a whole lot of other variables, specifically race; domestic carers who are white, for instance, earn a median wage of $12 an hour, while black and Latino workers earn $10, and Asians $8.33, according to research done in 2012 by the National Domestic Workers Alliance.[4]

On one hand, it's nice to see the American ladies getting cut some slack in the domestic department. On the other, it's pretty awful that that slack gets taken up by workers whose pay-rate depends at least in part on the colour of their skin.

Women do more housework than men do. This is the big picture, everywhere. Across all the countries of the OECD, men average 141 minutes a day of work in the home, and women average 273 – twice as much, basically.[5] This is not a regionalised statistic. It's a global one. I'm not trying to get you down. The truth is that no matter how fast things change outside the home, things inside the home don't change that fast.

In order to zoom in and have a closer look at the local situation, I'm now going to introduce you to one of the greatest things the Australian Government has done for nerds in the last thirty years. It's called the Time Use Survey, and it's carried out by the Australian Bureau of Statistics on a broad cross-section of Australian households, asking men and women to fill out detailed diaries recording how they spend their time.

The Time Use Survey is a fabulously nosy affair. It tracks what people do right down to the last minute, and keeps track of when they do two things at once. It is much more reliable than an ordinary survey, which is when house-holders are asked to estimate the amount of time they spend on various activities. This is because when human beings are asked on the phone to estimate how much housework they do, they exaggerate.

A national diary study carried out in the United States at the turn of the twenty-first century, for instance, found that everybody was pretending to do more housework than they actually did. Men claimed to be doing twenty-three hours of housework a week, when the diaries revealed they were really only doing ten. And women estimated they were doing thirty-two hours, but actually it turned out to be more like seventeen.[6]

Intellectually, this makes sense. If someone from the Australian Bureau of Statistics rings you when you just happen to be skiving off work and binge-watching *Game of Thrones* while the children amuse themselves with online gambling, then of course you're going to claim you are currently supervising maths homework, especially if you have any suspicion at all that your spouse is going to hear about this. People lie to surveys all the time. It's why the One Nation vote was always a bit higher than polls detected. It's why, despite everybody always saying when surveyed that they would be prepared to pay higher taxes in return for more spending on health and education, they usually vote the other way.

The Australian Bureau of Statistics' Time Use Surveys, which they conducted in 1992, 1997 and 2006, have been described by the US National Academy of Sciences as 'the Mercedes of time-use surveys'.[7] They are spectacularly detailed. The information that is winkled out in these diaries is a source of deep geek-joy, obviously, but it's much more than that. It gives us the only really reliable national estimate of work in the home, given that we don't account for that work in any of the other established ways, of which 'paying for it' would be the first to mind.

The tragic news, however, is that the study planned for 2013 was cancelled due to budget cuts the Bureau was obliged to make by the Gillard Government.[8] It's now not scheduled again until 2019, which means I will be using data from 2006, so if you've significantly picked up your game on housework in the past eight years and you feel it's been overlooked, you should go ahead and raise it with your local MP.

In the years between 1992 and 2006, quite a bit changed in Australian society. Significant economic reform took place. And the employment patterns of Australian women, of whom, in 1992, only 48 per cent were in some kind of paid work, changed too: by 2006, more than half of Australia's women – 55 per cent – were in the workforce.[9]

This movement of women into the workplace was considerable, but it was not counterbalanced by men moving in the opposite direction. And women did not decrease their overall contribution to housework to reflect the other jobs they'd taken on since 1992. In fact, between 1992 and 2006, women actually increased the time they spent on child care by nearly 20 per cent.[10]

Defenders of the traditional breadwinner/homemaker model argue that the lopsided distribution of paid and unpaid work within a couple makes economic sense. This is the system called 'exchange bargaining', in which one person – commonly the husband – earns money and supports another person – usually the wife – who in return agrees to take responsibility for bathroom grout and the Easter Bonnet Parade, and all the rest of it. There certainly are appealing aspects to this arrangement: no one is doubling up on tasks too much, and there is a fairly clear rule of thumb as to who does what.

And it's true that if you add up the total number of hours that everybody's worked, including all paid and unpaid work, the total number of hours done by men and women in couple families tends to be about the same. In the traditional family structure, he will take care of earning the income, plus lawnmowing, plus the removal of certain crawling pests, and it will add up to about the same amount of time as she is spending on cooking, cleaning, and child care.

What's really interesting, though, is what happens in those families when circumstances change. What happens when women move into paid work, and men move out of it? If the exchange bargaining model is to be believed, everybody should swap around tasks so that things stay roughly even, right?

But that's not what happens. According to the Australian Time Use Survey data, men on average do between fifteen and twenty hours of housework a week, no matter whether they work full-time, part-time or not at all. Men who are not in the labour force at all do about twenty hours of housework. Part-time working men do about fifteen hours, and full-time working men do sixteen.[11] Why do men working full-time do slightly more housework than men working part-time? I do not know.

Women, however, are an entirely different story. Women will do more housework if they are not employed, and drop it back as they take on more hours of paid work. There's a much greater range; on average, an Australian woman does forty-two hours of housework a week (excluding child care) if she doesn't have a paid job, but only twenty-five hours of housework if she works full-time. Still more than the average man – even the one who doesn't do any paid work at all.[12]

Keep in mind, these are averages. If you are a home dad, reading this in a quick break between taekwondo training, ironing, and the preparation of a healthy after-school snack of crudités, please do not cuss me out. Obviously, many men do more housework than twenty hours. But the statistics make it pretty clear: women do more housework than men, by quite a long straw, no matter how many hours of paid work they do.

While women's housework hours depend strongly on what else is going on in her life, there are only a handful of life events that change the amount of housework that men do, to a significant and broadly observed degree.

Moving out of home is one of them. A man aged between twenty and forty-nine who moves out of his parents' home to live either alone or in a share household dramatically increases the time he spends cooking and shopping.[13]

Another is divorce. According to Janeen Baxter, a leading academic in this field, who analysed data from a survey project of several thousand Australians called Negotiating the Lifecourse, divorce immediately adds about ten hours a week to a man's domestic workload. Divorce means something quite different for women, who do about six hours less a week after divorcing their husbands.[14]

What about the arrival of children? Surely all that extra washing, sterilising, shopping for magic swaddle suits that do not work and so on must make a difference to the domestic workload?

Baxter's research found that the birth of a first child jacked up a woman's housework considerably; she did about half as much again after that child's birth, and more again after the birth of a second child.[15]

The birth of a first child, however, generates negligible extra housework for men. And the arrival of a further child after that actually *reduces* the amount of time the supplier of its Y chromosome spends doing housework. Baxter, puzzled, advances two theories: 'It may be that additional children help to cement an already traditional division of labour in many households. Or it may be that additional children lead men to increase their hours of paid work in order to compensate for the increased expenditure associated with more children, or to compensate for their wives' reduced time in paid labour.'[16]

So women shrink their housework hours when they work full-time and increase them when they have children – they respond rather elastically, in other words, to all the changes life can bring. But men seem to be bound by some kind of unwritten national housework award which keeps them at about twenty hours a week, no matter what else is going on.

There is another factor that has an intriguing effect on the division of labour in the Australian home, and that's share of earnings. The historical male-breadwinner model assumes that men will earn all of the household income and that women will do most or all of the housework.

When you look at how women change their behaviour according to how much they earn, instead of how many hours of paid work they do, you notice something absolutely fascinating.

Janeen Baxter and Belinda Hewitt, in their 2012 paper 'Negotiating Domestic Labor: Women's Earnings and Housework Time in Australia', analysed information from Australian households harvested by the Household, Income and Labour Dynamics in Australia (HILDA) survey.[17] They specifically looked at the pattern of women's housework plotted against their contribution to the household's total weekly earnings. They looked at women in couple families only; no one would be surprised to learn that single mothers do all the housework in their homes.

Here's what they found: on average, women do seventeen minutes less housework a week for every 1 per cent extra they contribute to the household budget. So if a husband earns $99,000 and his wife goes out and gets a casual job that pays $1000, she will lop seventeen minutes off her weekly housework. Another 1 per cent of contribution ensues a further seventeen fewer minutes of work around the house, and so on. This, so far, is a rather beautiful demonstration of bargaining theory. Paid work is exchangeable for unpaid work; if you do more of one, you will do less of the other.

But this pattern holds only until the woman's contribution

reaches 66.6 per cent of total household income. Once she starts earning more than that, she actually starts *increasing* her amount of unpaid work again.[18] Once the woman is firmly established as the family's main breadwinner, in other words, she starts behaving in exactly the opposite manner from what the bargaining model would predict – as she earns more from paid work, she resumes more and more work around the house.

Now this is quite weird. Why would a woman making a bigger contribution to the paid work in any given household also feel obliged to increase the amount of unpaid work she does at the same time? And why does 66.6 per cent serve as a trigger-point for everything in a household to change? What is it, the Number of the Laundress or something?

'One explanation is that we have such a strong male breadwinner culture in Australia that in those households women are, if you like, re-asserting their gender identity by picking up some of the housework that's left over,' says Baxter.

This strange Australian pattern isn't just something that popped up in Baxter's study. It was first discussed in 2003, when a team of Australian and American researchers got together to compare Australian and American patterns of housework division between the sexes. That project – Michael Bittman of the University of New South Wales was the lead Australian researcher involved – also found that Australian couples changed their behaviour markedly when women started out-earning their husbands.[19] Bittman and colleagues plotted a graph showing how women behaved as their contribution to the household finances grew; it curved downwards until the women were earning about the same as their husbands, then curved right back up again as their earnings grew. The resultant graph is the shape of a slightly off-centre smile. The Bittman study also plots the contribution of husbands throughout all this; it remains – roughly as we'd expect given the other evidence previously discussed – pretty much a straight line throughout.

The researchers were puzzled. Could they have got it wrong? Could there be something else going on? After all, the number of households in which women out-earned their husbands was not huge; could something be skewing the results? They tried breaking the housework down into constituent elements: cooking, cleaning, and laundry. They tried eliminating households with unemployed husbands. Every way they cut it, the same parabola kept popping up.

American couples were different, interestingly enough. Over there, as wives earned more, they cut back on their housework hours. There wasn't any weird Number of the Beast reversal for the women, unlike in Australia. What happened instead was that their husbands went on strike. American men increased their rates of housework as their wives earned more, right up to the point at which their earnings were at a par. As their wives outstripped them in terms of income, though, the men then downed tools and decreased their housework again.[20]

Again, the researchers tried everything they could to explain the differences between what they observed in the US and what they observed in Australia. But, after fiddling about to account for possible differences in research methods and data analysis, they could find nothing that would erase the disparity. It was, they concluded, a genuine cross-national phenomenon. 'Australian women respond to earning more than their husbands by increasing their housework, as if to make up for the gender deviance of female breadwinning and their husbands' dependence on this,' they concluded, while 'Australian men's participation in housework is impervious to their wives' earnings.'[21]

In Australia, therefore, bargaining as an explanation of housework division only really works until it bumps up against our rather robust set of implicit national assumptions about whose job it is to earn money. I'm going to have a much closer look at this whole area in Chapter 9, 'Role Reversal'.

So we know that women expand and contract their housework hours according to all sorts of factors, and men's housework hours stay kind of static. What happens to all that housework that a woman stops doing when she goes into full-time work, if it's not being picked up by her husband?

This is a pretty significant question. Let's take a look at the busiest households of all; families with children aged under fifteen. In those households, a stay-at-home mum does an amazing sixty-five hours a week of combined housework and childcare, but she cuts that back to forty-one hours if she goes to work full-time. That's a whole twenty-four hours, every week, of housework she just stops doing. And her husband doesn't vary his hours much – he just keeps doing twenty hours a week or so, as per the national unwritten accord.[22]

What happens to all that cleaning, dusting, and cooking? Who does it? Where does it go?

Well, in some cases, some of it will be outsourced; the family might hire a cleaner, or eat more takeaway food. But in many cases, the work simply doesn't get done.

One imagines that the houses of these families just end up being grubbier. When women cut back their hours at home, housework is the first thing to go. They hang on to child care for dear life; mothers who increase their paid work hours maintain the same amount of childcare time, usually through cutting back in other areas, like leisure, or sleep.[23]

If houses just end up being dirtier, is that so much of a problem? Well, it depends who you ask.

New York Magazine's Jonathan Chait, in a 2013 essay entitled 'A Really Easy Answer to the Feminist Housework Problem', delivered on his headline promise with this simple recommendation: 'Do less of it.'[24] Chait – a home dad – is irritated by the tenor of debate about household division of labour. 'Viewing housework inequality as entirely a phenomenon of exploitative men free-riding off of female domestic labour makes sense only if you think men derive equal enjoyment from a cleaner and neater home,' he wrote. 'The assumption of much of the feminist commentary surrounding household chores assumes that there is a correct level of cleanliness in a heterosexual relationship, and that level is determined by the female. I think a little cultural relativism would improve the debate.'

Chait himself – by way of declaring his stakeholder interest in this matter – disclosed that in college he had lived 'in a group house with newspapers for carpeting and pizza boxes stacked to the ceiling'. Since marriage, though, he and his wife have settled on a standard: a bit neater than he would keep it, and a bit messier than she'd like.

The Canadian writer Stephen Marche enlarges upon the theme in a recent *New York Times* piece – rather excitingly entitled 'The Case for Filth' – in which he too agitates for grime.[25]

'The ancient Romans would have found Renaissance Europeans disgusting beyond belief (as their Muslim contemporaries did) and certainly my grandmother would find my house filthy,' he argues. 'The standards have changed. There exists no agreed-upon definition of "what has to be done" in a household.'

The solution to housework wars is not only clear, but refreshingly easy, in Marche's view: 'Housework is perhaps the only political problem in which doing less and not caring are the solution, where apathy is the most progressive and sensible attitude,' Marche writes. 'Fifty years ago, it was perfectly normal to iron sheets and to vacuum drapes. They were "necessary" tasks. The solution to the inequality of dusting wasn't dividing the dusting; it was not doing the dusting at all.'

Part of the problem, in the housework wars, is a definitional one. What is housework? And what is the baseline amount of it that needs to be done in order for a household to function without risk of septicaemia, structural collapse, vermin or juvenile delinquency?

To explore this further, I telephoned John Birmingham, who wrote the bible of share-house filth, the 1994 bestseller *He Died with a Felafel in His Hand*.

'This is completely politically incorrect, I know, but I suspect that men just have a much greater tolerance for filth than women do,' Birmingham says. 'For example, as I'm talking to you, I'm looking at two full garbage bags leaned like drunken sailors up against the wall in the entry hall of our house. I'll get around to putting them out sometime today. I'm cool with two giant bags of rubbish blocking the hallway. But I know for a fact that Jane – and most women – would be driven bugshit crazy by those things sitting there all day.'

Birmingham, who works from home, does plenty of housework by average male standards. But he admits that he feels extra heroic when he does it. 'Jane's very lucky in that I quite like ironing,' he says. 'I can put on my podcasts and work away, but even then, I only iron the easy stuff – shirts and jeans and stuff. She's got all these complicated lady-lawyer outfits; I don't go anywhere near that shit. But I'll do two hours of ironing and I'll feel – I feel it right down in my meat – as if it's worth about six months of other stuff.'

The degree of satisfaction after doing a task – or the feeling of martyrdom for having undertaken it at all – is an entirely subjective concept, Birmingham explains: 'A lot of men tend to define taking the kids down the park to kick the footy around as housework,' he says. 'They will see that as exactly as valid as the two hours of laundry that their wife did while they were down there.'

It's true: the definitions of housework and child care can be naggingly elastic. If I lie on a sofa for half an hour reading a book and my children are nearby building a block tower on the rug, for example, my Time Use Survey diary will quite happily accept that as half an hour of child care, every bit as valid as the half hour I spend sorting out their nit problem or making experiments with food colouring, vinegar and bicarbonate of soda. And in fairness, even though I am quite enjoying the book, I am obliged to be there; I couldn't just fang off down the pub, for instance, because I am 'minding' the children and everyone agrees that children need to be minded.

But what about the jobs that not everyone agrees are actually important? Sometimes, when we're going to visit friends, I decide we need to take them some home-made biscuits. The time I spend baking those biscuits is time I would probably – if prompted – record as housework. But Jeremy, who never sees the point of taking biscuits and is rarely an enthusiastic co-sponsor of the pre-visit biscuit-baking project, might have a good argument against including such housework in the register at all.

This asymmetry of belief can – in many households – be the source of much ancillary friction. How can an argument be had over fairness when each party has a different idea of what constitutes the necessary work requiring fair division? Is it fair for party A to be annoyed with party B for not doing half of the window-washing, when party B has never even noticed that the windows were dirty and in any event considers any attempt to wash them as at best Pyrrhic and at worst useless?

Smouldering hostilities may thus be established within two camps; party A is pretty much going to be washing the windows, probably in a sullen fug of silence, scented with the whiff of singed martyr. Party B's prior suspicion that party A is a tiny bit OCD about such matters solidifies – without any need for further discussion – into certainty.

Viewed from space, the world of housework looks pretty clear-cut. Viewed up close, it is a teeming microcosm of unspoken conventions, ancient grievances, and systems of exchange so baroque as to be practically incomprehensible. Here's one, outlined by Marche in his article:

> The mechanism of emptying the dishwasher in my house is typically elaborate. When I cook, my wife tends to be responsible for the dishes. But she hates removing the cutlery from the dishwasher. (To figure out why she hates removing the cutlery would require decades of deep analysis. I do not know.) Therefore emptying the cutlery is my responsibility. So if I unload all the dishes, it's a gift to my wife, but the cutlery is not. It is my marital duty. Every well-managed household is full of such minor insanities.[26]

Aha! This introduces a new and Byzantine complication to the calculus. In a world of assumed responsibility, you get credit for doing things that are viewed as additional to your usual beat, but no credit at all for things that are supposed to be your bag anyway. Hence the display of Yuletide wonder and awe when a school dad constructs a wise man outfit from a Starbucks cup and an old footy jumper, compared to the heartfelt round of indifference when a school mum produces actual gold, frankincense and myrrh, plus a donkey in flawless, anatomically correct papier-mâché. This is her job; to fulfil it adequately is more or less unsurprising. But for him to do it at all carries an element of surprise; that it should be done well is barely imaginable.

Patterns of assumption about responsibility aren't just annoying to the person who is more routinely taken for granted. They are also incredibly important in enforcing forms of behaviour.

Yes, women are more commonly assumed to bear the ultimate responsibility for housework and child care. This should not mean anything to an independently minded couple who live in a bubble. But that generalised assumption (and if you doubt that it exists, have a look at the people who appear in TV advertisements for floor cleaner, toilet cleaner, window cleaner, snap-lock lunch bags, nappies, nappy wipes, baby formula, sliced bread, two-minute noodles – do those people ever have penises?) creates a varying amount of unspoken pressure within a relationship of two otherwise sensible people.

That pressure is due to one reality: if these things are done badly, it is more likely to be seen as the woman's failure. If a child is not properly cared for, or a house is filthy, the opprobrium for such laxity will be directed at first instance to the woman. This explains why women and men might have differing institutional standards of cleanliness. They have differing amounts of skin in the game.

For a man, the question of how clean a floor needs to be is entirely a matter of personal comfort and utility. For a woman, the judgement is a little more nuanced; her own instincts may be leavened by the knowledge that a dirty house will be viewed as her dirty house, not his. Hence, her standards may be artificially inflated by community standards, or the incredibly clean house belonging to her friend up the road, or indeed the incredibly sparkling surfaces over which impeccably manicured TV mum's hands linger lovingly après application of Spray n' Wipe.

Perceptions that child care is ultimately the responsibility of mothers, meanwhile, influences all kinds of behaviour in ways that become obvious the second you start thinking about all this, but are often accepted without comment.

Both fathers and mothers have increased the time they spend in child care across the last few decades. This is mostly because we've all read too many parenting books, and are as a society now less inclined to count an afternoon spent with five other kids setting fire to things down the local tip as acceptable for a nine-year-old. More is expected of parents on both sides now.

But mothers and fathers do different types of child care. Mothers are more likely to do the bits that aren't flexible time-wise: the school run, for instance, or the child-care drop-off and pickup. Breakfast, dinner, bath-time, getting dressed, school lunches; these are all very typical mum jobs, whereas dad jobs are much more likely to include things like play-time, reading stories, sports and so on.

Because raising children is by definition a bewildering exercise, these divisions may be difficult to spot in your average home, where every day is a scramble. But the University of New South Wales professor Lyn Craig, who has spent many years looking at the way Australian parents manage raising children, has established some clear patterns.

One of the significant differences between the child care that women do and the child care than men do is that the woman is much, much more likely to be alone with her child for more of the time. When Craig and a colleague undertook a comparative study in 2011 of Australian parents with Italian, Danish and French parents, one of the most obvious distinctions, across all countries, was that mothers did a lot more by themselves.[27]

In their benchmark Australian family (two parents, working dad, no university qualifications, one child aged under four), the mother did eighteen times as much solo care as her husband, who was alone with his children very rarely.[28] The child care a woman does is more likely to enable her spouse to go out and do other things. But her husband's child care is overwhelmingly likely to be done while she's still there.

This doesn't mean that the stuff dads do is worthless, or that it's irrelevant; of course not. What it does mean, though, is that while 'shared parenting' is an extremely popular concept, the detail as to who does exactly what – and when – can still add up to a fairly restrictive arrangement.

A few years ago, a colleague of mine was overheard at work telling his buddies: 'Sorry, can't make the pub tonight. I'm babysitting!' A female workmate chimed in, dryly: 'Mate. You do know that it's not babysitting if it's your own kid, right?' And that's correct. It's not baby-sitting if it's your own kid. But the way women and men look after children in Australia absolutely reinforces the idea that it's mothers who are responsible for looking after children, and fathers who are helpers.

There are many implicit daily tests for this proposition. Whose responsibility is it to organise babysitting, if you're going out? If a child gets sick at school, who goes to the rescue? Who is responsible for organising holiday activi-ties? If both parents have a work commitment that clashes with a dentist visit or sports day, who is ultimately the person who will reschedule? And, most significantly, who pays for child care?

When mothers are making the decision about when or whether to go back to work, you will often hear something along the lines of: 'Well, I would like to go back to work, but my salary would barely cover the childcare fees, so we decided against it.' A tiny little part of me goes a tiny little bit crazy when I hear this. Not because I am enraged by the prospect of women staying out of the workforce in order to look after their kids; far from it. It's a perfectly reasonable thing to do, because of all the non-economic advantages such an arrangement entails. I also think it's entirely reasonable for men to do it. It just fascinates me that childcare expenses are automatically hypothecated against a mother's income. What other household expense is tied directly to one household member's earning capacity in this way? I can't think of another example. You don't hear women saying: 'Yeah, well, we'd love to live in a house, but my salary doesn't cover the mortgage, so we've decided to live in a tent in Centennial Park instead, just till things pick up a bit.'

I know, I know; it's a cost-benefit analysis, and an immediate one. When the decision is about whether a woman will go back to paid work, it's her job that hangs in the balance, and her salary that is stacked up against the childcare fees that will be incurred, should she choose to earn that salary. They are hinged together by the economic decision facing the household. I get that.

But cost-benefit analyses are regularly a close-run thing in matters of household strategy. People continue to buy houses even in ruinously overheated markets. Or spend vast amounts of money on private school educations, sometimes going in to debt or substantial short-term adversity to do so. They buy cars they can't afford. They put themselves in hock up to the eyeballs to establish a small business they believe in. Why? Because they have faith that the benefits, in the long term, will outweigh the up-front costs. But the calculations about women's salaries often exist in a different strategic space. A woman who takes leave from work to have a baby and then elects not to go back to work at all gives up more than the ticket value of the immediate salary she would have recovered on her return. She gives up her capacity to win further advancement. She gives up the personal professional relationships and networks that might otherwise have yielded opportunities for promotion. The salary foregone is far, far greater than the figure punched in to the household calculator at the point when the decision is made. Such is the cost of human assumptions.

Like I said at the beginning of this chapter, averages have their limitations. Every household is different in its own way, whether it's a bloke who actually likes ironing, or a woman who has an inexplicable fear of removing cutlery from the dishwasher. But the broader patterns of the Australian home are so distinct as to be undeniable; women, and especially mothers, do more housework than men. They do more housework than men even when they also have full-time paid jobs. And men do less housework than women, even if they're not working at all.

This is the wife drought's strange and seemingly unshakeable grip on us all. In an average Australian family, a woman will commonly behave like a housewife even if she isn't one. And a man will behave as though he's married to a housewife, even when he isn't.

5

A QUESTION OF COMPETENCE

I am standing in the kitchen of the man who is about to become Australia's twenty-eighth prime minister. He is throwing together a casual barbecue dinner; salmon for me, steak for him. He is lovingly, if inexpertly, encasing my salmon in foil. He gets some butter on a knife and butters the fish. After the fish has received its unguent coating, there is some fishy butter left over. He reaches to scrape it back into the butter dish. The salad-preparing Abbott girls – as tensed for paternal clangers as the Rudd progeny are for the electronic clack of an iPhone selfie – stare at what he's doing, eyes widened in discreet horror. 'Dad!'

This is a campaign of dad moments. Kevin Rudd's targeted use of the Aussie vernacular implies a rigorous, retrospective immersion course of *Kingswood Country* back episodes. His latter-day attachment to the building blocks of social media – the selfie, the Tweet – evoke the same feelings of complex affection and horror as are experienced by adults whose parents sign up for Facebook for the first time. Anyone who has been 'poked' on Facebook by their mother-in-law will immediately know what I mean.

And every day there's a new dad moment from the Abbott camp: Tony at a press conference heartily congratulating his candidate for Lindsay on her sex appeal, Tony hollering his encouragement to his daughter 'Go Bridgey babe!' during a staged netball game, Tony winking as a pensioner tells him she is working on an adult sex line to make ends meet. This is mild to borderline stuff; conduct that might win you a chilly audience before some kind of formal mediator if attempted in the workplace, and a spell on the back verandah if ventured at a family barbie. But they don't do him too much harm.

It's funny what people notice out of a show like *Kitchen Cabinet*. Sometimes I'll get a torrent of outraged correspondence about something I genuinely haven't noticed at the time. When the Abbott episode goes to air, for instance, the hottest topics turn out to be the fact that his kitchen fridge only has a two-star energy rating (this had escaped me entirely) and the fact that he prepared fish for me, and steak for himself. 'Fish for the lady, and steak for the man! What is this, 1956?' tweeted one horrified viewer. I did point out, several times, that he cooked fish for me as a courtesy, because I don't eat things with legs.

But the fact that the prime-minister-to-be was not, shall we say, at his competent best in the kitchen was not particularly widely remarked upon. The fish-buttering, which to me was extremely memorable, did not provoke significant comment.

Modern political image control is ceaselessly, twitchily alive to the risk of appearing incompetent in public. Media advisers take a hyper-conservative approach with their candidates: don't use chopsticks before the cameras, in case it turns out you're not as good with them as you thought. For God's sake, don't dance. Don't try a sport you're not familiar with. Don't arm-wrestle anyone. Don't chop wood.

But for men, there is a definite exemption for incompetence in the kitchen. The prime minister's fish-buttering – like Joe Hockey's appearance on our programme, in which the now-treasurer served an entrée of Dippity-Bix, could not find the drawer with the knives, and visibly blanched in fear when handed an iceberg lettuce – did him no harm at all.

These instances are clearly distinguishable from the national round of horror and garment-rending that ensued when Julia Gillard was, in 2005, photographed in her kitchen next to an empty fruit-bowl.

Gillard's empty fruit-bowl was not a sign of hypocrisy, nor had she been caught out. She has spent years in politics cheerfully acknowledging her complete uselessness in the face of anything culinarily north of a buttered Salada. I remember her telling me – in her customary self-deprecating drawl – about an incident in 2002 in which her electorate staff, rather evilly, had auctioned off a 'Dinner for Six at Julia Gillard's House' for a fundraiser. Gillard wheedled a friend into coming round to cook for the event, and had just cleared a large volume of papers from her dining table in advance of the guests' arrival when Labor leader Simon Crean – then her close ally – rang for a chat.

Cradling the phone twixt ear and shoulder, she groped around under the sink for something to clean the table with, and had squirted a generous amount of what she thought was furniture polish all over the wooden table before – in full declamatory flight on some question of political strategy or other – she looked down and realised she'd just coated the table with oven cleaner.

Male incompetence in the kitchen is almost a recommendation, from which it can be calmly inferred that the chap in question has better things to do: run the country, understand what the non-accelerating inflation rate of unemployment is, and so forth.

Female incompetence in the kitchen, however, carries with it a certain implicit suggestion of aridity, of a humanity strangled in some way that is not right, as Julia Gillard discovered. She is the only politician we've asked to appear on *Kitchen Cabinet* who consistently refused. She can't cook, and was not keen to pretend she could, or be filmed being rubbish at it. She realised, I imagine, that she would not be extended the indulgence of a dad moment.

Dad moments are rather a fascinating phenomenon. They celebrate instances of lovable male incompetence. Being unable to boil an egg, or get through a standard press conference without mildly sexually harassing a colleague, becomes a forehead-slapping occasion for a certain brand of fond ruefulness: oh, you devil, you. Dad moments are moments in which it's okay to be howlingly bad at something – in fact, it's more than okay. It's a good thing.

Dad moments are a powerful national force. Channel Seven's breakfast host David Koch, whose smart-but-daggy presentation style is supplemented by a constant Twitter-stream of dad jokes, is one of the nation's favourite broadcasters.

The 'Mere Male' column in *New Idea* has been published every week since its debut on 15 March 1950. It serves as a sort of national Dad Moment *Hansard*, and the tone and content – I gauge from the weirdly addictive compendium of Mere Male's first thirty years that I acquired from eBay at an extremely competitive price recently – have changed very little over the decades.

'I was sick in bed but feeling rather hungry,' reports Ginny, from Auckland. 'MM was rattling round in the kitchen and told me there was no need to get up and get the tea. He did – his own!'[1]

A correspondent from Shepparton offers this: 'As I ate lunch at my boyfriend's house, his mother remarked that he had made the salad. As soon as she began to eat it, she shrieked, "Are you sure you washed the lettuce properly?" "Yes!" MM replied. "I even used soap!"'

Ay-Mee, of Glen Waverley, chimes in: 'A very excited MM greeted me on my return from shopping. "They delivered your new automatic washer and I have done the washing for you, love," he told me. "The cycle is finishing now." So it was. There was just one snag – the dear man had forgotten to put the clothes in!'

Dad moments tend to involve near-criminal degrees of incompetence in an area largely independent from his professional life: household matters or, at a pinch, inter-personal relations. 'Dad! You forgot to fix the brake pads on the bus and now all those school children are horribly maimed! You crazy knucklehead!' is not a dad moment.

But 'Dad! You can't iron a shirt while it's ON YOU!' most certainly is.

I've always been fascinated by women's eagerness to write in to *New Idea* with these stories. How is having a husband who is thoughtless, or a domestic dunderplunken, anything to write home about? Mere Male is – as the publishers note in the foreword to my 1981 compendium addition – 'almost an institution within the structure of our society. While he has been around since the colonials decided to call themselves Aussies, his exploits have been reported faithfully by wives, mothers, friends and lovers every week for thirty-one years in *New Idea*. And despite this, he endures still.'

Mere Male has pottered along happily for more than sixty years now, soaping up lettuce leaves and popping electric kettles on hotplates, largely unmolested by the vast social changes that have occurred around him in that time. Feminism has not starved him of habitat, nor has political correctness done much to reconstruct him. His quaint antiquity itself is compelling.

In fact, the continuing existence of Mere Male is a valuable piece of anthropological evidence. The fact that a man trying and failing to do housework is still funny demonstrates how deeply we still believe that domestic work is a female sphere of competence. And there is nothing funnier, in the annals of comedic formula, as the 'Fish out of water' story.

Just ask Hollywood. It's funny when a kid inhabits an adult's body (*Big*, *Freaky Friday*, etc.). It's funny when a tough Aussie jackaroo ends up in slick New York (*Crocodile Dundee*). It's funny when an African chieftain is obliged to adapt to American life (*Coming to America*).

And above all, it's funny when a man is left to look after children. It's funny, because it's still kind of unusual.

There are two distinct types of full-time screen dads: Widower Dad, and The Bumbler. Hollywood is historically cautious when it depicts a man looking after his own children. Usually, there has to be a good reason for the mom not being around, and often the writers just take the cleanest route – killing her before the movie even starts. This approach has several advantages. Obviously, it saves on actors' wages. And it means viewers don't feel awkward the way they might if the mom was just at work or something. Plus, it leaves the dad uncomplicatedly free to date Cameron Diaz.

Dads whose wives have been killed are definitely the pick of the Hollywood fathers. They are wise (Gregory Peck in *To Kill a Mockingbird*), sensitive (Liam Neeson in *Love Actually*) and usually handsome (both of the above, plus Jude Law in *The Holiday*). This Widower Super-Dad meme also extends to animals, including fish: Nemo's dad, for instance, who trails his son all over the ocean, was widowed in dramatic circumstances when his wife was attacked fatally by a barracuda.

The death-rate among screen mothers who get hitched to warm, sensitive, handsome fathers and then conveniently expire is actually getting to a point where screen-marrying Jude Law should carry some sort of government health warning.

But Hollywood offers another, much dicier variety of Hands-On Dad. He's the Bumbler. The Bumbler's primary carer status is much less likely to come about due to spousal death; usually, it's conferred by some kind of Act-of-God-style external event.

Redundancy or recession is a popular one (*Mr. Mom*, *Daddy Day Care*), but occasionally it gets more exotic, like in *Three Men and a Baby*, where the chaps just find an infant on the doorstep (a development which seems to arouse negligible interest among responsible authorities). Or Gru, the unlikely dad in the animated hit *Despicable Me*, who borrows three girls from an orphanage (another maternal mortality event, alas) in order to exploit them for his nefarious schemes, but ends up bungling his way into adoring them. These dads are seriously clueless, and their ineptitude is the central source of laughs. The children may as well be puppets in these films.

Humour really is an incredibly useful diagnostic social tool. It's okay to laugh at a man being bad at bringing up kids or cooking, because it's not really an insult; we don't expect him to be good at either of those things.

All this explains why Mere Male is funny. But how does it explain why women are so prepared to expose the incompetence of their partners or sons, when in so doing they identify themselves firmly as the type of boob who would rather pick up after her husband all her life than teach him how to use a washing machine?

Perhaps it's because the existence of a spouse who is helpless in a particular field serves gently to enhance the status of the more expert spouse. Thus, a woman whose husband cannot boil an egg is – one subtly intuits – a woman who runs such a tight ship that boiled eggs are available to that husband around the clock, within minutes, without him needing to lift a finger. Just as it once was a male status symbol to have a wife who 'didn't need to work', it remains to some degree a female status symbol to have a husband who is charmingly unable to shop, or cook, or iron. The incompetence of her husband is actually a demonstration of her own super-competence.

Rebecca Meisenbach, in her 2009 paper 'The Female Breadwinner', ventured the theory that women who earn more than their husbands may exaggerate their husbands' incompetence in the home in order to retain a strong feminine identity despite their 'unorthodox' domestic arrangements.[2] A majority of the female breadwinners Meisenbach interviewed reported that they retained control over the housework. They either did it themselves or they directed their husbands to do the jobs that needed to be done. But even when they got the husbands to do the chores, they reserved the right to complain that he wasn't very good at it. Or to make generalised comments about how men just aren't as tidy, or don't notice when things need doing. 'By highlighting stories of how the men have to be told or asked to do specific chores in the home, these female bread-winners still fit gender boundaries of a wife as someone who manages the home and children,' Meisenbach wrote.

This certainly gels with the phenomenon from the last chapter, in which women pick up more housework again as they earn a greater proportion of the household's income. It seems crazy. Why would you deliberately hold on to chores?

And then I realised that I do exactly the same thing. As I'm writing this, I'm also using another part of my brain to plan the next forty-eight hours, during which period I will be interstate at a conference. I will be away for two nights.

I've planned what will be for dinner for those nights. I've cooked enough fried rice for everyone, and left the makings of another meal ready in the fridge. I have also procured some easy lunchbox items so school lunch will be easier for Jeremy to put together.

This is not because Jeremy cannot cook. He is a good cook. Nor does he, as far as I am aware, have any special impairment in the 'lunch box assembly' part of the brain. So why do I think it's necessary to carry on like he needs special help with these basic tasks? If someone trailed around me at work, pre-writing articles for me, I'd probably feel like punching them within about twenty minutes. Certainly, I'd find it patronising.

But that's how this works: it's okay to assume men are incompetent at domestic tasks, even if it would be quite offensive for the diametrically opposite assumption – that women are incompetent at work – to be vocalised in public.

Which is why you don't see the *Economist*, say, publishing a cheeky weekly column called 'Fragrantly Female', in which dopey women executives are fondly documented.

Imagine it: 'FF – newly appointed chief financial officer – appeared at a board meeting with her CEO to provide a detailed briefing on the company's expansion plans. She was tapping away at her laptop, but exclaimed "YES!" when the CEO mentioned that some redundancies would probably be a part of the company's five-year plan. The chairman turned to her, puzzled. "Do you have something to say, Miss Brown?" FF blushed. "Sorry," she mumbled. "I just won this great handbag on eBay!"' John Topjob, Hunters Hill.

And you don't see movies whose central gag is a woman going to work. This is partly because we actually don't see women in the workforce as unusual any more. Women have infiltrated the workplace to a much greater extent. There may be a great howling dearth of women near the top of the heap, but down around middle-management level there are plenty of women, so most workplaces are accustomed to having ladies around. Women at work, it's now finally fair to say, are not remarkable. But a man turning up to a mothers' group is still remarkable, and consequently a viable subject for situation comedy.

Just incidentally, movies continue to present a skewed version not only of what women do but also of how many of us tend to be around the place as a general matter of course. Researchers at the Geena Davis Institute on Gender in Media (yes, I know, but this is interesting, I promise) watched 129 top-grossing family movies released between 2006 and 2011, and found that women only had 28.3 per cent of speaking roles. The researchers also totted up the percentage of women who had powerful or significant screen jobs, and found that they constituted only 3.4 per cent of screen CEOs, 4.5 per cent of high-level screen politicians, and 21.9 per cent of screen doctors. They constituted zero per cent of investors and developers.[3]

Movies are commercial undertakings, with a rock-solid financial incentive to appeal to the viewing audience's existing prejudices rather than shaking them up. Poking fun at someone doing something different isn't just safe; it's also more likely to be profitable.

The other reason it's still perfectly acceptable for women to disparage men's domestic competence is because the domestic sphere is gloriously unregulated. Extensive sex discrimination laws make it illegal to express – in the workplace – the view that chicks are hopeless. Workplaces are regulated; anyone circulating a series of ribald tales of serial female incompetence at work can look forward to a lengthy and potentially quite upsetting encounter with the relevant workplace tribunal.

Homes, though, are a free-speech stomping ground, which means that any woman can whine at length about how bad men as a general class are at picking up dirty laundry, replacing caps on toothpaste tubes, or organising children for school, without feeling that they are committing any sort of offence against the broad notion of gender equality.

My panic-cooking to compensate for an imminent absence, with its casual implied assumption that my partner is a simpleton who cannot make a Vegemite sandwich unsupervised, is exactly the sort of high-handed and patronising conduct that would annoy a woman at work, were all the circumstances reversed. I imagine myself obliged to mount a defence before the Human Rights and Equal Opportunity Tribunal.

'Your Honour, I do accept that in making these meals ahead, I may have created a circumstance from which the complainant may have inferred I thought him incompetent. On reflection, I also understand that my fried rice – well-intentioned as it was – might have interfered with any independently formulated plans the complainant may himself have made, including but not limited to pasta carbonara, which the kids really like. But in my defence, I always do the lunches. And I know how annoying it is to have three starving kids milling about and whining while you're trying to cook dinner from scratch. Your Honour: I meant well.'

Is there something else involved, though? Is there a Meisenbachian hidden bid for power in my meal prep? I think it's a bit more complicated than that. If I'm honest with myself, I think the fuss I make about going away (making a footy-team-sized lasagne, finding presents for the kids for my return, and so on) is partly to create the plausible illusion that my absence is an unusual event – a blip in what is otherwise a blameless and sustained maternal presence. This is, of course, ridiculous; I go away overnight for work at least once a month, and everybody copes. But I would rather flap about in an overstressed and rather inaccurate demonstration that I do it all than simply vacate the field to someone else who is actually capable of replacing me. At one level I don't want to be replaced, because I don't want anybody else to be *as good at it as I am*. Also, I feel guilty about leaving. And staying up until 1 am to cook meals when I've got to be on a 7 am flight feels like appropriate penance.

This is what 'Mum moments' tend to be – moments of supercharged and twanging overcompetence, in which the heroine dashes about, rescheduling appointments with one hand and steering a toddler bike with the other, offsetting the resultant hike in blood pressure with the soothing balm of martyrdom. *Look how much I got done at once. I must be doing something right.*

I was once asked to speak in a debate about workplace flexibility and whether it was or wasn't the key to equality. It's a subject I'm very interested in, obviously, so I was looking forward to it.

By the time the actual date for the debate rolled around, though, I was in serious overload. I had a standard busy work week, plus a nasty cluster of speeches I had foolishly agreed to deliver, and a houseful of visitors in town for my brother-in-law's birthday, for which I had agreed to bake a birthday cake. It was also my daughter's birthday. So when I sat down to write a speech about work–life balance the night before the debate, I found myself in such a state of exhaustion that I burst into tears.

In the end, I went to the debate and just told the story of my stupid week, including the moment at the end of it where assembling some thoughts on flexible working turned out to be the task that tipped me over into panic attack.

Afterwards, I fell into conversation with Marian Baird, who is one of Australia's pre-eminent experts in the area of women and work; a woman of such pulsating intelligence that I always feel a little under-researched when I am around her. Compulsively, I apologised for backloading my contribution to the debate with tales of 'my own domestic incompetence'. She looked at me evenly. 'Tales of competence, don't you mean?'

And she was quite right, of course. I had thought I was being self-deprecating. But actually, viewed in retrospect, without the mitigating context of panic, I see that what I was actually doing in that speech was boasting. Check out how amazing I am. I can do all this stuff at once. And still turn up with my hair brushed.

I also met Lisa Annese that night – she is the possessor of the best mum moment I have ever come across, bar none. Lisa is the CEO of the Diversity Council Australia.

She came back to work for the organisation when – not long after the birth of her third child – she was promoted.

Shortly after starting her new job, Lisa was required to be on a 5.30 am conference call with experts based in New York, Singapore and Utah. It was all going swimmingly until she heard – elsewhere in the house – a commotion of some kind break out. Kids shrieking, joined swiftly by the frenzied yapping of the family dog. Lisa manipulated the phone's mute button strategically, so as to minimise the audibility to her international colleagues of this mounting, and at this stage unclassified, family crisis. The shrieking escalated. It was coming in waves now. Suddenly, the dog plunged into Lisa's office, barking hysterically. Diving under the desk, it became entangled in the nest of cords and leads there and, despite Lisa's best efforts with the mute button, the sounds of the hysterical chihuahua began to bleed across into the transatlantic calm of the teleconference.

Then the children started coming in. At first, they tried – in the face of stern shushing from their mother – to express in rudimentary sign language what was going on outside. Then they came back with bits of paper on which explanatory messages had been hastily scrawled in a juvenile hand. Increasingly concerned for her international credibility, Lisa waved them away. Finally, Lisa's second daughter re-entered, carrying the maimed remains of a baby guinea pig. It turns out one of the family's guinea pigs had been – unbeknownst to all – pregnant. The delivery of the babies had been the first source of excitement outside; the next was the father's surprise decision to celebrate the event by partially eating one of the babies. Lisa silently absorbed this development, while continuing to be a full participant in the business of the meeting.

A final delegation of children delivered a written ultimatum about five minutes later: 'We've named the baby Coconut, and we're having the funeral NOW.'

'I got through the meeting,' Lisa recalls. 'I have no idea what they thought of me.'

Now, she says, she has learned to stop worrying about her private life bleeding into her work life. 'I'm not apologetic about anything any more. If I'm in a doctor's surgery with my kid, taking the call, I'll say where I am. I find once you stop apologising, people stop expecting you to apologise.'

Compartmentalising work and family responsibilities so as to display a flawless face of competence to both worlds is a common female tactic. Lisa recalls a fellow executive – also a mother – telling her: 'When I go and pick my kids up from school, I always walk out with a briefcase so it looks like I'm going to a meeting.'

But what does this tactic achieve? Usually, the privilege of going crazy in the echoing privacy of your own skull, with no one else but you understanding exactly how hard you're actually working.

In October 2013, I filled in for Leigh Sales for a few weeks as host of *7.30*. One of the weeks was a special kind of hell; I flew with the children to Adelaide at the weekend so they could hang out with their grandparents while I spoke at my old school, did three sessions at the Adelaide Festival of Ideas, then on Sunday my mother and I and the baby drove to Port Pirie – shrieking with laughter at my idiocy in having got myself into this mess – for a speech to the SA Rural Women's Gathering, before packing everyone up and heading back to Sydney for another week of *7.30*. I had agreed months earlier to speak at a dinner for the Sydney University Debating Union, so Tuesday found me cursingly, at 8 pm, after a gruelling day and a live interview with the treasurer, climbing into a frock and a cab, and heading for the university.

The event was in full swing when I got there; beautifully dressed young men and women tossing aphorisms at each other. I accepted a glass of champagne and tried to perk up, while making conversation with a charming young man. I explained why I was late: work, too many children, and so on. 'You must be busy!' he chirped. 'Still – I guess you can't be that busy, if you've got time to come and speak to us!'

I felt a bit sick when he said that. But it was a useful thing to hear. It made me realise that my obsession with super-competency – my determination not to break engagements and to simply absorb pressure indefinitely – was nobody's fault but my own. Who could I blame for this beside myself? Whose fault was it that I was entering my sixteenth waking hour for the day doing a favour for a bunch of people to whom I owed absolutely nothing? Why would this kid ever realise that getting here nearly broke me? Why should he? What was I expecting? A tiara? Given that I had bent over backwards to make the whole thing look easy, why should I feel aggrieved that someone took me at my word?

The smiling face of female super-competence is an advertising regular. The Harpic ad campaign for its 'Two-In-One' toilet freshener tablets opens with the mother of a newborn receiving a surprise visit from a swarm of buddies. 'Can I use your loo?' one of them asks. The woman's face creases in horror. What if it's not clean? But then, her brow clears. Of course! Thank the baby Jesus, she has had the foresight to hook a gaudily coloured compacted brick of baking soda and overpowering lavender-fragrance over the ceramic lip of her dunny, so she's totally in the clear. Whew! 'What does your loo say about you?' inquires the ad cheekily, as a closer.

One would hope the most a loo would say about a person is that that person has mastered peristalsis. But this is the home, where key performance indicators are not listed in the employment contract. And nature abhors a vacuum.

In November 2012, British supermarket chain Asda broadcast a commercial in which a smiling blonde super-mum prepares for her family Christmas. Against an upbeat soundtrack, the camera tracks her as she buys a tree, strings lights, wraps awkwardly shaped presents, bastes a turkey, peels potatoes, chocks a wobbly table up with books, makes beds, installs festive napery, is roused at dawn by squealing children, prepares lunch single-handedly, allocates herself the footstool at the corner of the table when the chairs run out, then concludes as she stands happily, at the end of the day, surveying a silver paper-strewn lounge room in which a dozing mass of humanity satedly watches TV, and smiles. 'It doesn't just happen by magic!' advises the voiceover. 'Behind every great Christmas, there's Mum. And behind Mum, there's Asda.'

After a number of complaints, Asda issued a partial apology in which it acknowledged some people were upset by the stereotyping in the ad, but insisted they had had a lot of positive feedback.

'We do two things to women in advertising,' says advertising creative director Dee Madigan. 'We play on their insecurity about their looks, and we play on their guilt about their children; if you love your children, you'll keep them safe from germs with this new disposable wipe.'

Among men, though, the dad bungler is as common in advertising as he is in the movies. Kia's 2010 ad for its Sportage wagon features a tracksuited dad cruising the streets miming to a Grandmaster Flash song. His reverie intensifies as members of the actual band materialise and rap along with him, and by the time he eases the car into a suburban driveway, he's developed a serious White Man Overbite. At this point, his wife, a drained-looking blonde woman holding a garden hose, with which she is seemingly using her last drops of human optimism to water some shrubs, asks him unsmilingly, 'Did you get the nappies?' He grimaces: 'Ah. The nappies!'

Men and nappies. In the advertising world, the nappy is a vile nemesis to modern man. It is Apollo Creed to his Rocky Balboa. It is Gollum to his Frodo Baggins. Its ways confound him. Its velcro tabs are a tactical labyrinth. Its sizing system is a Rosetta stone of incomprehensibility. Its posse of baffling accessories (scented disposal bags, pilchers, wipes with or without perfume and moisturiser) may as well have been designed by a vengeful ex for all the comfort they bring to modern man in advertising.

Huggies – one of the most recognisable global faces of Big Nappy – in 2012 aired an expensive TV ad campaign in the US, in which the company announced it had put its product 'to the toughest test imaginable: dads. Alone with their babies. In one house. For five days.' The ad featured highlights of dads racing about with soiled toddlers held aloft, and watching entire sports games while their kids dragged about in dirty pants.

In this case, there was an immediate backlash against the ad's outdated and insulting attitudes. 'Kimberly-Clark also makes products that are used by doctors during surgical procedures,' read one online petition. 'Would they ever feel that advertising those products based on "The Ultimate Test: Female Surgeons" was in any way appropriate? Would they defend it as actually "celebrating" the important role of women in the medical field? No. Never.'[4]

So many parents wrote in to the company's Facebook page complaining about the ad's outdated assumptions that Huggies staged an immediate and unconditional surrender. The company scrubbed all evidence of the 'Dads watch sport while their kids wallow in ordure' sequence and replaced it with adorable footage of dads giving their kids a bottle and rocking them to sleep. 'To prove Huggies can handle anything, we asked real dads to put them to the test. With their own babies!' the new ad burblingly announced.

The oldest defence in the book to this kind of stuff is that women are just better at babies.

In 2013, when British journalist Peter Hitchens was a guest on the ABC's *Q&A* programme, he denounced feminism for remaining silent on the modern exploitation of women in poorly paid jobs while continuing to engage in 'ceaseless denigration of the most important and responsible task most of us will ever do . . . the raising of the next generation'.

'Wait!' interrupted another guest, the US writer Hanna Rosin, author of the menacingly titled *The End of Men* and very likely near the top of Mr Hitchens' hit-list of problem feminists. 'Why do the women have to do it if it's such an important job?'

'Should I tell you a very simple reason why?' asked Hitchens, not for the first time that evening raising his voice to be heard over a mutinous rumble from the *Q&A* crowd. 'It may not apply to you, but in a lot of cases: they're better at it. Anybody who's been involved in raising children knows that women are better at it.'[5]

Ah. I feel this is a question we have been dancing around. Are women better at it? Are they just more competent at bringing up children? Is that why they end up doing more of it?

It's a tricky one to answer. It might well be that in some sort of Nappy Olympiad or Structured Playoffs, mothers would thump fathers. But does that mean women are inherently better at all this stuff than men are? Or does it just mean they get more practice? I think I am a good writer. I can write a thousand-word column in a couple of hours and, in most circumstances, I would back it to be a better column than one drawn at random from a small group of average Australians, so long as that group didn't include Laura Tingle or anything. But I was pretty rubbish when I started being a writer. And as much as I might privately fancy myself as the repository of some sort of innate gift, the truth is far less comfortable: the fact that I am good at writing is not entirely unrelated to the fact that, in professional terms, I do nothing else the whole time.

When men and women produce a baby together for the first time, it's an absolute festival of mutual incompetence. Unless you're one of those people who has raised younger siblings as your own or had direct experience in a child-care centre, odds are you will have no idea – regardless of your chromosomal configuration – which way up the damn baby goes.

When Jeremy and I had our first child, we were in London, where the National Health Service favours a brisk release-to-the-wild system for newborns and their radically underqualified parents. We were given our discharge forms when Audrey was six hours old, at which point we wrapped her with inexpert reverence in rugs, carried her to the car park and then stood around for approximately ninety minutes arguing over how the baby capsule fitted into the car we had rented for the occasion, during which time I swear I saw the baby trying discreetly to flag down other more experienced passers-by. Eventually we jerry-rigged the thing and drove home, whereupon it was discovered no one knew anything at all about what to do with babies. We had tickets for a Yo La Tengo gig just up the road, and actually considered taking the baby along. That's how dumb we were.

How do men and women get from this situation of mutual incompetence to one in which it is wordlessly assumed that the chick is better at babies? Let's not pretend this is a simple 'Men want to get out of it; women get conned into it' situation. Expertise in parenting is like expertise in absolutely anything else; you collect it as you go along. And when one parent is given early opportunities to amass competence (let's call this parent, for ease of reference, 'the one with the breasts') then that parent quickly becomes the expert. And once that person is the expert – the one with a legitimate initiation into the arcane world of colic and settling and swaddling and all of that seriously non-intuitive stuff – then it takes quite a bit of application for the other parent to keep up. It's like – oh, I don't know – being a woman executive in a company where all the training sessions are held over lunch in a local topless bar. It's technically possible to remain competitive in that environment, it's just not terribly easy. And before you know it, because life is busy, and because humans cleave towards economic efficiency in most technical areas with the possible exception of automotive manufacturing, you'll hear this: 'That's not how you do it! Oh, for God's sake. Give it here. We haven't got all day.'

One of the most common responses to having a baby is the feeling that you, and only you, truly understand just how momentous this feeling is, just how extraordinary this particular mewling infant is, and just how completely all previous perceptions have been atomised by this small and needy hostage to fortune.

Which makes it doubly ironic that this is – of all life's junctures – the one at which men and women are most apt to default to incredibly conventional approaches. This is the beauty of humanity; our ability to form broad and reliable social patterns while staunchly maintaining the belief in our own originality. Dad will go back to work, while Mum pursues her new area of expertise. You might hear things like: 'Oh, yeah, Patrick is really keen to have some time away from work with the baby, but his job's super busy at the moment. We're definitely going to split things evenly, but it makes more sense for me to do the home stuff right now; it's his turn next time!' And next time Patrick will be earning more, and it will make even less sense for him to take time out, and in any event he won't be the parent who knows what to do with Farex, and on it goes. Social patterns might be as big as the Northern Lights, but we only see them in our own time; and by the time we realise how deeply we fuel them, it's already too late.

In these circumstances, there are plenty of people besides Peter Hitchens with an interest in women being 'better at it' than men. For a father ceding nappy duty – whether in puzzlement or guilty relief – it's a comfort to know he's leaving things to the expert. And for a mother seeking a rational underpinning to her new existence, which might otherwise be all aswim in a hormonal soup of existential fears and delights, 'I'm better at it' is as good a stake in the ground as any.

What would happen if we could artificially extend that initial period of equal-opportunity incompetence? If we could keep mothers and fathers at the same level of expertise just that little bit longer? Would it help to keep both parents more involved?

This is the point at which we turn, with a practised sense of resignation, to Norway. Damn those Norwegians, with their foresight and sensitivity, with their well-timed sovereign wealth fund to intelligently invest the proceeds of their resources boom (we blew ours on big tellies) and their relentlessly high quality of life. Wouldn't you know? It was Norway that in 1993 introduced a coercive model of paternal leave that actually pushed men into taking time off.

Norway already had a generous paid parental leave system, and since 1977 it had been available to fathers too. But only 3 per cent of fathers were taking it. So in 1993, the Norwegian government decreed that a chunk of the standard paid parental leave would only be paid if it was the dad taking the time off.[6]

This system rather fiendishly re-engineered the assumption that men's primary usefulness in the early days of parenthood was as a provider. By introducing a 'use-it-or-lose-it' financial benefit, the Norwegian system means that fathers who fail to take leave are worse off financially, rather than better. For a few weeks at least, the compulsion to provide is working with the concept of hands-on fathering, rather than against it as is usually the case.

Today, 90 per cent of Norwegian fathers take paternity leave. And fathers spend on average an hour a day more on child care and family time than they did ten years ago, and two hours a day more than they did in 1970.[7]

The Norwegian experience suggests that men and women can both be good at bringing up children, depending on the options and incentives, and the opportunities they have to get in at the ground level. Of course, they also have bullet-proof child care, which helps.

But even in Australia, where paternal leave is significantly less evolved than the Scandinavian model, there is evidence that for fathers, taking time out of work early on makes them more engaged parents in the long term.

Australian fathers who took ten or more days off work around the birth of their child were more likely to be involved in childcare-related activities when their children were toddlers. Only 19.3 per cent of fathers who hadn't taken paternal leave put their toddlers to bed regularly, for instance, but that rose to 27.9 per cent among dads who had taken ten days or more, according to a 2013 OECD study of four countries including Australia.[8]

We have historically looked at paid parental leave as a measure to increase women's participation in the workplace; more recently, Prime Minister Tony Abbott has talked about his paid parental leave scheme not as a welfare measure, but as an employment entitlement like any other.

What if we looked at things the other way up, though? And saw paid parental leave as a way of giving fathers the chance to become expert at looking after babies at the same time mothers do?

Our system doesn't just allow fathers to be hopeless. It expects them to be. It encourages them to be. And it is perpetually surprised when they aren't.

6

WHAT'S A
WIFE WORTH?

Edith Brown was fifteen years old when her father was hanged. It was 1876.

Her mother had died in childbirth when Edith was seven, and the young girl was sent off promptly thereafter to a Perth boarding school run by the Misses Cowan. But even as Edith undertook her education, her father – pastoralist Kenneth Brown – addressed himself assiduously to his own self-destruction, drinking himself into madness, beggaring himself on the horses and eventually shooting dead his second wife, Mary Tindall, a crime for which he was crisply sentenced to the ultimate sanction then available under Western Australian law.

Now, one might ordinarily expect a teenager subjected to such Gothic detail in her early years to take things relatively quietly for a bit. But Edith rallied. Three years after her father's execution, she married James Cowan, the brother of her schoolmistresses. They had four daughters and a son, between which happy events Edith also immersed herself deeply in charitable work, and in 1921, much to everyone's surprise and by a margin of only forty-six votes, Edith Cowan became the first woman to be elected to any Parliament in Australia.

When I say 'to everyone's surprise', I include Edith, and most certainly I include the man she deposed in the seat of West Perth, Mr Thomas Draper, who was WA's attorney-general at the time, and had moreover been primarily responsible for the legislation allowing women to run for Parliament in the 1921 election in the first place. Mrs Cowan's election remains a small but reverberant matter of national pride; keep in mind, another twenty-three years would pass before Frenchwomen even got the vote.

Her campaign was reasonably orthodox. She concentrated on law and order, industry assistance and reduction in the cost of living. Her husband James assisted by knocking on doors and handing out pamphlets; he was at one point ushered into the drawing room of a lady who assured him earnestly that this Mrs Cowan was neglecting her children (the youngest of whom was by then thirty) and that her poor husband was dying of a broken heart.[1]

Edith – an inveterate campaigner, suffragette and activist – in the end spent only three years as a state politician. But during that time she gave Australia the closest legislative run we've ever seen at a minimum wage for housewives.

The question arose rather elliptically, in the course of an established parliamentary debate about whether domestic servants and – of all things – insurance brokers, should have access to the arbitration courts. At the time, there was no formal regulation of servants' wages, though it was a common joke in the periodicals of the day that the rather emancipated servants of the Australian colonies tended to set their own terms, and did well owing to the high demand for their work.

Mrs Cowan was still a newcomer to the Parliament. The *Bulletin* had not yet exhausted its cartoon series 'The New "House" Wife', which depicted the Member for West Perth variously scrubbing the despatch box, mopping the floor of the chamber, polishing the mace, and taking her parliamentary seat behind a copper of sudsy water and a washboard.[2]

So when she rose to outline her amendment to the Industrial Arbitration Act, the whole country was already predisposed to mirth on her account; what she had to say only exacerbated matters.

'The interpretation of the term "worker" is further amended by adding the following words,' proposed Mrs Cowan. 'So far as this Act extends to persons engaged in domestic service, a husband shall be deemed an employer, and his wife, if living with him, shall be deemed a worker employed by him, with regard to work done by the wife for the household which is commonly done by persons engaged in domestic service.'[3]

'Why should not married women have a union?' the first woman elected to an Australian parliament continued, in address to the chamber. 'Why should they be cut off from the same privileges? I do not think members of the Opposition would wish that their wives should be cut off from the same standing and privileges as a domestic worker would enjoy . . . If it is good for the housemaid and cook to go to the Arbitration Court, if it is good for the washerwoman to go to the Arbitration Court, it is equally good for the wife to do so. That is my reason for giving notice of the amendment,' she declared.[4]

'We shall have a revolution!' exclaimed Mr Frederick Teesdale, Member for Roebourne, a former pearler later eulogised as one of Parliament's 'most picturesque and lovable characters'.[5]

Replied Mrs Cowan: 'That is perfectly true. I have heard it stated in this House that there are some things which can only be put right by a revolution . . . but let it come by degrees, if possible. I stand for the women of this State.'[6]

Hansard records that at this point members chorused in unison: 'No!'

Mr Marshall, of Murchison, who entered the Assembly at the same time as Mrs Cowan and seems to have spent much of his time spluttering in outrage about one thing or another, was especially empurpled by his colleague's effrontery. 'You do not stand for my wife's cause, anyhow, and I will see that she does not go to the Arbitration Court!' he declared.

Mrs Cowan responded evenly. 'The honourable Member, judging by his tone and the remarks he made here one night, is probably one whose wife might be most happy and pleased if brought under the Arbitration Act.'[7]

History is mute on the intoxicating question of Mr Marshall's marriage.

But Mrs Cowan's amendment prompted an excitable

and national exchange of views as to the implications of a minimum wage for housewives.

Some, like *Australian Woman's Mirror* journalist Gwen Spencer, felt it was more in the interests of a family that money be given to the wife rather than retained by the husband, who was just as likely to fritter it away on 'drink, hobbies, racing or investments which might possibly turn out a failure'.[8]

Others felt that a regulated wage might assist women by formally recognising an existing arrangement that very much favoured men. *Leader* writer Helen Normanton argued that the reason 'many a man can earn a high salary and can sustain heavy mental and moral loads of business anxiety is largely due to the fact that he has in the background a silent partner whose name does not appear on his business stationery'.[9]

The industrial implications of Mrs Cowan's amendment, however, were lost on no one. A poet for the *Herald* summoned the spectre of the work-to-rule housewife:

Father:
I say, come quick, Maria!
Here's little baby Ted!
He's fallen in the fire
And burned his pretty head!

Mother:
I cannot help it, Father.
It's after union time
Besides, I would much rather
Read Marx's work sublime!

Father:
This chop's a little underdone
I'd rather have some steak.
It really is but little fun
My teeth on it to break.

Mother:
The Board's determination
Is ninepence for a chop.
'T'would cause you aggravation
If my work should stop.

The price of steak's a shilling
If you chose to pay,
To cook I'd be unwilling –
Because I'm off today![10]

Obviously, the prospect of a work-to-rule housewife was both novel and terrifying. What if she downed tools in the middle of dinner? Or amid the execution of some more intimate duty?

The accountability question ran both ways, of course.

Gwen Spencer, already on the record as advocating the redistribution of earnings from feckless men to their entirely more blameless wives, further considered that formalising a housewife's wages would bring a pleasing symmetry to the obligation.

Wages, she wrote, would 'have the effect of shaming certain married shirkers into doing their fair share of home-making, by emphasising the fact that they are cheating if they wear a man's ring and take what they can get from him while doing as little as they possibly can in return'.[11]

And perhaps husbands – newly chastened by a dose of industrial accountability – would begin to evaluate the quality of domestic work more stringently, and consider suing for specific performance should they awake to a congealed breakfast.

Sir James Mitchell, WA's premier, trod extremely carefully. 'There is some proposal, I believe, to make the wife an employee of the husband. I do not suppose there are many of us who are not controlled by our wives. If the Member for West Perth were successful in getting an alteration made to that effect, I do not think it would very much alter the position.'[12]

In the end, Mrs Cowan's amendment came to naught, as did the rest of the bill, which staggered through the committee stage and expired, largely unlamented, before the Council; Mrs Cowan was voted out in 1924, and the matter was not formally revisited.

Australia – still only in its infancy as a nation, and still working out which way was up on all sorts of fronts – already had a rather erratic national sense of what wives were worth, at any rate. In the early days of the colonies, it was felt that women were a burden rather than an asset: extra mouths to feed, in an alien and inhospitable environment. George Megalogenis, who is always on the lookout for such things, alerted me to a fascinating 1796 dispatch from New South Wales Governor John Hunter to the Duke of Portland, in which the viceroy records his preference that a new shipload of convicts bound for Botany Bay contain no women at all. 'I must express my hope that the three hundred are all men and not part men and part women, for of the latter we have already enough,' Hunter wrote. 'We have scarsely [sic] any way of employing them, and they are generally found to be worse characters than the men; if we had more work for them it would often be difficult to employ them, for we generally find those of a certain age taken up in the indispensable dutys [sic] of nursing an infant.'

But circumstances changed very quickly as enterprise blossomed in the new settlements, and by the 1850s, with hordes of prospectors flooding into the tent city of Ballarat hoping to retrieve the gold nuggets that were internationally reputed to litter the ground there, wives became quite the commodity. Wives helped keep tents liveable. They supported their husbands with their small business enterprises. Sometimes, when the hefty licence fees outpaced whatever miserable specks of gold their husbands had managed to coax out of Ballarat's notoriously fickle subsoil, they became the primary breadwinners.

In fact, the 'wife rush' that seized Victoria in the early 1850s was no less fevered than the gold rush, for all that it is less well-remembered. Clare Wright, in her Stella Prize-winning book *The Forgotten Rebels of Eureka*, describes the years during which wives enjoyed a seller's market in Victoria; diggers flocked to Melbourne's wharves to pay enthusiastic suit to any disembarking women. Newly arrived women wrote excitedly to their friends and sisters in the old country, advising them of Australia's husband-glut and encouraging them to come over. The prospect of adventure, not to mention independence from family and church, was intoxicating.

In 1850, Victoria recorded 2668 marriages. Within two years, that number had nearly trebled. But then something odd happened. The marriage rate plateaued.[13]

'Although it was a seller's market, women were choosing not to put up their wares,' records Wright. 'There's no doubt that women in Victoria felt a power in the marriage stakes that they had never experienced before.'[14] The high demand for domestic servants meant even the poorest of arriving women had choices; they could earn a good wage by themselves, and did not have to depend on a man.

Starved of actual brides, a certain cohort of men pioneered a bohemian new craze – the 'Digger's Wedding'. 'A newly cashed-up digger would pay a woman to act as a model bride,' explains Wright. 'He would deck her out in the finest wedding couture a nugget could buy, hire carriages and coachmen in gaudy livery, and purchase half the stock of the nearest pub. A crowd of intoxicated digger mates would march alongside the carriage all the way to the bayside suburb of St Kilda, where there would be a champagne dinner for all.'[15]

Wright also records that during those scant years of wife rush, there was a short-lived spike in the registration of illegitimate children. 'Registering the birth of a legally ille-gitimate child was an extraordinary public disclosure and suggests that women were less eager to cover the tracks of ex-nuptial conception, and less likely to see another man's child as an impediment to future marriage prospects, at a time when it was a seller's market.'[16]

The wife rush, like the gold rush, didn't last. But this awkward question surrounding the usefulness or other-wise of wives, and of how – if at all – their work should be recognised or recompensed, is one that remains stubbornly unresolved.

Lots of external events have influenced the way women work, and the sort of work we expect them to do. World War I introduced women to nursing and low-level political activism. The Great Depression taught them to be responsible for the whole household, and to make rudimentary furniture out of fruit crates that would – eighty years later – sell for vast amounts in inner-city antique stores. World War II entitled them to work in factories, and to wear trousers. Recessions, world wars, and waves of feminism have changed and sculpted the shape of women's enterprise. But accurately valuing the work that women do in the home? It's still a pretty sticky area.

Housework doesn't count towards the best-known measure of national productivity, the gross domestic product, even though women spend an average thirty-three hours a week doing it.[17]

And it's not paid, unless you count the slightly tangential efforts from the federal government, like the weekly five shillings per child that Robert Menzies introduced for mothers in 1941, which grew and mutated across the decades since, periodically augmented by one-off gobs of money like the Baby Bonus, star of John Howard's 2004 campaign launch.

The first and most commonly invoked method used when attempting to value housework is the 'replacement model'. This is the one where you calculate how much it would cost to hire someone else to do all the jobs that housewives do.

This is fairly easy for the big stuff, like cleaning and child care, where standard rates of underpay are clearly ascertainable from the formal economy. (These areas also most clearly demonstrate the brain-snapping weirdness of domestic labour's elastic relationship to the economy: when I vacuum my house, it's worth nothing at all, but when somebody else does it, it's suddenly worth twenty bucks an hour.) Things get a bit more ticklish, however, the further you go. When calculating how much it would cost to hire a cook, what kind of cook are we talking about? Some sausage-fingered graduate fresh from a two-day hospitality course, or Heston Blumenthal?

In 1967 the Chase Manhattan Bank established that a housewife was worth $8300 annually (about $60,000 in today's terms), based on her twelve distinct jobs: nurse-maid, cook, housekeeper, dietitian, food buyer, dish washer, laundress, seamstress, practical nurse, maintenance man, gardener, and chauffeur. 'It's an awesome thing for her to keep in mind when she asks for a new fur coat!' twinkled the *Gettysburg Times*, reporting the findings.[18]

Nearly fifty years later, we haven't really messed with the replacement model too much. The US website www.salary.com offers a dinky online calculator which computes that, in 2013, an American stay-at-home mom's ninety-four-hour work week is worth an annual pay packet of $113,568 – which seems perfectly reasonable (apart from being imaginary).[19] The website's calculation includes three 'CEO' hours and seven 'psychologist' hours, which bump up the pay-grade, but is dropping Steve Jobs or Sigmund Freud into a home a persuasive analogy, or just profoundly awkward for all involved?

Like most assessors in this economically tricky terrain, neither Chase in 1967 nor salary.com in 2013 venture into the *full range* of amenities a substitute wife might need to offer in the interests of completeness. Let me put that more bluntly. 'Prostitute' is not on the list.

The other main way in which the work of wives has in the past been valued is called the 'opportunity cost' method. This method was pioneered by the Nobel Prize-winning economist Gary Becker, who reasoned that the value of a wife's unpaid work in the home can be calculated by establishing what she might have earned out in the world if she didn't have to ice thirty-six cupcakes, devise a wire hook device to get a LEGO fireman out of the bathroom drain, and convey four profoundly ungrateful nine-year-olds to footy practice.

This has a certain rudimentary appeal, if you overlook Becker's persistent habit of referring to children as 'non-market household commodities'. If a woman is, for example, a qualified lawyer able to command $200 an hour in professional fees, then the hour she spends cleaning the awkward bit behind the bath with Exit Mould and a toothbrush gaffer-taped to a wooden spoon should also be worth $200, because that's what her time is valued at by the market, and it's not like the market is paying so much attention to what women do with their time that we can afford to pass up a straightforward valuation when one presents itself.

Another advantage of this method is that it begins to offer some kind of unsophisticated tracking-system of women's professional skills, some of which are reactivated after a stint in the home and some of which aren't. At present the national resources that go into educating and training millions of women who don't go on to attain comparable seniority with men seem to be lost to the system; they simply blink out, like the radar signal of a light plane entering the Bermuda Triangle. At least the opportunity cost method delivers some kind of account-ability: 'Don't be silly. That lawyer has not dropped out of the system. She still has all that learning stuff in her head; it's just that right now she is making a viking helmet out of papier-mâché and aluminium foil.'

To be honest, though, there are cracks in the opportu-nity cost method you could drive a truck through. Firstly, and most obviously: the cost of an hour of housework isn't necessarily its value. As any cab driver who used to be a banker will tell you – and in my experience most of them will indeed tell you – they don't get paid like bankers any more. Why would we perform this switcheroo especially for housewives, and for no one else?

Secondly, there are no market constraints in place governing the quantity of hours worked. Our lady lawyer could easily put a load of washing on, then fanny about on Facebook for ninety minutes. No one is going to hold her accountable for inflating her own hours, which introduces a rather unsatisfactory degree of elasticity into the whole shebang.

And neither of the above-mentioned models really does anything at all about assessing the quality of work in the home. This is quite a difficult – not to mention emotionally charged – area. Is one hour of seriously ramshackle house-hold work undertaken by a slatternly bungler worth the same as an hour of multi-tasking perfection wrought by some Martha Stewart-style domestic goddess in an orderly home that always smells of freshly baked bread?

When I deliver my daughter to school, and compare her general turnout (hat mauled but vaguely present, hair at nape forming the discreet but unmistakeable beginnings of a dreadlock, dress hem still stapled up in what was, last week, initially conceived as a temporary measure) with those of her friend (intricate braid, shiny shoes, lunchbox tenderly crammed with nourishing treats), it is something of a bulging question.

The replacement model would put the same value on my work and that of the friend's mum, roughly speaking, though if you were going to be fussy you would probably budget for a hair stylist and a personal groomer for her kid a pay-grade or two above the one for my kid. On the opportunity cost model though, my morning's cursory attentions would be worth far more, as I am better paid than the other mum is. And that doesn't seem right.

This is a hard area to discuss, not least because we have a lasting societal taboo that prevents us from calling some mothers good and some mothers bad. It's one of those things that's okay to think but not really okay to say out loud, and really quite scorchingly not okay to incorporate into any kind of work-valuation model, no matter how many PhDs in economics you might have.

Competence or otherwise is at the very heart of our modern employment economy; if you're especially good at something, you'll probably end up getting paid more to do it than your workmate who is only so-so. But your worth as a mother is a far more nuanced affair, delicate and robust at the same time. If we're honest, casual valuations of motherhood are often more about just being there than they are about competence.

Maybe it's a bit harsh to be introducing a whole bunch of key performance indicators in this field anyway. We should keep in mind that no matter how intricate our economic model for determining how much a wife's work is worth, it's still only imaginary pay at the end of the day, so getting fussy about standards could seem a bit unreasonable.

While wives are productive, busy and in good health, the valuations of their work remain strictly theoretical; thesis-ballast for special-interest economists, column-fodder for feminists, pub talk for tight-lipped couples on date night. You can argue till the cows come home about what wives *should* be paid, but let's not pretend that under any of these models, stay-at-home spouses actually *will* be paid. It's all Monopoly money, in the end, which should rather lessen the angst about whether you end up on Mayfair or Old Kent Road.

It's not until they die, or get divorced, or horribly maimed, that wives, and the work they do, experience the acrid yet compelling tang of real money; for that intriguing set of ex-post-facto calculations, we now turn to the court system.

As Joni Mitchell reminded us, you don't know what you've got till it's gone. And in legal terms, one of the surest ways of working out what something is worth is to lose it in an accident that was someone else's fault.

Tort law has a special history here. When a working person is injured or killed, there is a calculus – framed loosely by legislation, and honed into precision by generations of plaintiffs and defendants, inhabiting archaeological layers of loss and grief – that instructs us as to what those accidents are worth; what that loss is worth, what is properly claimable. Pages and pages of tables, regulated under workers' compensation schemes, exist in most states to tell us how much a finger is worth, how much for an eye, how much for a broken neck. How much income is foregone? What can the injured person now expect, by way of future employment? How can the gap most fairly be compensated?

When a person who works at home is injured, however, things work rather differently. Loss of ability to work in the home after an accident is viewed as a 'non-economic loss', which is legal-speak for 'not very much money'. It is an acknowledgement, rather than a formal compensation. In tort law, a housewife rendered incapable of vacuuming is treated in the same way as a man who can no longer go kayaking, or run in the City to Surf. Her inability to do housework is often cited, in such cases, as damaging to her general happiness; Justice Reynolds in a 1982 case called *Burnicle v Cutelli*, for instance, found that an injured housewife had 'lost part of a capacity, the exercise of which can give to her pride and satisfaction and the receipt of gratitude, and the loss of which can lead to frustration and feelings of inadequacy'.[20] Because housework is unpaid, it is grouped with recreation.

The other kind of compensation historically available when a housewife is injured is compensation to her husband, under a doctrine called 'loss of consortium'.

Loss of consortium is adapted from a Latin phrase and refers to circumstances in which a man loses the society and services of his wife. I do not blush to use the gender-specific pronouns here, as inherited British law always intended this term to refer to wives, and indeed in many jurisdictions these damages were, for a long time, only claimable by men in relation to awful accidents befalling the women to whom they were married. In the 1970s, the states of Queensland and South Australia amended their legislation to make loss of consortium claimable by wives, too. New South Wales abolished the legislation entirely in 1984.

The good news is that loss of consortium tots up all the stuff that both the replacement-value model and the opportunity-cost model were too shy to canvass; whereas practitioners of the dismal science pull a discreet curtain around the marital bed, the courts wade right in there, in order to compensate for loss-of-nooky when something happens to a man's wife. (It also covers stuff like not having anyone around to do the ironing any more; this element is called 'loss of servitium', and yes, it does mean exactly what it sounds like it means.)

The bad news is that loss of consortium is payable to the chap. And the prospect of a man not being able to have sex any more does seem to have excited slightly more empathy on the bench, historically, than the premature expiry of a woman's capacity to scrub things.

The feminist barrister and academic Reg Graycar has made rather a study of the courts' special solicitude for men whom circumstances have deprived of sex. She notes that damage to women's sexual organs tends to attract rather cursory judicial attention; if an injury makes sexual intercourse painful, it is interpreted as unfortunate but not necessarily compensable.

A damaged penis, on the other hand, is more compelling; Graycar cites a half-million-dollar initial award to a man whose penis was damaged in a botched circumcision as a baby but could still have sex, and $535,045 in 1997 for a man who lost his libido after being attacked by a crazed pig.[21]

But we digress. The relevant and interesting thing about tort law for our purposes is that the valuation of a housewife's work is very much calculated in terms of her usefulness to the people around her, whether that is as a sexual partner or servant.

The other point at which the legal community gathers to consider the worth of a homemaker is another of life's grimmer way stations: divorce.

Divorce, while unfortunate, is a marvellous clarifier. It enables husbands and wives to conduct – in court, and before a professionally indifferent arbiter – all the arguments they might secretly have rehearsed in ostensibly happier times.

'You had nothing when I married you!'

'Think of what I put up with, you cheating couch potato!'

'You've spent a small fortune on shoes. How dare you!'

'What sort of grown man can't pick up his own pants?'

There is a deep psychological reckoning in divorce. All of a sudden, the emotional discounts people afford to each other when they are in loving relationships (*He's a good dad, so I don't mind that it's always me who gets up with the children. She works hard; what does it matter if she is addicted to* Gray's Anatomy?) are summarily cancelled. Instead of the emotional division of labour implicit in most relationships, couples move to a mandated division of labour, by agreement or by order of the court.

All of a sudden, matters of care, custody and maintenance are written down on a piece of paper, the way they hardly ever are when things are still going okay.

In some cases, divorced women find that their husbands become more domestically productive than they were before. Which would be great, if it wasn't for the loneliness and heartbreak and so on.

But there is also – importantly – an economic reckoning in divorce. It is one of the only circumstances in which a woman's domestic contribution to a household is calculated and the result is that *actual money changes hands*, rather than just citation credits or Nobel Prizes.

Western divorce law is a fabulously serpentine affair. In England, until the year 1857, divorces were only awarded with the direct approval of Parliament. Obviously, they weren't very easy to get, given that you had to summon a simple majority on the House of Commons just to get shot of your spouse; unsurprisingly, it was only the rich and influential who managed it.

And even if you were rich and influential, it helped to be male, as the rules about what constituted a divorceable offence varied for men and women. A single act of adultery committed by a wife, for instance, was grounds for her husband to divorce her – no questions asked. But in order for adultery to be a divorcing matter for a woman, her husband needed to be a serial, irrepressible and shameless pants man, preferably with goats, before Parliament would even think of getting involved.

The reasoning behind this imbalance was summarised rather fragrantly by the estimable Dr Samuel Johnson: 'Between a man and his wife, a husband's infidelity is nothing. Wise married women do not trouble themselves about the infidelity of their husbands. The difference between the two cases is boundless. The man imposes no bastards upon his wife. A man, to be sure, is criminal in the sight of God, but he does not do his wife a very material injury if he does not insult her; if, for instance, he steals privately to her chambermaid; Sir, a wife ought not greatly to resent this.'

So, wealthy people got divorces through Parliament. Ordinary people just went about ridding themselves of annoying spouses in less administratively difficult ways – murdering them, bigamously marrying someone else, or nicking a loaf of bread and emigrating to Australia.[22]

Things were democratised slightly by the Divorce Act of 1857, after which a woman was entitled to a divorce if her husband sodomised her, committed bestiality or was trenchantly and serially unfaithful, but a single national standard for infidelity for men and women was not achieved until 1959.[23]

In Australia, meanwhile, the states took the English position and evolved at their own speed. In cosmopolitan New South Wales, a lady could get a divorce from 1892 onwards if her husband had been a drunk for three years, but South Australian women had to wait another thirty-six years for the same right.[24]

Divorce and marriage laws were a curious admixture of solicitude for and discrimination against women. The stout ties that bound wives to abusive husbands also nominally obliged those husbands to provide, and this was the source – in the legislative eye, anyway – of considerable comfort to women. As we know from the parliamentary debates around the public service marriage ban, marriage was the principal social welfare unit the nation had to offer its lady constituents.

So when Gough Whitlam sought to introduce no-fault divorce in 1973, the legislation was utterly revolutionary. Husbands and wives would no longer have to declare whose violence or inconstancy or abandonment had been the cause of the marriage's disintegration. Husbands would not be tied to an inflexible and lifelong system of alimony; property settlements would be made on the basis of both parties' contribution to the marriage, both as breadwinners and as homemakers.

Among the enthusiastic backbench participants in this particular slice of the action-packed Whitlam years were two future prime ministers – Paul Keating, the Member for Bankstown, and John Howard, the Member for Bennelong.

'There was no more important piece of social legislation debated in the time that I was in federal Parliament than the Family Law Bill,' recalls Howard in his memoir, *Lazarus Rising*.[25] 'All parties allowed their members a free vote, and this exposed real fissures and bitterness within the Labor Party.'

Howard spoke in support of much of the bill, and was particularly enthusiastic about the new mechanism for recognising the contribution of homemakers. 'I believe that that provision is the first legislative expression which has been given to a growing demand in our society that, in adjudicating on and assessing financial relationships between a husband and a wife, both in a divorce situation and in an estate situation, proper and adequate recognition be made of non-financial contributions made to the relationship and to the acquisition of the matrimonial assets,' he told the House of Representatives on 28 February 1975.[26]

Paul Keating's reservations were much more in evidence,

and expressed with a pungency for which the young western Sydney MP was already known.

'Without wishing to be offensive to anyone,' he began (so far, so good), 'I suggest that the bill in its present form is pretty much a playboy's bill and does not pay much concern at all to the welfare of women. I believe that many supporters of the bill are people who do not want to have their conduct exposed and who never want to be named in divorce proceedings.'[27]

Keating's views were far from isolated. In the months and months for which the bill would be debated, its strongest critics argued that the legislation abandoned women; that it left them unprovided for, and that their husbands would readily take the opportunity to skip town, probably with some fast little unit from Accounts.

It was the provisions awarding no-fault divorce that generated, by far, the most heat and light during the parliamentary debate; hardly surprising. But it was the innocuous sections 75 and 79, which won praise from a young John Howard for recognising for the first time the contributions of stay-at-home mothers, that would provide a long-burn struggle for the Australian court system.

The framework set by Parliament is pretty broad. Section 79 simply obliges courts to 'take into account' contributions, both financial and non-financial, made by husbands and wives to the shared wealth and property being divvied up at the end of their union.

This is typical of the relationship between the Australian legislature and the court system – a 'frenemy' arrangement if ever I've seen one. At the end of two years of sobbing debate, Parliament had finally agreed that a value should be put on the contribution of homemakers. The ticklish task of working out exactly how to compute that value was then tossed to the courts themselves. This is a common sort of circumstance; judges are obliged to enforce the laws that Parliament makes, even the ones it rushes through late at night when everyone is drunk or overtired or so sick of the sight of the legislation that they leave gaps. Part of the judicial process is combing back through *Hansard* to work out what the politicians were really meaning to do. Judges, I often think, cannot enjoy this very much, and I wonder if they get a little revenge-thrill when, from time to time, they do things like declaring whole chunks of refugee policy unconstitutional.

And what did the courts do with this spanking-new requirement that the contributions of homemakers be formally taken into account in divorce property settlements? How did they work it out? Did they employ the replacement-value model, to figure out a homemaker's bill for services rendered on the basis of what it would have cost to hire somebody else to do all that stuff? Or did they invoke the opportunity-cost model to figure out what the homemaker might otherwise have earned, had she (and yes, the homemakers in these cases are still usually chicks) not been so incautious as to get hitched to that damn fool of an ex-husband?

They did not. After a certain amount of post-legislative head-scratching and rummaging through *Hansard*, the courts agreed that Parliament had definitely intended for homemakers not to be diddled out of property rights just because they had not earned money over the course of their marriages.

But it was felt that Parliament did not intend for courts to go trawling through people's marriages and calculating exactly which wives made how many school lunches and which husbands always slept in on Sundays even when it was her birthday.

The late Justice Nygh, of the Family Court, made the point with some force:

> It has been suggested from time to time that the Court must assess in some way or another the contribution made by a party, for instance, as a breadwinner on one hand and as homemaker on the other, on a scale which presumably ranks from the perfect to a total failure . . . it is not, I think, the function of this Court. It has never done so and I trust will never do so in the future, to assess the quality of each party on a scoring-board which, so far as breadwinners are concerned, would give top marks to the Holmes à Courts of this world and bottom marks to the unemployed roustabout and, I suppose, in the homemaker and parenting stakes, would give top marks to those ladies who in the age of the great dictators would have received the glorious mother-hood medal, and bottom marks to those ladies who – it is alleged – spend most of their time in the tennis club and the coffee klatch and waste their precious time in idle leisure. I take the view, based on the traditional marriage vows, that the parties take one another for better and for worse.[28]

What has emerged instead is a rather different rule of thumb. The courts look at the property the couple has accumulated together and simply credit the homemaker with a chunk of it; the very fact of her existence is the relevant factor, not the quality of her work.

Here's Justice Dawson's view, from a pivotal 1984 High Court case concerning the divorce of a Mr and Mrs Mallet: 'The contribution of a homemaker or parent is to free the other party to the marriage – usually the husband or father – to devote his time and energy to the pursuit of financial gain and so to make a real and substantial contribution to the acquisition, conservation or improvement of property where the monies gained are used for any of those purposes. There can be no doubt that this is a correct explanation of the policy which lies behind this aspect of the legislation.'[29]

Here we see the sniff of a new model for valuing the work of housewives, where the relevant consideration is not whether she is a good mother or housekeeper, or what she could otherwise have been doing with her time, but the extent to which her very presence frees her husband up to go and make money. The value of her work is thus tied directly to the value of his: if he goes out and makes a million through hard work and strategic investment, then her homemaking duties are richly rewarded. If he is a small-time bungler, her share of the property won't be any the larger for the fact that she was more competent a housewife than he was an earner.

The interesting thing is that the courts have regularly made exceptions for male breadwinners with exceptional skills.

When Brett Whiteley and his wife Wendy divorced in 1989 after a 25-year marriage, for instance, the marital property of about $11 million was acrimoniously contested. Both were artists, and Brett Whiteley had often said he considered his wife to have been born with the greater talent. But it was his commercial success that generated the sizeable fortune, bolstered by Wendy's role as his muse, model, adviser, and the mother of their child.

Justice Alwynne Rowlands, of the Family Court, nominated a 67.5–32.5 split Brett Whiteley's way. 'Because of his special skill as an artist, he made by far and away the major contribution to the substantial assets the parties now have,' Justice Rowlands ruled. 'While giving weight to the wife's contribution in the various areas to which I have referred, it is clear that it has been the husband's industry and talent which has been substantially more significant of the two.'[30]

In 1993, another landmark case, *Ferraro v Ferraro*, found that a special talent for business entitled the husband to a greater share of the property even though his wife, it was acknowledged by the court, had made a substantial contribution to the business. Again, her contribution was important because of what it allowed her husband to do. 'The facts are that the husband, particularly in the latter years, devoted his full-time attention to his business activities and thus the wife was left with virtually the sole responsibility for the children and the home,' found the judgement. 'That latter circumstance is significant not only in relation to the evaluation of the wife's homemaker contributions . . . but is important because it freed the husband from those responsibilities in order to pursue without interruption his own business activities.'[31]

So, according to the courts, a homemaker's contribution to family wealth isn't gauged by his or her skilfulness in homemaking, nor is it gauged by calculating how much it would cost to hire someone else to do their job. Nor do the courts, it seems, pay any mind to the opportunity cost model; Justice Rowland wasn't the least bit worried about how much Wendy Whiteley, for instance, could have earned as an artist under her own steam had she not been busy having a baby, advising her husband, and lolling about in bathtubs with her pants off in order that Brett Whiteley should never be short of a shapely bottom for one of his squillion-dollar canvases.

No: the courts, working with the structure the Parliament gave them back in 1975, seem to have arrived constructively at their own model for calculating the value of a housewife. The relevant consideration is not what the homemaker herself does, but *what her work enables her husband to do*, of which she is usually entitled to roughly half, unless he has been especially brilliant.

At first blush, this is an extremely old-fashioned approach. Even to talk, in the twenty-first century, of 'housewives' feels rather antique, and I apologise for doing it; the fact is that when the Family Court considers the role and contribution of homemakers under the Family Law Act, the majority of those homemakers continue to be women. There are hardly any cases in which a bread-winning woman and her stay-at-home husband litigate on the breakdown of their marriages. And to receive half of jointly accumulated assets is generally held to be a reasonable deal, so you don't hear too much squawking about it. But the curious logjam remains in our ability, as a society, to put a proper value on domestic work.

I'm reminded of a book I have by Dorothy Carnegie, entitled *How to Help Your Husband Get Ahead in His Social and Business Life*.[32] It was published in 1953, and its author is billed on the dust jacket as 'Mrs Dale Carnegie'. 'This is a book which every woman will want to read – and which no man will want his wife to miss!' Dorothy was, in fact – as browsers were no doubt intended immediately to suspect – the wife of Dale Carnegie, the American motivational speaker and author of *How to Win Friends and Influence People*. He is significantly to blame for America's $12-billion-a-year self-help book addiction, but that is hardly his wife's fault.

Mrs Carnegie's own tome is a handbook of the wifely arts, over the course of which she enjoins her readers to work with their husbands, rather than against them, reminding women that if he fails, so does she. 'Make mountains of his virtues, and molehills of his faults!' is one of her chirpier pieces of advice, along with quite a lot of prescriptive material about how you should always put makeup and a nice dress on in the afternoons, and not start banging on about everything in the house that's broken the minute he's walked in the door.

'Helping a man attain success is a full-time career in itself,' Mrs Carnegie advises. 'You just can't hope to do it unless it is important enough to claim all your attention.'

Most of Mrs Carnegie's recommendations are about careful handling of one's husband's fortunes and psyche: be interested in his work, but not too interested. Be a social asset. Also, make friends with his secretary (this last is especially authoritative seeing as the author, before she was Mrs Carnegie, was employed as Mr Carnegie's secretary).

It's a very funny, quaint old book, soaked in the assumptions of a 1950s-era domestic apartheid. The world of home and the world of work are almost entirely separate, joined only by the sinew of marriage and obligation. Are a wife's efforts of value? Only to the extent that she enables and invigorates her husband's professional capacity. The only thing that slightly crimps one's ironic enjoyment of such a volume is the deep and not-quite-unfounded suspicion that it is not yet entirely out of date.

7

PUBLIC LIFE?
NEED A WIFE!

One winter morning in 2012, I ran into Tanya Plibersek in a Manuka coffee shop. It was about 7 am. She was having a breakfast meeting with Greg Combet. I was finding new and diverting ways of entertaining my son, who at age two was accompanying me on this trip to Canberra, and had decided to respond energetically to his new environment by waking up at 4 am.

Combet left, and we sat down with Tanya. My boy is the same age as her youngest, and I could see, on her face, that look so common to the separated-from-child parent, which is to say I could see she was performing the mental calculation of how weird it would be for her to actually sniff my kid's hair.

We had the usual 'how do you manage it' exchange. 'I guess we're both pretty lucky to have partners who pull their weight in the parenting stakes,' I concluded, as my son lovingly inserted a croissant into my left ear. 'Yes,' Tanya said, knitting her brows in that serene, reflective way she has. 'I really hope, though, that we're the last generation of women who have to feel lucky about that.'

I've thought about that observation many times since. She was right. Why *do* women with a helpful spouse often feel like they've won the lottery, while men with a helpful spouse seem unremarkable?

Helpful spouses are useful in any circumstance, of course, but nowhere are they more useful than in federal politics, which involves compulsory travel to Canberra for up to eighteen weeks a year.

Every time the nation lurches into a new bout of head-scratching about why there aren't more women in federal politics (this sort of spasmodic debate receded while Julia Gillard was prime minister because with a lady in the Lodge it was generally assumed, and fair enough, that we might have sorted it out; it resumed smoothly the day that Tony Abbott hammered into place a Cabinet with just one woman) I genuinely feel like stabbing myself in the eye with a rusty fork.

Seriously, if I have to hear one more expert talk on radio about how Question Time is blokey or how women don't put themselves forward for preselection, I shall begin to scream and never stop. It's perfectly obvious why there aren't more women in federal Parliament. Sure, it's got to do with political culture and factions and preselections and so on, but to a large and understated yet sky-writingly self-evident extent it's because if you are a person who wants to use your productive years pursuing a political career with energy and rigour, but you don't want to sacrifice the idea of having a family, then you will usually need a wife. And female politicians don't get wives, on the whole. They tend to make do with husbands, instead, who are in many cases lovely and accommodating and very, very helpful, but are almost never the practical equal of the political wives who have for so long been an invisible suspension bridge under the Parliament of our nation. Women who have raised children largely unaided by their husbands. Women who have tolerated that awful domestic pincer-movement in which the more successful her husband becomes at work, the less help he will be at home, and the more deeply he belongs to the nation, the less he will belong to her. Women who are so used to being the only parent at the parent–teacher interview that they don't even bother to check the dates any more. Women for whom spousal success brings not only even more prolonged absences, but sometimes the kind of scrutiny that is heartbreaking and traumatic, and all the more so because she must endure so much of it on her own.

Women like Margie Abbott, a private person with her own career who raised three lovely girls and then was forced, simply by virtue of her husband's career, to endure months of thrilling public discussion of the child that husband believed he had conceived in his teens.

The online dating profile of your average MP would read like this:

Hi! I'm an ambitious 40-year-old who enjoys walks on the beach, factional backbiting and micro-economic reform. I'm looking for that special someone to settle down and have kids with. I will be away for about half of every year, so it would be great if you could either not work at all, or restructure your entire life so that you can be responsible for pretty much everything to do with the kids, while also having to explain to their tear-streaked little faces why I'm never there and then also not being resentful when they're all over me like a rash when I do drop in and give them lollies and bugger up their sleep patterns and so on.

When I am home, I will be on the phone pretty much the entire time. When I'm a minister, I will be unbelievably busy. When I'm not a minister, I will be resentful and paranoid. Oh, and the odds are that at some point in my political career, Michelle Grattan will phone while we're actually doing it.

The political spouse's job is a tricky one, but there always seem to be women who are up to the challenge: men have been combining political careers with family since representative democracy's year dot, and things show no signs of slowing down.

Tanya Plibersek has had three children while serving as a federal MP, and is generally viewed as something of a phenomenon. Christopher Pyne has had four kids during his career, and it's barely mentioned. The difference? Pyne has a wife, Carolyn, who not only raises the children largely single-handed but also works hard to insulate their lives from the madness of their father's job.

'I don't want their lives defined by their father,' Carolyn Pyne says. 'We don't have the TV on during the week. We don't watch *Q&A*. There was something on during *The Project* one week – Felix had turned the TV on and this guy did a parody of Christopher. Aurelia, our six-year-old, just burst into tears.

'We prefer not to take Christopher anywhere! People will come up to him and say, "I see you're with your family and probably want some privacy, but . . ." and then they just talk to him anyway. It's hard on the children.'

There's another dimension to political families, too: what happens when a parent who has been absent all week being – say – a minister, with staff scrambling to his every instruction, comes home?

'Ah, the re-entry issue.' Carolyn Pyne laughs. 'He'll come home with his 1950s book of parenting, and ask "Why aren't you doing this?" "Why aren't you loving me?" "Why aren't you doing more homework?" And Eleanor Pyne, who's nearly fourteen, will roll her eyes and say "How long is he here for?"

'It's hard for him, because he comes back to re-establish his place in the family and, of course, we've been here all the time, getting along without him.'

Politicians – especially the very successful ones – run to a schedule with which no normal household can practically keep pace. 'Christopher's up really early and he just goes all day long. He never stops. He goes at 100 miles per hour, every day, every weekend,' says Carolyn. 'Just the talking! Sometimes, particularly in the lead-up to an election, he'll talk from 5 am until eleven o'clock at night. Political spouses often feel they are married part-time, but on the other hand, he's so full-on that if he was here 24/7, we'd be in danger of going insane.'

Carolyn's personal sanity provisions include a return to university study, and relentless teasing of her husband, whom she describes as 'easy to laugh with . . . and at'. After the 2014 Budget, amid a groundswell of student protest at her husband, she was among the first wave of students due to graduate in the newly straitened tertiary environment.

'I won't let him come to my ceremony. He said he was going to come disguised as Cyrano de Bergerac and hide in the wings, but I absolutely refused. I'm not being mean to him, but I hate being the centre of attention. I got two tickets to the ceremony and I'm taking the twins. It's about me that day, not about him. He said "But I'll have a police escort! I'll be fine!" I said, "It's not about you. I worked really hard, and now I just want something for myself."'

Political 'wives' are largely invisible, but they are indispensable to the political process, and this is something that begins long before the candidate gets anywhere near Canberra. It begins with preselection.

The degree of difficulty involved in getting preselection as a candidate for a major party ranges from tricky to diabolically difficult, depending on which seat you're going for. If you're contesting a seat your party deems as unwinnable, especially in a time of rampant team despair, it can be refreshingly easy. If you're after a safe seat in a party that is in Government or about to be, you are almost certainly in for a long and potentially bruising campaign. It's like trying to get a seat on the ferry in a storm. Anyone can get a wet seat. But getting a dry one involves foresight, early arrival, and sharp elbows.

Things you can do that might help you get preselection for a nice safe seat include, but are not limited to: buying a house in the electorate. Living with your mother in the electorate, at a pinch. Having a photogenic family with no obvious tattoos, unfortunate political opinions, demanding careers of their own, or substance dependencies. Going to every tedious meeting and chook raffle your branch coughs up for years on end, starting well before the incumbent has developed the faintest impulse towards either gracious retirement or career-ending indiscretion. Becoming a person of influence in the party, either by working for a union or for an existing politician and establishing yourself – via a complicated series of social exchanges involving late nights, duck pancakes and travel to obscure policy conferences – at the centre of an existing power structure. Being a famous athlete, rock star or existing public figure.

The above-mentioned capers are not for everyone. They suit thrusting young men and women with no family commitments, or people with extremely understanding spouses who are prepared to look after things at home while the candidate is out late leafleting in deep suburbia. They often do not suit women who have working husbands and children and who are trying to do several things at once.

Karen Andrews, the former engineer and IR consultant who won the safe conservative Queensland seat of McPherson for the Liberal National Party in the 2010 election, started her campaign for preselection several years earlier. 'It's like a job in itself,' she says of the preselection process. 'In our party, to get preselected you need to have a majority of votes from eligible members who live in the electorate. It does take time, because you need to be well-known to the members, and you need a good level of support so that when the preselection comes around they will actually come out and vote for you. Party members do not appreciate the blow-ins, so you need to do a lot of work in advance.'

For several years, Andrews immersed herself in party work, organising party meetings and fundraisers and attending countless local events, and working the phones to party members whenever she had time. Her husband, Chris, with whom she ran an industrial relations consultancy, was happy to support her; she had carried a heavier load at home while he completed a doctorate, and they had agreed that it was her turn.

But when the preselection happened – and it was a contested one, as you would expect in a safe seat – the couple's three young daughters, then aged seven, ten and fifteen, did become an issue. 'I was really surprised by the strength of some of the opinions that were put to me,' Andrews recalls.

'I only had one comment to the effect that "we really need a man for the job", and that was out of a couple of hundred people, but then there was some other feedback about my role as a mother,' she says. 'There was an email, for instance, from a preselector who wrote to tell me that he would never allow his own wife to leave their children at such a young age. I didn't reply, as I didn't think there would be much point. But I must say I was taken aback that someone would put that in an email, and then send it. I mean, it was clearly a considered view.'

Political career planning is necessarily a dicey affair. Winning preselection is one hurdle; winning the seat itself is the next. Much can go wrong. The funniest federal elections are the ones where fortunes change considerably between preselection season and election day, and a high electoral tide brings all sorts of strange fish flapping onto the shore. The Howard landslide of 1996 was one of those.

A good chunk of the preselections had been done back when Alexander Downer was leader the previous year, and everyone was still politely assuming that Downer had a better chance of being made Pope than prime minister. When the 1996 election went resoundingly the Coalition's way, there were some extremely surprised new MPs. Coalminer Paul Marek, for instance, having been selected by the Liberal Party to contest a safe Labor Queensland seat, disappeared back down the mines and had to be hunted down days after the election to receive the news he had achieved a 6.9 per cent swing and was the new Member for Capricornia.

In 1997, industrial officer Anna Burke was preselected by the Labor Party to contest the suburban Melbourne seat of Chisholm. There wasn't much competition for the preselection; Chisholm was held by the high-profile health minister Michael Wooldridge. 'It's all right,' Burke told her husband, Stephen Burgess. 'I can't win!'

'I think it's fair to say that her noble ambition was to knock a couple of per cent off his margin and make him really sweat for it,' remembers Burgess. But then Wooldridge leapfrogged to the safer seat of Casey, and all of a sudden Anna Burke was a chance.

She won the seat. The couple's life was rapidly very different, and their plans for a family seriously compromised. Nevertheless, Burke was pregnant within a year of her election. She remembers breaking the news of her impending confinement to her leader, Kim Beazley, and Labor Whip 'Leaping' Leo McLeay.

'They just about fell off their chairs,' she says. 'I'm not sure any of us realised how difficult it was going to be.'

She took no maternity leave. 'I came back to Parliament with a six-week-old baby. There's just so much stuff you don't anticipate. I wanted to put a cot in my office, for example. "Sorry: OH&S. You can't have a cot." Trying to get a capsule into a Comcar. Going to a committee hearing in Sydney and being told: "You can just hold the baby in your lap."'

'We just sort of played the cards we were dealt,' says Anna's husband Stephen, who was an intensive care ambulance paramedic. He quickly realised that his shift work and her regular absences in Canberra were not going to add up to a manageable life. He applied to his employer for parental leave, and received a hostile response. 'I was the first bloke who had ever asked for it,' he explains. 'We moved into a protracted . . . well, negotiation would be a polite way to describe it. They insisted that the reference in the agreement to "parental leave" actually meant "maternity leave" and was only available to women. Intensive care paramedics weren't exactly thick on the ground and I guess they didn't want to open that Pandora's box . . . what if all sorts of other blokes wanted to do it too?'

After some sustained pressure, Stephen got his year's leave. 'All I had to do in the end was rattle the sabre . . . I didn't have to do anything formal. Just this sort of war of attrition of correspondence, and meetings where I'd pull out the Macquarie Dictionary and check the definition of the word "parental".'

During his leave, Stephen travelled with baby Maddie to Canberra, where Anna was 'like the sun in the solar system, and we were sort of in her orbit'.

'I got on first-name terms with the switchboard staff. They'd page her, and she'd whip back to R296 from wherever she was, she'd feed and then Maddie would sleep, or I'd take her for a walk. In some ways, it wasn't hard at all because MPs are well looked-after in the workplace. They're well-paid, they have an office, they're in charge in that office and their diaries are their own to manage. It's like being a franchisee.'

The difficulties Burke had as a parliamentary mother are really only due to one factor: she was only the second woman to give birth while serving as a member of the House of Representatives. Only the second, in nearly a century of federation, a period in which countless men sired countless children while working as MPs and ministers.

Ros Kelly was the first, in 1983. Because Kelly was the Member for Canberra, she didn't have the prohibitive travel barriers that still make the whole motherhood-and-parliament deal so tricky for her successors. But she didn't have a 'wife' either; her husband was former child star, footballer, senior treasury official and then super-banker David Morgan, who had a few irons in the fire himself.

Kelly went back to work less than a week after leaving hospital. One of her parliamentary colleagues, Bruce Goodluck – the Liberal Member for Franklin, and himself the father of five daughters – opened the batting by saying publicly that she should have stayed home longer.

'Her husband's got a good job and I'm sure Parliament would be only too happy to give her maternity leave,' he said. 'If children are put into child-minding centres from birth, God help us. Who wants the socialisation of babies?'[1]

During the treasurer's budget speech that year, Kelly left the chamber briefly. History does not record exactly why; perhaps it was to feed her baby, or perhaps it was to do the sorts of things that MPs leave the chamber for hundreds of times a day, but Goodluck chanted 'Where's Ros? Where's Ros?' until she returned.[2]

(Mr Goodluck, whose 18-year stint in the House of Representatives appears to have been complicated neither by formal paternity leave nor – indeed – higher duty of any kind, is best known for an incident in November 1994, in which he appeared briefly in the chamber wearing a chicken suit. Questioned many years later, he confirmed that he had forgotten exactly what the issue was at the time.)

For her part, Kelly explained that she was simply trying to balance her responsibilities as a parent and a public representative. '. . . I've got a responsibility to my child and myself too, and I think I'll be a much better mother through being happy with the job that I'm doing.'[3]

A rash of births has since swelled the ranks of parliamentary new mothers to the point where you can no longer count them on your fingers, and now need to remove your shoes as well.

Those who do have babies in office tend to have a very different experience from their new-father colleagues, no matter how supportive their spouses.

For one thing, there is a lot less automatic acceptance of a mother who leaves her children for a third of the year to attend Parliament in Canberra than there is of the time-honoured formula in which it is the parliamentary dad who does the scarpering.

The new fathers in Parliament fly under the radar; they

might have a cigar with friends when the happy event occurs, but they hardly ever miss a beat at work, and the lovely little bundle generally only materialises in Canberra if there is a corresponding event at which its mother is also required. Joe Hockey was the first minister to take paternity leave when his son Xavier was born in 2005; a move of which, he recalls, Prime Minister John Howard approved because 'it made him look modern'!

But paternity leave for men in Parliament remains rare, and short.

In Hockey's case, his wife Melissa Babbage juggled three children and a demanding job as Deutsche Bank's head of global finance during his absences, with the aid of family and a battalion of nannies.

Carolyn Pyne, who has been married to Christopher for twenty years, doesn't get to Canberra much to socialise with other spouses; just getting there is an endeavour.

'I remember bringing the children to Canberra when Aurelia (the youngest) was a newborn,' she says. 'I had Aurelia strapped to me in the papoose and the other three had all had cereal with that UHT milk and, as we landed in Canberra, they all started vomiting at once. It was unbelievable. You know those cloth things velcroed on the back of the seats? I was even grabbing those to try and clean the kids up. Eventually, it turned out the father of one of our babysitters was up the back of the plane, and he came to the rescue and helped me get them all off the plane.'

Tanya Plibersek has had three babies in Parliament and never had more than two weeks off. She also breastfed all three until they were twelve months old. Travelling back and forth between Sydney and Canberra myself, I would often see her boarding flights with baby Louis in a sling. I know the mechanics of how she probably did it, but still – my imagination blanches at the equation. One baby, two siblings, one Cabinet job. Unbelievable. Now, it's good to have extraordinary people in Parliament; that's the idea, and a truly extraordinary person in Parliament is an exhilarating thing to see. But surely it's a sign of trouble that a woman can be extraordinary for doing something that wouldn't rate so much as a footnote in the CV of any comparable man. 'Personal: Raised three children with the help of a loving spouse.' Yawn.

Plibersek's view is that standards are different for women. 'It's a practical advantage for men to have children; in politics, you're regarded as more rounded if you have kids,' she says.

'There's more ambivalence about women with children. There's a lot of people who regard it positively, but for every person who feels that way, there's someone else saying, "How could you leave your children, you must be a heartless automaton".'

Plibersek herself has been on the receiving end of all kinds of feedback; some, from women who had been anxious about taking on extra work because of their children but view Plibersek as an inspiration, are grateful notes of thanks. But of the others – and the deputy Labor leader is clearly emotional about these, as she declines to describe them – some are very hurtful indeed. Plibersek's husband, Michael Coutts-Trotter, is a senior state bureaucrat who has headed the departments of education and finance, for successive NSW governments, of either hue.

Does she envy her male political colleagues, who are

able to do their jobs without being accused of neglecting their children?

'Oh, I don't know. Having a really equal relationship is a much greater recipe for happiness than a relationship where one person gets to pursue their professional dream and the other person gets to support that dream. We try to support each other in what we want to do professionally, and share what we do at home. One of the benefits is being able to talk to someone who actually understands exactly what's involved – "I'm going to the Expenditure Review Committee tomorrow." "Oh. Okay. You'll need to be left alone with your papers tonight." I think you understand the pressure on each other.'

'On the other hand, you don't get the option of slacking off or doing less than you should because "Oh, my job is so hard and what are you doing? It's your job to stay home." Not trying to lighten your load is a great recipe for happiness as well. I prefer it the way it is, for us.'

'Of the blokes who are the partners of female MPs that I have met, some of them take the path that I did, which is to put their family obligations ahead of their professional development,' says Stephen Burgess, Anna Burke's husband.

'But a substantial number don't. Whereas I think that for many men who are in the Parliament, the female partners – if they have any children – do that to a much greater extent. Partly that's social conditioning, but I also think that a lot of men derive their identity from working, not just an income.'

The difficulty of combining motherhood with a parliamentary career is borne out by the numbers. Andrew Leigh, who is the Member for Fraser and a relentlessly curious economist, recently dug around for some statistics on his colleagues and the rate at which they reproduce.

For his forthcoming book *The Luck of Politics*, Leigh researched the children of MPs and senators in the 44th Parliament using publicly available sources including *Who's Who*, Wikipedia and party websites.[4] Leigh's particular focus was on child gender. He had a funny little idea (economists are like that) about a correlation between parents' political beliefs and the gender of their children. And indeed, he found that Coalition women were more likely to have sons, while Labor men were more likely to have daughters.

But the broader patterns he identified were pretty striking, too. Leigh worked out how many children the male and female politicians in the 44th Parliament had, on average. Male MPs and senators had 2.1 children each; a shade over the national household average of 1.9. Women parliamentarians, however, averaged only 1.2 progeny.

Put that another way: there is a one-child penalty for women in federal politics.[5]

It's not just an Australian accident, either; similar research in 2012 by the UK's Political Studies Association reveals a spookily matched pattern in Westminster. Male politicians there averaged 1.9 children, while women fielded 1.2 each.[6]

Some female politicians, of course, don't have children at all; that's what keeps those averages down. And the brutal truth is that childlessness is still probably the biggest natural advantage a woman can give herself in terms of dealing with the demands of a successful career in federal politics. For some, indeed, it is the price of entry.

In the 44th Parliament, four in every ten female representatives are childless – twice the childlessness rate found among their male colleagues.[7] It's a similar story in the UK, where 45 per cent of female MPs are childless, compared with 28 per cent of the men.[8]

I've spelled it out as if the decision not to have children is a strategic one; or that it's even a conscious decision, which is not always the case. Sometimes, it just doesn't happen. Sometimes, by the time you get into politics, it's just more or less impossible. If you come from Western Australia, it's actually just about impossible; none of the women from WA has children who aren't grown up, and the two Coalition women ministers who come from there – Foreign Minister Julie Bishop and Michaelia Cash, Minister Assisting the Prime Minister for Women – are both childless.

When the Coalition senator Bill Heffernan expressed his suspicion of childless Julia Gillard in 2007, it was because she had chosen that course.

'I mean, anyone who chooses to remain deliberately barren . . . they've got no idea what life's about,' Senator Heffernan told the *Bulletin*. 'We've got a few on our side as well.

'One of the great understandings in a community is family and the relationship between Mum, Dad and a bucket of nappies.'[9]

Is childlessness a deliberate choice? For Gillard, it was – more or less.

'If I'd met a man that I was tremendously in love with, and one thing in life he wanted was to have kids, then obviously maybe I might have made a different set of decisions.

I mean, who knows with the "what ifs"?' she told *Australian Story* in 2006.

'I suspect if I had made a different set of choices I would have been a very conservative parent. I'm kind of full of admiration for women who can mix it together, working and having kids, but I'm not sure I could've. There's something in me that's focused and single-minded and if I was ever going to do that, I'm not sure I could have done this.'[10]

A woman's peak child-bearing years extend – it is generally agreed – between the ages of twenty and thirty-five. And from what we know publicly about that particular slice of Julia Gillard's life, it was spent like this: at twenty-two, she became the second woman to lead the Australian Union of Students. At twenty-five, she graduated from her law degree and was hired by Slater and Gordon. At twenty-nine, she was made a partner of that firm. At thirty, she started a relationship. At thirty-four, having tried at length to get preselection for various seats, she failed to get the nod for the Senate, found out her boyfriend was facing allegations of defrauding money, broke up with him and lost her job and then worked like buggery to rescue her political career, and kind of surprisingly actually succeeded and at thirty-seven won the federal seat of Lalor, and ten years later found herself getting roused on for having no kids.

This is the rather horrid double rabbit-punch politics can dole out to women. You give up all sorts of opportunities to get there in the first place – some women do choose to be childless, but others don't, they just run out of time or become aware of the spectacular paucity of dating options or realise they can't face the juggle, or suddenly remember that they live in Perth. Having come to that real-isation (and let us never assume that that peculiarly private epiphany is businesslike, or swift, or without tears) they rather quickly learn that they are now to be marked down for relinquishing what they felt they could not claim.

'You actually cannot win,' is Tanya Plibersek's conclu-sion. 'So many of the criticisms of Julia Gillard were about the fact that she was unmarried and childless. But on the flip side, if she'd been exactly who she was only married, and a working mother, the criticisms about neglecting her children would have been just as strong . . . possibly, they would have come from the same people.'

'You cannot begin to please people with your personal arrangements. You have to be content with your own personal arrangements. You and your own family have to be happy – that's all.'

Heffernan's 'deliberately barren' remark isn't an orphan, by the way. And it's not even a sentiment restricted to his side of politics. Gillard's predecessor in the Labor lead-ership, Mark Latham – her former great friend – wrote dismissively of her in 2009 that she could not hope to be a decent education minister owing to her personal failure to reproduce.[11]

This was not, interestingly enough, a critique Latham had extended to himself in his capacity of shadow educa-tion minister between 1997 and 1998 under Kim Beazley, a role he undertook without the benefit of any children at all.

This critique is altogether sharper, and more thrombosis-inducing, when it comes from men who themselves – like Senator Heffernan – have had the privilege of wives, meaning that the joy and fulfilment of family has come for them at something of a discount, whereas for women it is exorbitantly priced.

Perhaps the test, for any male critic of a childless female MP, is this: 'Ah. But would *you* stay at home, and change the nappies, as your wife did for you, if the roles were reversed?' In very few cases could one imagine the answer being 'yes', although Latham – who clearly was changed profoundly by fatherhood and on retirement from politics became a stay-at-home dad – is an honourable exception.

Men in politics who don't have families get marked down too, by the way; it's not just women. Bob Carr, who managed to be Premier of New South Wales for a decade despite not having children, not driving a car, not liking meat pies and not enjoying organised sports, was in 1992 evaluated by Liberal leader John Hewson thus: 'You've got to be suspicious of a guy that doesn't drive and doesn't like kids and things like that.'[12]

Dr Hewson, whose Ferrari informed voters in the most reverberant way imaginable of his licensed status, had three children at the time from his first marriage (he has since had two more children, one with each subsequent wife). One of his children, with his first wife Margaret, gave a television interview explaining that Dr Hewson had in any event always put politics first even before he left the family.

Tim Fischer, the Australian diplomat and former Nationals leader and deputy prime minister, married at the age of forty-six and later told the *Age* that his extended period of bachelorhood had occasionally raised eyebrows.

'There was a fair bit of hypocrisy around during the '70s and '80s in relation to marital status,' he told the paper.

'It seemed there was a question mark over being a party leader and being single or being a frontbencher and single. The same people [who questioned me] were married but having affairs all around Canberra.'[13]

Thirteen years after Bob Carr acquired a political asterisk on account of not having any kids, his successor Morris Iemma was criticised for spending too much time with his. Iemma, who took six weeks of private leave from his job as health minister in 2003 when his wife became ill just before giving birth to twins, was subjected to a near-audible whispering campaign from colleagues on the grounds that he lacked commitment to the job.[14]

When Labor senator and numbers man Mark Arbib announced his resignation from politics in March 2012, citing the grief of his young children over his regular absences, the hot rumour around Canberra was that he was secretly facing troubles with ICAC – a rumour that subsequent years have proved entirely unfounded. So unbelievable was it, in other words, that a parliamentary father might sincerely want to be with his family that substitute explanations were automatically generated by the gossip-sphere.

The expectation of parliamentary fathers is clear: be one, by all means – you will be thought unusual otherwise – but don't go overboard or anything. Parliamentary fathers are required to keep their families within an acceptable range; helpfully visible, but not intrusive. There is no requirement for you to talk about them.

Mothers in politics, however, are required to talk about their children all the time. It's not enough to have children, like the men do; if you're a mother in politics, this status will also oblige you to have a position on all sorts of particular matters, like breastfeeding, or child care, or the photography of Bill Henson. Plus, people will constantly ask you where the children are. And every single thing you do, and the enthusiasm and grooming with which you do it, will be combed for significant indicators as to whether women can have it all. Part of this deal is that if you ever stop doing your job – hell, even if you just move to another job – it will almost certainly be construed as rock-hard evidence that combining career and family never pays.

When Nicola Roxon resigned from politics after fifteen years in Parliament – five of them as a Cabinet minister, raising a young child with her Melbourne-based partner Michael Kerrisk – her departure was widely construed as an acknowledgement that she couldn't 'have it all'. Roxon herself, exasperated, wrote an article for *The Monthly* explaining that it was 'rubbish' to suggest her resignation meant anything at all for working women beyond that she had done a job, done it well in her own estimation, and now had decided to do something else.[15]

When Roxon was sworn in as minister for health after the 2007 election, her daughter Rebecca was two years old. She became, at that moment, the first woman in Australian history to serve in the federal Cabinet while raising a preschool-age child.

For a man to serve as a Cabinet minister in a demanding portfolio like Health while raising young children is perfectly unremarkable; some of Tanya Plibersek's longest-serving predecessors, like Tony Abbott, Michael Wooldridge, and Labor's Neal Blewett – combined successful political careers with children of primary-school age and younger. In fact, lots of men, over Australia's 112-year recruitment history with Cabinet ministers, have served on the nation's board of directors while blithely reproducing, and *nobody ever really noticed*.

Up until the moment at which Nicola Roxon was sworn in, Australia had had ten female Cabinet ministers. Just ten. Of those, three were childless: Julie Bishop, Kaye Patterson, and Amanda Vanstone. All of the others had older children by the time they got to Cabinet; not that I'm suggesting for an instant that life would have been without complication for those women, especially in the case of Enid Lyons who had eleven children and came from Tasmania and was a widow by the time she arrived in Cabinet, which pretty much would be enough to make anyone opt for a simpler career – say, hiding in a cupboard under a damp towel.

Roxon, as a minister, introduced a number of rules that gave her the best chance of giving her family some normalcy. She made it be known that she preferred meetings to dinners. She blocked out time between 6.30 am and 9 am for her daughter, even though staff sometimes found it frustrating. She installed a 'one-week rule' for submissions – they needed to be with her one week in advance of the deadline for a ministerial answer, to allow her time to absorb and process them. She worked late at night, after Rebecca was in bed. 'Some new staff were really freaked out because I'd send an email at 11 pm and they didn't know whether that meant that they were supposed to still be at work as well,' she says.

'I really had to tell people – I'm going to send an email when I'm working, but it doesn't mean I think you should be working then, too.'

Roxon was involved with what history will recall at the very least as an eventful period in government; she was deeply involved in the first Rudd Government's headlong tilt at health reform, including the lengthy 'Mob Cap' tour in which she and Prime Minister Rudd pinged back and forth rather pointlessly from operating theatre to scrubs room in hospitals across the continent. As health minister, and as the grown-up daughter of a father lost far too soon to cancer, she saddled up against the tobacco companies to pioneer plain packaging.

But the questions about how she 'managed' the job were always front of mind.

'If you look at the good and bad things I was involved in, there is still more stuff about my work–life balance,' she recalls. 'Of course it's hard, and of course you should talk about it. But every dinner function you'd go to, it'd be "How are you doing it? How old did you say your daughter was?" And so on.'

'How do you manage?' is the question, often kindly extended, to which many parliamentary mothers learn to take polite exception. The late Janine Haines, who led the Democrats for four years in the 1980s, had a 'wife' – her husband, Ian, who cared for the couple's two children when she was away in Canberra. But Haines was gradually driven mad by constant questions about how she – and he – 'managed it'. Haines' husband was asked repeatedly whether he felt neglected or emasculated. He began to be known as 'Mr Mum', or 'Denis', in honour of Denis Thatcher.

'When people say to me "How do you feel about leaving your husband and children at home while you go to work?", I tell them that I will answer that question when it is asked of a man first,' Janine Haines finally told the *Canberra Times* in 1987.[16]

When asked how she 'managed', she replied: 'Probably the same way men manage to be both senators and fathers . . . Ian is how I manage it. Every politician needs a supportive spouse . . . He is placid, easy-going with a very secure sense of his own worth. He runs the whole thing. I don't even interfere when I am at home.'[17]

This constant attention exacerbates the guilt that is never far from the surface among parliamentary mothers. 'Sometimes I think I'm failing at motherhood,' wrote Greens Senator Larissa Waters in 2013, after her four-year-old young daughter became ill during a sitting week.[18] 'Since becoming a mother and a senator my life has become infinitely more rewarding and also a hell of a lot more complicated . . . I feel like I'm performing a constant juggling act and with my hand-eye coordination I'm bound to drop a ball from time to time.'

'I think everyone in politics hides how hard it is,' says Karen Andrews, who – like Waters – once had to monitor her ill daughter by text message from Question Time as she was taken to hospital by her grandmother. Andrews told me the story, then asked me not to publish it, then changed her mind. There are so many sensitivities involved; being thought an absent and thus careless mother, being thought an inattentive participant in the nation's primary interrogative event. Anxieties run deep. 'I don't think it's spoken about very openly. Women feel very uncomfortable in talking about any issues they have because we are concerned about how that will be perceived, or that people will think our priority is our family when we should be focusing on our jobs.'

The political wife drought isn't just about children, though, and whether or not you can have them without going mad. The usefulness of political 'wives' is not restricted to their ability to keep the kids quiet while the prime minister's on the phone, or artfully distract a child who has not clapped eyes on his father for a week. In some circumstances, a political spouse can become a potent campaigner in their own right.

But it's the ones who work part-time, or not at all, who are more likely to be able to oblige; and that's usually the wives, not the husbands.

'I think it comes down to the not-working thing,' says Karen Andrews. 'Those parliamentary wives who don't work can actually attend women's functions, can stand in at community functions and so on. As a parliamentarian, you probably have about three-to-one in terms of functions you are invited to and functions you can attend; a wife can sometimes go along instead; they're being there, they're being supportive and they're being a presence, and I think that's great. But if you have a working partner they just can't do that. I can't recall my husband ever going out to represent me.'

Anna Burke says the idea of a spouse as a 'political asset' is usually a wife-shaped one, which doesn't often survive the transition to husbands. 'I take my husband nowhere. Nor would I ever send him as my representative, which I hear of male politicians doing from time to time. It's my job, not his.

'For a spouse, it's hard, traumatic work. Do you really want to come to a Chinese restaurant to eat fatty food and hang out with a bunch of people you don't know while your partner abandons you for the night? Plus then you're also paying for a babysitter.

'As a politician, you'll have people coming up to you on those nights saying: "Where's your husband? Thought you might bring him along to social occasions?" And I think, well – you might be at a social occasion, but I'm at work.'

In fact, the enlistment of male partners for ambassadorial roles has a short and unhappy history. Tim Mathieson, the only man ever to be issued the Lodge's second set of keys, was in 2008 appointed as an ambassador for men's health, back when he was merely the deputy first bloke. The announcement was greeted with a degree of harrumphing about 'jobs for the boys', despite the fact that the gig obliged Mathieson to drive himself – unpaid – from country town to country town, talking blokes into having prostate examinations.

Therese Rein's sheaf of responsibilities, meanwhile, as patron of everything from the National Portrait Gallery to the Indigenous Literacy Project, were never questioned in the same way; neither were the similar activities of many of her predecessors.

Weirdly, it seems that male political spouses not only are not expected to be useful; they're viewed with something between panic and suspicion when they actually attempt to be.

We shall not speak of Mr Mathieson's professional skills; he was a hairdresser, which on one memorable occasion emboldened a radio host to ask Julia Gillard directly whether her boyfriend was in fact gay. Elsewhere, his job was viewed as a great joke, though not – I suspect – by any professional woman who has ever been required to attend a breakfast function or appear on morning television, by whom a hairdresser boyfriend might properly be viewed as money in the bank.

In a properly functioning democracy, a parliament should reflect its people. And while the number of women in federal Parliament does not reflect that women are a shade over 50 per cent of the population, the parliamentary culture has done rather a better job of accurately reflecting our culture's expectations of men and of women. Of men: work hard, and don't expect any sympathy if you're separated from your families. Of women: work, by all means. But there will be strings attached, and they will be fiendishly hard to sever; a mother's absence from her children, in politics as much as anywhere else, will be viewed much more critically than a father's.

When Edith Cowan became Australia's first female parliamentarian in 1921, the *Age* sounded a note of caution in its editorial pages. 'A Parliament composed wholly or mainly of woman politicians is not a prospect to be regarded with enthusiasm. Were political office to become the ambition of the fair sex, and were standing for Parliament to become the latest craze of fashion, there would be many dreary and neglected homes throughout the country sacrificed on the altar of political ambition.'[19]

Nearly a century later, significant remnants of those attitudes remain; the guilt of creating a 'dreary and neglected home' still weighs heavier on the shoulders of women in Parliament, even though by rights the partial loss of either parent to politics is a significant forfeit for any child. 'Every politician is a selfish parent,' says Graham Perrett, Labor MP for the Queensland seat of Moreton. 'You have to be, to get on in politics. Your partner and your children suffer, and that means your partner has to sign up.'

But when female partners sign up in greater numbers than male ones, the effect on Australia's representative democracy is unmistakeable. Male politicians get wives, and female politicians tend not to. What flows from that is a greater natural hesitation – among women – to take on a political career.

When I interviewed Greens leader Christine Milne for *Kitchen Cabinet* in 2012, she was full of enthusiasm for political life, with its unmatchable opportunity to engineer social change. The only juncture at which she showed any hesitation was when talking about the impact of politics on her two sons.

'I missed significant things in their lives,' she said. 'One of my boys was Christopher Robin in a children's play at Christmas time and I couldn't be there because the Parliament was sitting and, unlike now, when people get pairs relatively easy in the Senate, there was no such thing in the Tasmanian Parliament at that time because the numbers were tight. There was just no way you could get a pair for a children's play, so those sorts of things I missed out on.'

'There is a stage when the feminist movement . . . where we all thought we could have it all. Everything we wanted to do we could achieve; we could do the university thing, we could go into careers and do that well, we could do the mothering well, we could do what we wanted in the community and we could volunteer and so on, and the reality is – you can't.'

Milne's advice to women considering a political career was blunt: 'I wouldn't say avoid it, but just go into it with your eyes open and think about how you are going to stage your career. How long are you going to be there? What role? What level of responsibility would you like to take? Is this the best time to do it? Have you got that level of support in your own relationship and family that will enable you to do the job well? These are serious questions, but I think women have gotten to the point where they know that you can't have it all any more.'

'Having it all.' It's such a totemic phrase when used with reference to women, and it's so loaded. 'Having it all' sounds greedy. Unreasonable. Impossible, too. And you will never hear that phrase used about a man, even though men – particularly in politics – very commonly combine demanding careers with young families. For them, having it all is perfectly possible because they're not doing it all.

If 'having it all' means 'doing it all', then of course it's never going to fly. Tanya Plibersek doesn't have a 'wife'. But she's got a pretty useful composite alternative: a husband who juggles, and help where she needs it. I have those things, too, and until such time as they become common-place, I will continue to feel lucky.

8

ROLE REVERSAL

One of the most comfortable things about assumptions is that they don't feel like assumptions at all. Mostly, they just feel like the natural way of things. Take fathers working long hours, for instance, or male politicians spending eighteen weeks a year away from their young children without anyone really batting an eyelid. Or mothers looking after young children for long days while their partners are at work – or even for weeks on end if there's business travel. The assumption that a boss makes when an employee is sent on a snap business trip is that there is someone at home to work around that unexpected event. If a child is taken ill at school or child care, in most cases staff will call the mother first. That's an assumption, and often it's a reasonable one.

How can you test whether something's an assumption? Try this: switch things around, and check how bananas everybody goes.

For the last eight chapters, more or less, we've looked at what happens to women and men when they behave in ways we generally consider to be normal; the expectations of what they will do when they have children, and the consequences for their lives and jobs. Now, just for our own entertainment and for a dirty great slab of confirmation that these assumptions actually do exist, we take a look at what happens when people do the unexpected.

The first thing that happens when you start behaving in a way that is contrary to expectations is that you get a lot of questions. This is pretty normal human behaviour. If you're walking a bunch of kids to the park and one of them wanders off down a side street or starts balancing on a wall, what's the first thing you yell? 'What are you doing? Come back here!' And at work, if someone wears high heels when normally they don't, or turns up in a suit, or brings a packed lunch when they normally buy a hamburger up the street, the first response from colleagues will ordinarily be a question. 'Going on a date?' 'Got a court summons have you, mate?' 'Ooo! Economy drive, is it?'

Questions are human beings' cheapest and most direct technique for dealing with things that are not quite right. There are questions that are regularly asked of working mothers, but would rarely, if ever, be put to a working father. And there are some others that are fired daily at fathers who look after their children full-time, but would never be levelled at a stay-at-home mum. Questions are ostensibly demands for information, but they can run both ways; sometimes, their purpose is as much to deliver intelligence as to elicit it.

How do you do it? This is a golden regular for working mothers, especially those who have obviously demanding jobs. Usually, it is not a hostile question; it's just that the questioner is genuinely baffled to some degree by the actual mechanics involved in a mother working long hours. Instinct tells them that mothers spend a lot of time with their children; the fact that this mother is obviously also spending a lot of time working creates a sort of conceptual logjam, from which the questioner is requesting to be released.

Much as a woman might occasionally be tempted to answer 'Parapsychology', or 'Jedi mind control', the answer is usually pretty basic. Either the dad is doing more than the average male allotment of stuff around the house, or some kind of third party is involved: grandparents, nannies, formal child care, and so on. People don't ever ask working dads how they 'do it'. That's because they already have a pretty good idea how he does it, and they're usually spot on.

How can *you* do *it?* This is a variation on the first question – a slightly more emotionally loaded one.

Jane Morrow, a Sydney publisher, was given a significant promotion at work when she was thirty-two weeks pregnant with her third child. In order to take the job, she knew she would have to come back to work pretty quickly after maternity leave. She and her husband, Nathan, a human resources manager in the energy sector, discussed the matter (she really wanted to take the job) and decided that he would take three months' parental leave. On his last day before going on leave, his company told him he would be made redundant on his return.

So when Jane went back to work, she was the sole breadwinner.

'We had a relative come round to drop off some stuff when I was going back to work,' she recalls. 'Audrey was four or five months old, and we were borrowing her breast pump and all sorts of paraphernalia. She said to me: "It's amazing that you're doing this. It's not in my nature to leave my babies."'

This is another, slightly more sophisticated use of the question; here it is used not principally to elicit information, but to deliver a message. It combines a shot of admiration 'You're amazing!' with a Bob-Hawke-sized chaser of disapproval. It reminds the target of the natural world order, and her place outside it. At heart, it really means: 'I so admire you for being able to do something of which I, with my fundamental decency, would be entirely incapable.'

Jane, for her part, was gobsmacked. 'I was like: "I'm leaving them with their DAD, for God's sake." It wasn't even like I was leaving them at a childcare centre, which I don't think there's anything wrong with, by the way. An actual parent was going to be looking after them.'

Where's the baby? This isn't one that mothers get asked by their ordinary workmates – she might get it when people know she's had another baby recently, or maybe by professional associates she hasn't seen for a bit. Because our assumption is implicitly that children will be looked after principally by their mother, confronting visual evidence that this particular mother seems to be without her children may prompt an episode of childlike confusion in the questioner.

An amusing way to answer this one is to widen your eyes, clap your hands to your face, scream 'Oh my God!' and run out of the room. Again, there are not actually all that many possibilities here by way of serious answer. Logic tells you that if the baby is not with its mother, and assuming it has not been put on eBay or left on the train, it will either be with its father or with a third party. If the baby is with its father, there will be more questions.

Fiona Sugden is the woman with the long blonde hair you have seen a million times walking behind Kevin Rudd in campaign footage. She is one of the rare Rudd staffers who found a moment to breed during her time working for him; three children in five years, all born when Fiona – a typical Rudd staffer in at least this respect – was aged under thirty. When Rudd took back the leadership in June 2013, she had a four-year-old, a two-year-old, and a six-month-old baby. He asked her to come back for the campaign, and she said yes. Leaving young children and disappearing for months on end is a familiar part of the life of a campaign staffer; it's the same sacrifice politicians make, only with none of the pay, fame, and selective adulation. It's far more usual to see fathers doing it, though; Sugden faced a lot of questions.

'I just literally left my home for four months,' she says. 'I had to accept that I would be judged. Even within the Labor Party. Constantly, every day, I would get it: "Where are the kids? How are you managing this? Are you okay? Are you mad?"'

In truth, Sugden didn't always know exactly where the kids were. She knew they were being looked after, capably, by her husband with the help of a nanny. They were fine. But lots of people assumed Sugden was not.

Aren't you lucky? This is one for the mothers with 'wives'; partners who do stay at home, or work fewer hours, in order to take care of children. A working father with a stay-at-home partner is a perfectly ordinary proposition. A working mother with a stay-at-home partner, however, is lucky. This question, more than any of the other questions, involves a confusing and intimate clash of impulses in the breast of the woman being questioned. Usually, she does feel lucky. But she might also feel a bit stabby.

While Sugden was treated like something of a freak for leaving her three young children to travel with the prime minister, her husband – who worked, and had the support of a nanny – became something of a hero.

'He had much more help than I ever had,' says Sugden, bluntly. 'But people were all over him. "Can I help?" And to me: "Oh my God. You're so lucky." Even the childcare educators – "You're so lucky that your husband can even do this!" Well, he had those kids too. Of course he should be able to look after them. It was as if he was some kind of male god. Of *course* I was grateful that he was supportive, but . . . my God.'

Look around you. How many mothers do you know who routinely wrangle two or three children by themselves while the fathers are at work, or travelling? It's so common as to be utterly unremarkable. And no one would ever track down the dad and remind him of his good fortune. *That* arrangement isn't lucky. It's just normal.

Aren't you amazing? Men who stay home and look after their kids, rather than working, can occupy an extremely strange neural landscape. It's a landscape of extremes, in which they experience either the chill winds of exclusion or the hot breath of overpraise, but precious little in between.

'There are daily comments like "Isn't he amazing?" and "Isn't it wonderful how he manages all the kids?" in a tone as though he were a charmingly bumbling Hugh Grant character,' says Jane Morrow of her husband. 'He feels patronised. I feel like shouting: "Yes, he is. But no more so than all the mothers out there juggling the same!" I did it for six years, and no one told me I was amazing.'

A man who answers 'I'm a full-time dad', when asked the inevitable question at a backyard barbecue, can expect two broad responses. First, he may be viewed with suspicion or even contempt by other men. Secondly, he may be in distinct danger of being kissed to death by the women present.

Daniel Petre, whose book *Father Time* was written about his active decision to put his family and children first, says he gets very distinct reactions from men and women. He had hundreds of letters from women when the book was published; most lamenting their inability to reconnect with their overworked spouses. And mothers he met at school and elsewhere were hugely enthusiastic.

'I'd get it all the time: "You're such a great dad!" But I would just think, well, how would they know? And I'd say: "Let's see. Wait till they're twenty, and then we'll see where I fucked up."'

Among fathers, though, Petre's terrain was distinctly rockier. 'You're ostracised, because their wife thinks you're a better father than he is. Men who had read my book would say, "You're a dickhead. You've caused me more stress in my life."'

The hero–zero complex entangles men because – even after all these decades of change for women – we're still not entirely sure where a man who does housework actually fits. Is he a failure, or a triumph? It depends who you ask. But its daily impact is more pernicious. Caught between two dizzying extremes – silently thought a failure by some, and wildly over-applauded by others simply for remembering to put socks on a child – a father doesn't ever get a clear sense of how he's *actually* doing.

The American comedian Louis C. K., who has built his own TV show around his life as a full-time dad, is angered by the constant assumption that when looking after his children, he is just taking a break from his proper job.

When I take my kids out for dinner or lunch, people smile at us. A waitress said to my kids the other day, 'Isn't that nice that you're getting to have a little lunch with your daddy?' And I was insulted by it, because I'm like, *I'm fucking taking them to lunch, and then I'm taking them home, and then I'm feeding them and doing their home-work with them and putting them to bed*. She's like, 'Oh, this is special time with daddy'. Well, no, this is boring time with daddy, the same as everything.

If I do something for my kids, I get a medal, because most fathers don't. If a mother makes a tremendous effort for her kids and does incredible things, no one gives a shit, because she's a mom, and that's what she's supposed to do. It's like giving a bus driver a medal for driving straight ahead. Nobody's interested. And that's really not fair, but it is the way it is.[1]

What are you *doing here?* This is a question that fathers are asked all the time. Sometimes, it's not a direct question. Sometimes, it is a question wordlessly and yet no less insistently posed by circumstance. When a gathering is called a 'mothers' group', it frames itself immediately as a group to which fathers are not invited. There might as well be an electric sign flashing 'What are you doing here?' if ever a bloke walks through the door.

Sometimes, the question is more direct than that.

Damien Walker lives in Launceston with his wife and daughter, and is a full-time dad. He used to be a national operations manager in the pay-TV industry, a job that consumed his attention around the clock. He'd come home at 7 pm and have dinner – if he was lucky, he'd see his child – and then by 8 pm he'd be on the couch, back on his laptop, continuing the day's work. One day, he noticed that he was missing his daughter's life.

'Before my daughter was born, people told me all that stuff like, "You'll see. Things that matter to you now will stop mattering. Everything will change,"' he says. 'What I found, though, was that everything that mattered to me still mattered just as much as it had, it was just that something else now mattered more.

'It occurred to me that one day I would just come home and find that my daughter had grown up. I couldn't continue to think about the future when I would have more time to spend with my daughter. Things happen for the first time every day – you can't have that again. It had to be now. So I made the choice.'

Damien quit his job, and the family moved to Tasmania. His wife worked part-time. When his daughter went to school, Damien joined the crowds of mums dropping their kids off at school for the first time.

'You know what happens, all the parents mill around with their kids; they're tiny so you take them into class, make sure their bag's hung up, and they've got a little friend to sit next to,' he says. 'I used to do it every day, and I got a really strange vibe off some of the mothers; like I shouldn't be there or something.

'Not very far into the school year, I said to the teacher that I'd love to get more involved – maybe come in and do some art, or something. She said: "I really don't think that's a good idea. I don't know if you've noticed, but some of the other mothers aren't really comfortable having you around. The classroom really is a special place for mothers and children, and perhaps it would be best if you didn't come in so much."'

This story isn't typical, of course; or I hope it's not – most schools are thrilled to get offers of help from any parent. But the pattern of assumptions about who the helpful parent is most likely to be is amazingly resistant to change, and the reflexive view of schoolrooms as a 'special place for mothers and children' is reinforced, silently, every day. In my daughter's classroom, there is a roster for school reading: it has fifteen names on it, all mothers' names except for Jeremy's. (He put his name down anyway, because he's *amazing*.) It's not that fathers aren't allowed to come in for reading – far from it. It's just that they're not really expected to, and if they don't, no one is going to think any less of them. Wordlessly, the reading roster – with its oestrogen-soaked line-up – poses an implicit question to any bloke who turns up: 'What are *you* doing here?'

Do you come here often? 'I got hit on all the time,' says Damien Walker. 'When I was younger I used to love taking my puppy out for a walk – a baby German shepherd, because girls would always come up. But, man. Pushing a baby around? There are a lot of women who think that it's really sexy for a man to take time out from work to raise a child.'

Of all the things you have to navigate as a mother, tricky dating etiquette is not usually one of them. And yet dads who turn up in the female-dominated school-gate community can find themselves in awkward situations from time to time, arising from being the only bloke in the area. And a bloke giving off powerful 'good with children' pheromones at that.

It's not always sexual, of course. 'You know that look when you've got your toddler in the pram, maybe asleep, and you'll catch the eye of a lady and she sort of puts her head on one side and gives you a little smile and says, "Oooohhhhh"?' says Tom Slee, a business development manager in the superannuation field. 'I got it all the time, from sixteen-year-olds to 96-year-olds. At first, I found it kind of amusing, but then after a while I thought: God. Just stop it.'

There are upsides to this wave of lady-love – 'You could get away with murder in a shop,' admits Tom – but there are downsides too.

'At the local playground, you'd see all the same faces quite regularly – mainly it was just mums, but on school holidays the dads would be there too . . . the mums would come over and say "Hi", like usual, and you'd see the dads checking you out, and thinking "Who's this guy?"'

And when I say 'downsides', I include anything from mild embarrassment up to off-the-dial awkward. My friend Greg Cousins, an Adelaide-based teacher and artist, looked after his daughter Ruby when she was little, and was routinely the only dad at various playgroups, reading sessions at the library, and so on. He fell into regular conversation with one of the mothers; they talked about art, architecture – anything rather than kids' clothes, developmental milestones, and the rest of it. After a while, they agreed to have lunch at her house – a perfectly normal sort of thing that parents who meet through their children do all the time.

But when Greg and Ruby arrived for lunch, something was weird. 'As soon as she opened the door, she looked really, really embarrassed and uncomfortable,' he says. 'I couldn't work it out, but then suddenly she said something about how she hoped I wouldn't get the wrong idea about lunch, and that it was just lunch and nothing more. It was weird, but also sort of hilarious. I mean, my kid was there, and two of her kids, and these two enormous dogs that she had jumping around; how exactly were we going to pull it off if we did decide to leap into bed anyway?

'The lunch was great; it was really nice, but it was funny, like she needed to set things straight.'

Are you okay? Or *When are you going back to work?* This is another implicit question, often hovering in the minds of people who are awkward around stay-at-home fathers. Another way of putting it is: *What happened to you? Can't you get a job? Can't you keep a job*?

The writer John Birmingham, who works from home, lists the assumptions about stay-at-home dads: 'They're considered half-men. Less men than they should be.

They've lost their job. They can't get another one. They're just not up to it. They've gone for a lazier option.

'I am almost shamefully grateful that I worked from home for many years before I became trapped here by family necessity. If I didn't have a bunch of books and articles to be taking up with every day, I'd feel exposed to the same criticism.'

Assuming that there is something wrong with a man who stays home is not just a casually occurring piece of thoughtless discrimination. It's so hard-wired that it can enter professional pathology, as an American study of therapists revealed in 1990.[2] In this study, two groups of therapists watched a simulated video counselling session with a man, who played the same person with the same problems in each version but was introduced to the first group as an engineer whose wife stayed home and looked after their children. The second group was told that he was married to an engineer, and it was he who stayed home with the children. The therapists in the first group did not proffer any questions at all about the man's domestic arrangement and whether it generated any stress or difficulty for the client. But in the second group, nearly all the therapists asked questions about his home arrangements, as well as deeper ones like: 'What messages from your childhood do you have about what a man is?' The man insisted in both video versions that he was happy with his work arrangement, his wife, and his family.

But the second group nonetheless rated him as severely depressed, and made recommendations including: 'You probably need to renegotiate the contract that you've got at home.'

The power of Australia's strong male-breadwinner culture is almost elemental. It's not impossible, illegal, or even particularly impractical for a woman to be the main breadwinner in a family, or for a father to stay at home with his children. It's just that the gravitational pull of the orthodox arrangement is very, very strong.

Things change, of course; the standard family arrangement from fifty years ago was that a family unit had one main breadwinner – the man. And part of that arrangement has broken down, certainly. Mothers are much more likely now to be in employment of some kind. In 1983, only 40 per cent of couple families were dual-income. By 2013, that proportion had risen to nearly 60 per cent.[3]

Simply having a job, though, is only one step for women. Working in a full-time job is another, and only 22 per cent of mothers do that. Earning more than your husband is another step, and only 14 per cent of mothers do that.[4] Being the family's sole breadwinner, as a woman, is the most confronting step of all. And only 3 per cent of mothers do that.[5])

Why is it confronting? Because however modern we have become, or think we have become, we retain presumptions – rebuttable though they may be – about which job probably belongs to whom, in an 'average' family.

And that is why questions are asked of families in which mothers earn and fathers don't; to some extent, some people will struggle with the idea that it isn't all just a big hoax, and that everybody won't at some point burst out laughing and go back to their proper jobs. What are questions such as 'But where are the children?' and 'When are you going back to work?' after all, if not thinly disguised and plaintive entreaties for the reinstatement of normalcy?

Jane Morrow, the publisher and family breadwinner, lives in Sydney's inner west, the organic foodbowl of Australia's most cosmopolitan city. Instinct tells you that a working woman out-earning her husband there should barely raise an eyebrow. But the questions, the comments and the reactions to her family's arrangement indicate otherwise. 'They add up to a persistent, daily feeling that we are doing something very countercultural and that a role reversal is still freakishly rare for this day and age,' she says. She is genuinely puzzled. Even her parents – both feminists, both of whom raised a daughter to believe that there were no limits to what she could achieve – baulked initially at the idea of Jane's husband leaving his job, even though Jane had left hers twice before without adverse comment.

'Role reversal' – that's what these arrangements tend to be called, because they are the brute inversion of what we accept to be the standard model. And when men get teased for working in the home, the jokes are all about inversion: *Pop on your pinny, mate! Got your hoover?* Even the labels 'house husband' or 'Mr Mum' are cheery reworkings of terms originally designed for women. A mother who works is a 'working mother'. A father who works is just a normal guy.

'Trading places' can be complicated, for a number of reasons. The first is that there will always be people hanging around asking incessant questions, or giving you an Order of Australia for remembering the sunscreen. And it's hard to feel normal in those circumstances; 'normal' mothers and fathers don't get questions.

The second reason is that men and women usually have entirely different routes to becoming the breadwinner or the homemaker. If you dig through the information from the Census, and find the people who mark 'Not in the workforce' when the Census forms ask them what they do: that's where your stay-at-home parents are. They're not unemployed, because they're not looking for work. They're working at home, and very busy they are too. But there is a crucial difference between stay-at-home men and stay-at-home women. About 80 per cent of 'Not in the workforce' women say that they are there by choice, or because they have family responsibilities. But only about 20 per cent of the men give that reason for being out of the workforce. They are much more likely to say that they are there because they can't find the right job, or because of health reasons.[6]

This is the genesis of the 'Are you okay?' question. And the origin of the strongest stereotype of stay-at-home dads, which is that they are there because they lost their job. In truth, a lot of stay-at-home fathers do start out there because of an external shock of some kind – redundancy, illness, or sudden change of circumstance. Whereas women take time out of work to look after children because that's what's expected of them; they don't need the extra push. Childbirth is the thing that happens to them. Men need something else, as a general rule.

Daniel Petre's 'push' came when his sister was killed in a car accident. The shock of her loss, and the realisation that life was both short and fragile, triggered a significant rearrangement in his thinking, and a determination not to lose time with his family.

'I think, sadly, you get a massive wake-up call that brings into focus the frailty of life and the short amount of time you're going to have,' he says. 'You develop your relationship with your kids between the ages of zero and nine. After that, it's pretty much set.'

But he can understand why stay-at-home dads might not classify themselves as such. 'I do think men are reluctant to admit it. "I'm still looking. I'm still in the game. I'm still a player." You see them – you see the stay-at-home dads and they do look and feel ostracised. There isn't a social network for them. That's where playgroups came from – it doesn't exist for men. Men who are working don't really reach out to men who aren't working.'

The third reason is that even when men and women 'swap places' – if we assume for a moment that the orthodox arrangement is the standard one – it's hardly ever a clean job-swap. Women who earn the household's main income don't let go of their other roles at home. Men who stay at home with the children hardly ever behave like classic housewives. And in some instances, all parties involved start exhibiting some very strange behaviour just to cope with and compensate for the fact that everybody around them thinks that they're freaks.

Housework first. You will remember from Chapter 5 that some weird stuff happens when you look at women's housework plotted against her earnings. As wives earned more and more of the household's total income, their housework hours dropped away . . . right up until the point at which they earned 66.6 per cent of the income, whereupon they started to increase their housework again.

Women who earn all the income in a family, in other words, are likely to do more housework than women who earn the same amount as their husbands. This appears to be a special and unique Australian arrangement.

What explains this seemingly crazed behaviour? Well, the orthodox assumption that still governs Australian families today, for the most part, is that the father will earn more of the money, and the mother will do more of the unpaid work. Simply inverting those two things is not as simple as it sounds. Actually, given all the sensibilities and matters of pride involved, there's a fairly intense degree of diplomacy involved in shifting any of it about. And when a woman upsets one part of the orthodox equation, by earning more than her husband, one of the things she may try to do – either consciously or subconsciously – to correct the balance is to strengthen her commitment to the other part of the equation.

Put it this way: a woman who earns more money than her husband may be worried that this makes her less womanly. This will not usually manifest itself as a classic Martha Stewart panic attack about the state of the curtains; more usually, it will be a fit of the guilts about being away from the children, or not cooking enough nutritious meals, or persistent secret worrying that everyone thinks she is a Bad Mummy. Guilt about not being very good, in other words, at the job that the majority of universal opinion still identifies as *your* job.

Or, of course, she may not give a flying fork about it. But then there is the ancillary question of her husband's feelings. That might be another matter entirely. If she is already earning more than him, and thus exposing him to real or imagined opprobrium on that account (taunts, whispers, hilarious remarks about being a 'kept man', for instance), then she might feel on some level that having him do the vacuuming as well is a bridge too far. So maybe she'll just do it, to smooth things over. This might sound silly, when laid out in black and white. And maybe it is silly. But it's also real; the pattern in which higher-paid wives pick up a bigger share of housework is beyond dispute.

PhD student Karen Reeves, from the University of Sydney, undertook an in-depth study in 2013 of Australian female breadwinners and their experiences.[7] On the question of housework, she found that in about two-thirds of the homes she looked at, cleaning was either outsourced, shared, or argued about rather than largely undertaken by the 'house husband'. Reeves argues that these couples are 'managing the threat to masculine identity'.

'There was a sense in many families that the domestic and childcare role was not seen to be the man's role,' she wrote. 'The man, as a father, engaged in primary caregiving but not – as a man – in any cleaning or domestic duties.'[8]

One of Reeves' subjects, a solicitor who earned upwards of $200,000 a year, praised her husband for doing all sorts of jobs around the house including cleaning, but noted that he would not iron, because ironing was not a man's job. 'He does stamp his foot every once in a while and say "I am not going to be a house husband",' she reported.[9]

It is a tribute to the depth and complexity of the human spirit that ironing could become a sophisticated sociological oar with which a man could hold back a rising tide of imagined emasculation. But there is a nuanced language in tasks, and not all tasks change hands when men and women 'swap roles'.

I talked to Elisabeth, a partner in a large professional services firm, who is the family breadwinner for her husband and three children. She explained that her home-based spouse is different from her male colleagues' wives.

'Just by way of example, my female friends and I who are primary breadwinners agree that asking your male primary carer partner to drop off or pick up your drycleaning is just a line that cannot be crossed,' she says. 'When the gender roles are reversed, tasks to do with the children are acceptable but anything otherwise straying into the "wife" spectrum of tasks is either too demeaning to ask of a man or they just don't see it as being in the job spec.

'In isolation, it doesn't sound too onerous that the female primary breadwinner should deal with her own drycleaning. But when added to the multitude of other household/ family tasks that still fall to the female primary breadwinner (such as organising gifts, dealing with family finances/ admin, a fair whack of childcare) it means that the double shift is truly oppressive, and in a way that is not for male primary breadwinners who have wives who happily do all of this.'

If male 'wives' don't work the same way as female ones, female breadwinners don't function like male bread-winners either, as Reeves discovered.

First, they tended to downplay the importance of being a provider. They were all financially supporting their husbands, and yet none of them would put it like that. 'Often the male partner interviewed experienced a keen sense of being dependent on their partner, and yet for the women, they did not demonstrate an awareness, or interest in, "providing" for their partner,' Reeves noted.[10]

Some simply did not define themselves as breadwinners at all. 'The way I typically describe my situation . . . is I refer to my husband as primary carer,' said another woman, a corporate social responsibility executive. 'I don't like to use terms like he is the home carer or anything, because I think that there are some terms which can be disempowering . . . I prefer to use a term that empowers him and talks about him and his role and then people can infer what that means in terms of what I do, rather than calling myself the breadwinner.'[11]

A barrister, who works full-time and earns just under $200,000 a year while her tradesman husband looks after their three children, was especially cautious. 'I don't go around saying to people outside the workplace, "Oh, I am the breadwinner", I don't do that because I think that would be . . . I don't think my husband would like me to do that and I feel embarrassed as well – it's just when I'm sending stiff letters of reminder to pay bills that I do it. I mean he still wants to feel like he is the man and he doesn't want people to know, I mean they know he is at home, but I wouldn't go around saying it.'[12]

Some of the women Reeves talked to redefined the whole concept of 'supporting' the household to accommodate the unpaid work their husbands did; renovating the home, perhaps, or supervising the household finances. 'Broadly, in our family I earn cash and my partner builds capital,' says a chief executive officer, of her arrangements. 'I have been the main money earner through our relationship, but during that time my partner has studied law and economics including a PhD, he has built our two houses, he undertakes occasional consultancies and he is the primary caregiver for our two children including homeschooling.'[13]

Several of the female breadwinners interviewed had taken conscious steps to shield their husbands' sensibilities. The corporate social responsibility executive, for instance, had actively sought advice from a female mentor about how to ensure her husband did not feel emasculated. 'Her advice to me was, empower your husband, let him be the one who manages the money even though you are the one earning it because you don't have time, and if you are in a secure relationship or marriage . . . then you should trust them to do that.'[14]

When men and women move outside the structures that society establishes for them, they build funny little cubby-houses of their own. It happens in every family to some extent – it's what makes everyone different. A dad who loves ironing or does an exceptional chocolate cake, for instance. Or a mum whose job it has always been to kill spiders. But when a complete 'role reversal' takes place, vaster and grander edifices may need to be improvised.

Some of these structures will be built entirely of silence.

In Reeves' study, one family simply did not ever mention the fact that the wife was the main breadwinner. Everyone accorded that role to the father, even though he worked fewer hours and earned less than his wife.

How does such a salient detail simply never get mentioned? Easy. Every relationship has its no-go zones, its blind spots. It's very difficult to be entirely objective about a relationship of which you are a constituent part. And when you spend an enormous amount of time with someone, it's quite usual for even obvious stuff to go unnoticed or unmentioned. My favourite 'marriage blind spot' story was told to me by the Sydney arts executive Rachel Healy, who once was driving the family car with her partner, the composer Alan John, in the passenger seat. 'Do you think I should shave off my beard?' asked Alan, conversationally. Rachel kept driving, her eyes on the road. 'Do you have a beard?' she asked, with genuine interest.

In long-standing relationships, the paths of least resistance are resignedly well-trodden. 'I've given up on arguments about housework now,' says one respondent, a chief executive officer in her forties.[15] 'I said this to my women's group the other day who are all very strong feminists and one of them – a single woman – just said: "I can't believe you actually said that, that you are going to give up on the arguments and just do all the cleaning." I just don't want to have the argument any more. You just live your life being resentful. I figure that it's better than being a single parent. Everything he does is a bonus on top of being a single parent; I take it like that. If I have to spend five hours cleaning on Saturday, fine. Do it without complaining.'

It's easy, on hearing potted case histories or even (let's face it) going round to people's places for lunch, to arrive at a stern view one way or another as to how another family has organised their lives. Other families' arrangements always have the stamp of immutability: 'Aha! So that's what they've decided to do, the idiots!' But the truth is that families often don't make concerted decisions about how they're going to deal with certain circumstances; the circumstances arise, they make some ham-fisted, piecemeal attempt to deal with it, and that's what sticks. This goofball lack of strategy is what makes human beings interesting. It's also what makes us human.

Reeves' study identifies some of the things that Australian women and men trade between themselves as they adjust to running their households in a manner still thought unusual by the society in which they live. Some of the bargains, stalemates and concessions at which they eventually arrive may seem strange.

But the global shift of women into paid employment has caused renegotiation in households all over the world, with bargains being struck to allay the fears attached to change. It's an anthropologist's dream, this stuff. In her splendid global romp through the knock-on effects of women's employment across the world's households, Naila Kabeer noted that the advent of working wives has created anxieties for husbands all over the world.[16] In Bangladesh, husbands worried that a working wife increased their chances of being cuckolded. In India, some middle-income groups viewed a working wife as a blow to her husband's prestige. In Chile, men worried that their wives would become 'machista', or blokey, and that their friends would think them lesser men as a result. In Kenya, husbands worried that their household authority would be under threat if their wives worked.[17]

How did the women cope with these fears? They bargained, in many cases. The Bangladeshi women handed over their wages to their husbands in order to preserve his status as the family's breadwinner. Wives in Chile convinced their husbands that their domestic work would not suffer. In many of the anthropological studies canvassed by Kabeer, housework is used as a bargaining chip.

The weird little trade-offs and no-speaky deals impro-vised by Australian female breadwinners and their partners, in other words, are par for the course, globally, whatever our quaint regional specialities.

What about the central fear underlying all of this horse-trading, though – the fear that the whole marriage might just blow up if a satisfactory deal cannot be struck? Are marriages where the woman becomes the primary earner more likely to end in divorce?

For some worrying news on this front, we turn to Hollywood, a town that provides – it turns out – not only nonstop gossip and intrigue, but also a real live laboratory for examining what happens to the marriages of women who suddenly earn more than their husbands. Every year a crop of five actresses experience the exorbitant career bump that comes with an Oscar best actress nomination. Nomination brings all sorts of goodies – more fame, more attention, more magazine items reporting that you are defi-nitely doing it with George Clooney, and so on.

Keen observers, however, have noticed over the years that lady Oscar winners often got divorced soon after taking delivery of the bauble. The 'Oscar Curse' seemed to persist through the generations; way back in the 1940s, Vivien Leigh's Oscar left her suddenly single when she divorced Herbert Leigh Holman the same year. Jane Wyman, who won in 1948, immediately split up with Ronald Reagan. Some of cinema's most famous women – Ingrid Bergman, Audrey Hepburn, Sophia Loren, Joan Crawford, Jane Fonda – discovered that intense stardom and super-inflated earning power did not necessarily a happy marriage make. Even in recent and – one would assume – more emancipated times, the Oscar Curse continues to blight the lives of the successful: Halle Berry, Hilary Swank, Kate Winslet, Emma Thompson, Reese Witherspoon and Sandra Bullock have all divorced in Oscar's afterglow. Their marriages – for whatever reason – did not long survive the wife's sudden blast-off into global celebrity super-orbit.

A team of American and Canadian researchers decided in 2010 to quantify just how significant the Oscar Curse was.[18] Was it only winners who were cursed? Or were nominees a little bit cursed too? They counted up every Best Actress nominee between 1936 and 2010, and investigated how many of them were married or in a de facto relationship at the time. Of the 265 women who were in a relationship when nominated, 60 per cent later divorced; a hefty marital casualty rate.

But women who actually won the Best Actress Oscar were even more likely to get divorced. The median marriage length for winners was 4.3 years, the researchers established, while non-winners were looking at about twice as long – 9.5 years. Meanwhile, nothing like this pattern was observed for the men who won or were nominated for Oscars; non-winners and winners alike had marriages that lasted a median twelve years.[19]

On one level, it might seem fatuous to turn to Hollywood for a lesson about the dynamics among typical relationships. But the Oscars have a quota – there are five female and five male candidates every year, all of whom feel the invigorating and sudden career benefits of nomination. What other professional endeavour offers such a high-profile level playing field for high achievers? In other areas, the crop of astronomically successful women is often too small to permit a decent comparison.

In any event, affairs with George Clooney are neither here nor there when it comes to the marital destiny of successful women. Earning more money than your husband introduces complications for many women, whomever you are.

In the economist Gary Becker's famous formulation, stability in marriage comes from specialisation – one partner earns the money, freeing the other partner to take care of things at home. Or, if you choose to put it the other way, one partner's unpaid work in the home liberates the other to go out and prosper in the workplace. Now, if Becker's theory really was just about time and labour management, it would make no difference whether the earner was male or female. But, of course, it does make a difference – for about a zillion other sociological reasons.

In a 2009 German study, researchers analysed a spread of families and established that marriages were more likely to end in divorce where the wife earned more money.[20] They were more likely to end in divorce in the 'role reversal' scenario – when women went out and earned the money and their husbands stayed home with the children – than in the traditional male breadwinner situation. They were more likely to end in divorce when women earned the main income for the family and then came home and did all the housework too. The link between female breadwinning and escalated rates of divorce has been established by a series of such studies.[21] So – it's not just Oscar winners.

But human behaviour is riotously insubordinate to sensible analysis. Do people get divorced because they are unhappy? Or because those around them convince them that they should be unhappy? We are horribly susceptible to the opinions of others, and the thought that others pity us for getting a raw deal often burns more deeply than the supposed wound itself.

The truth is that doing things differently from the norm does tend to feel weird, and to look weird to others, and that's why most of us avoid doing so. I keep thinking about that Canadian study I wrote about in Chapter 2 – the one finding that men who left work early to pick up their kids copped more flak than women who did the same thing. That study also found that women who didn't have children were more likely to be harassed than women who did. The deep suggestion within that research is that the lead indicator for trouble at work is less to do with whether you are a man or a woman, and more to do with whether you behave the way people expect you to behave.

If workplaces were equally accepting of men who take time out for family, there would be no reason for men to feel awkward about asking. And if men were as common as women on the playgroup circuit, then the assumption that raising children is women's work would be less dominant.

We are shaped by assumptions, after all. But they needn't be set in stone.

CONCLUSION

One of the things that has surprised me most over the course of writing and researching this book is how powerful the male breadwinner model still is, even in our modern society. It seems like a dominant, ancient instinct that wordlessly underscores the patterns of a nation.

But the weird thing is, the male breadwinner model isn't even all that old. The idea that families could afford for only one parent to be in paid work is not an ancient model; it's a convenient one, popularised largely in post Industrial Revolution societies experiencing periods of relative affluence.

Ah – the Industrial Revolution: one of humanity's more effective revolutions. Less bloody than the Russian. Less pointless than the Whiskey Rebellion. More memorable than the Pastry War (a four-month conflict in the late 1830s between Mexico and France, arising from the claims of a disgruntled French pâtissier in Tacubaya that a bunch of Mexican officers had trashed his shop).

The Industrial Revolution got a lot of stuff done. It changed the way things are made, obviously – goods are now mass-produced in factories, rather than handmade by local artisans with shocking occupational health and safety conditions.

It started our global love affair with coal. It made life easier for horses, who were decreasingly relied upon for the agrarian work that had occupied the majority of the poor and working classes. It triggered, in time, an extraordinary burst of economic growth that established a sizeable middle class, enjoying not only reliable wages, but the fruits of the labour-saving devices they were employed to make. The car. The refrigerator. The washing machine. The tumble dryer. (Such is the irony of the human condition, of course, that in 2014 some of the richest beneficiaries of these labour-saving devices use their spare time to make cheese, spin wool, or grow their own vegetables. A magazine devoted to artisanal hobby coal-mining cannot be far away.)

Middle-class prosperity by the mid-twentieth century made it possible for many families to support themselves on the earnings of only one breadwinner. The new class of jobs – manufacturing, labouring, mining, bookkeeping – also changed the way a working day looked. Rather than working in and around the home, or on farms, men arrived at a new pattern of labour – leaving the home for a long work day under supervision at a large workplace, with hundreds of other men.

This standardisation of working hours had many

consequences. The rise in packed lunches, for one example: the Cornish pasty thrived. Organised labour, for another; so much easier to bargain collectively when you were all working in the same factory, rather than straggled across fields, probably in the rain. But it also had significant and lasting consequences for our expectations of men.

In the hardscrabble centuries before the Industrial Revolution, life for a vast proportion of the population was about trying to survive long enough to reproduce, without dying in childbirth or getting cholera while you were at it. In vast sections of the Third World, things are still like that. But the organisation of the developed world into orderly, regulated workforces of men heading off every day to factories or offices for a standard working day also established a dominant, and easily adjudicated idea of what an ideal man is.

An ideal man is a good employee. He goes to work five days a week, from nine to five, except if he is especially diligent and ambitious, in which case he will do copious overtime. Possibly he will do shift work, but these hours will be regulated and he will do his required allotment without absence, complaint, or shirking. Nothing that happens at home will interfere with his productivity. In some cases, he will wear a tie. Why will he wear a tie? Why, when he is in a hurry each morning, would he stop to select a long, thin strip of fabric, providing neither warmth nor protection, and knot it around his throat in one of a small range of internationally recognised knots? No reason at all, beyond the fact that that's just what men do. The tie is one of those special human things, like TV makeup or the Winter Olympic sport of curling, that would make no sense at all to a visiting alien, but are nonetheless permanent fixtures for homo sapiens.

Having children makes men better-thought-of as employees, as we established in earlier chapters. And the corollary belief – that men are better fathers if they are employed full-time – is also quite a powerful motivator. This creates a rather fascinating difference between what we expect of mothers and fathers. Being a good mother is a quality associated with constant presence. Being a good father, in the twenty-first century, still is correlated with being absent for much of a child's daily life.

Now, I'm not suggesting that before the Industrial Revolution fathers were any kind of model, or that being roped in to do ploughing or chicken-gutting at the age of seven, or dying in freak threshing accidents, was a good thing for children either.

I am just observing that men were removed from the home, effectively, by an immense structural change that overtook the nature of work and production, organising it in vast patterns for the first time.

Some of the patterns are especially elaborate. Look at the professional services industry, for example, where a truly anachronistic method of time management continues to reign supreme.

In Australia, lawyers and accountants in large firms are governed by a system of 'billable unit' charging. Their days are divided into six-minute chunks, and each six-minute unit is charged to whichever client is getting the benefit of their attention for that slice of time. A partner – who is very well paid – wins the business and is responsible for the client, but the grunt work is done by junior lawyers or accountants, beavering away at a certain hourly rate, measured out in six-minute chunks.

'In order for it to work,' explains Janna Robertson, a partner at KordaMentha, 'you've got to have a partner and – sitting underneath them – a team of juniors whom you're paying a lot less than you make off them. The more junior people are, the more you make off them.'

That's the business model, and the model for advancement is equally simple.

'You get success by having really high billable hours; by getting yourself rostered on to large and profitable jobs, and by making senior people – who make those decisions – like you enough to give you the work.'

Measuring out your time in six-minute units sounds like – and according to many accounts, is – a miserable sort of arrangement. But the most forceful equation here is that hours spent is the primary predictor of advancement. Not value to the client, not efficiency, or innovation, but time spent, with partners functioning as contemporary feudal lords, commanding swathes of overworked and underpaid serfs.

There are chinks appearing in this system, it must be said. New firms that charge a fixed price are springing up, capitalising on the pool of annoyed clients and a workforce of skilled professionals fed up to the back teeth with billable units.

But you can see, in this model, how an employee's capacity to work long hours is firmly tied to the measure of how competent and successful they are. You can see why a working dad in one of these firms would be loath to take time out to do stuff with his family. You can see why having a wife, in these jobs where working a seventy-hour week is the key to success, might be bloody handy. And you can therefore see why women – who are so much less likely to have a wife, and much more likely to be one – do not wind up getting to the top of these firms at anywhere near the rate that men do.

Like I said: the Industrial Revolution. One of our more influential revolutions. How fascinating to think that machinery could bring about such profound patterns in the way humans think about themselves and their roles. What could possibly change these assumptions and behaviours? Well – can you think of any other vast structural revolutions that might be underway right now?

The digital revolution, a global insurgency still new enough that it has not yet acquired proper noun status, is even now in the process of unpicking some of the patterns that were cemented by its revolutionary predecessor. When men began to travel in great numbers on a daily basis to workplaces containing the tools required for their labours – be they factories or offices – then the forty-hour work week was a sensible and rational response. How could a car worker build cars anywhere but in a car factory? To imagine a working day arranged in any other way was impossible.

But the Australian workforce has been changing for decades now. Manufacturing represents now only 7 per cent of gross domestic product; half of what it was twenty years ago, according to the World Bank.[1] The growth of the service economy, coupled with the explosion in communications technology, means that for many workers the orthodox working week doesn't necessarily make the best sense.

Why spend an hour each way on a bus through choked capital-city traffic to sit in an office doing work you could feasibly do from anywhere? There are many jobs, of course, in which it remains impractical to telecommute; bricks and mortar retail staff, bus drivers, hairdressers, swimming pool attendants, massage therapists, paramedics and police are among the long list of workers for whom not being there in person would be distinctly awkward.

Advances in communications technology, however, have already wrought extraordinary changes in many jobs. Big companies are beginning to experiment with flexible working. Laptops and smartphones mean that office workers are rarely genuinely out of reach.

Higher education has been transformed by technology. Back in the 1990s when I was accruing my HECS debt and spotty academic transcript at the University of Adelaide Law School, attendance was more or less mandatory. If you missed a lecture, or a tutorial, your only option was to try to cadge a set of Penny Wong's notes (popular on the photocopy black market, owing to her fine brain and neat handwriting). These days, you can download lectures, lecture notes, and reading materials online. There's none of the lurking about you used to have to do in order to get an audience with a course coordinator; now you can just email them. Students are at liberty to do other things instead, like take on four part-time jobs to defray the escalating cost of their degrees, plus buy off-brand sardines to live on. There's even a global network of courses called MOOCS – Massive Online Open Courses – which take the idea of democratised, virtual education to its current outer limits of possibility. These phenomena have taken about a hundredth of an evolutionary heartbeat to blossom, and those who have experienced them will never work in the same way that graduates did even a decade ago.

It gives me a chill to think how different my own life would be had I had children ten years earlier. As it is, the ability to watch Parliament live online – not to mention Senate estimates sessions, press conferences and the like – has meant that I can work from practically anywhere. Ten years earlier, I would have been either tied to Parliament House, or doing a different job, or doing no job.

I'm sure there will be heart attacks all round in some quarters when – in time – the suggestion is inevitably made that federal Parliament could meet virtually instead of in person. Can you imagine all the travel costs you'd eliminate, and how the group dynamic inside the big parties would change, if MPs were required to stay in their electorates and advocate from there, rather than busy themselves with factional intrigue in Canberra? I would bet you any money there'd be more women getting involved, too. Obviously, there are also good reasons for not having a virtual Parliament – scrutiny and accountability of the national decision-making process is easier when everybody's in one place, for example, besides which you'd be instantly murdered by Canberra's taxi drivers if you ever seriously suggested politicians stayed home – but things are evolving pretty fast.

The past half-century has been a time of extraordinary change for women. Rising levels of education, smaller family sizes, the decline in manufacturing, the rise of the service economy; these are developments that have seen women take on work and accomplishment in a way that has radically changed the expectations we have of ourselves and for ourselves.

The paid work that women do has expanded. But so have the expectations of motherhood. A 2006 study of American women found that modern mothers who work full-time actually spend more hours one-on-one with their children per week than their stay-at-home mothers had in 1976.[2] They just feel far more inadequate and guilty.

Men, too, are now expected to be better fathers than their own fathers were: more hands-on, more present, more attentive. But they're still expected to do all the old stuff too.

I read an interview with the feminist historian Stephanie Coontz in the *Atlantic* recently, and was struck by one particular passage. 'In some senses, men are where women were thirty years ago,' she told the magazine.

Fifty years ago, women were told, This is your place, stay in it. But about thirty years ago, it was, Yes, you can do other things, but you must not compromise your femininity in doing it; you still have to be attractive and sexy. A lot of women have learned that you can throw out the old ideas about what makes you feminine. Men are at the point where they're beginning to discover that there are things beyond the old notion of masculinity that are rewarding. Yes, intimacy is important. You ought to share housework with your wife. At the same time, they're being told – and not just by society but by women who subscribe to these conflicting messages about masculinity – that they should be disclosing but not weak. They should be gentle but still willing to kill a mouse. They're getting these messages that somehow they have to live up to a norm of masculinity that includes all the old protective, provider roles, but also the new ones.[3]

Being yanked one way and the other by conflicting expectations is not a comfortable place to be. And the emerging stress and strain on fathers – expected at once to be more present for their children, and yet still omnipresent at work – is the belated male version of the 'having it all' question.

Perhaps it's men's turn now to change. To harness the elemental force of another technology-led revolution that changes the very structure of their lives, and brings with it new ways of measuring what success is, what being a good father is, what being a good worker is.

I don't want to oversimplify this. Technology doesn't solve all our problems. And to a significant extent, it can create new problems too: workers who never stop working, whose smartphones make them available for duty twenty-four hours a day. But if I've become convinced by anything over the course of writing this book, it's that it often takes an external event for an average man to change his behaviour. Perhaps it's a recession. Perhaps it's being made redundant. Perhaps it's having a mentor or a boss who demonstrates that it's acceptable to work flexibly. Perhaps it's a wholesale disruptive technological revolution; who knows?

The certainty is this: as long as we continue to study, debate and agonise about what happens at work as if it is an entirely independent sphere from what happens at home, then we shall get no farther. For years, we have argued about quotas and affirmative action and all the ancillary techniques to move women up through leadership ranks, but we've taken our eyes off the other half of the equation. In focusing so hard on encouraging women to lean in, we've neglected to convince men of their entitlement to lean out once in a while. The men who already do – who have the confidence to stare down the expectations of them that lace invisibly but unmistakeably through the world of work – will perhaps be the advance riders of change.

Perhaps the last half-century, this window of history over which women changed significantly and men hardly at all, will be viewed as a brief window of awkward evolution-ary adolescence. Like one of those old fossils of creatures caught in that embarrassing interregnum between fishdom and swamp-thingdom, and immortalised in primordial mud for the interest of archaeologists some 200 million years hence.

Perhaps, in our ferociously joined-up new world, in which unthinkable volumes of information and intelligence are available from anywhere at a keystroke, we will finally realise that the worlds of home and work can't make sense until you look at them side by side. That a drought in one place creates a drought in the other. And that rain is good for everyone.

REFERENCES

Introduction: The Wife Drought

1. Australian Bureau of Statistics 2011, *Census of Population and Housing*, ABS, Canberra, 2011, analysis provided by Jennifer Baxter, Australian Institute of Family Studies
2. Ibid.
3. Fitzsimmons, Terrance William, 'Navigating CEO appointments: do Australia's top male and female CEOs differ in how they made it to the top?' PhD Thesis, UQ Business School, University of Queensland, 2011
4. Ibid., p. 205
5. Baxter, Jennifer, 'Parents Working Out Work', *Australian Family Trends No. 1*, Australian Institute of Family Studies, April 2013, at http://www.aifs.gov.au/institute/pubs/factssheets/2013/familytrends/aft1/
6. Australian Bureau of Statistics 2009, *Australian Social Trends – Trends In Household Work*, cat. no. 4102.0, ABS, Canberra, March 2009

7. *OECD Factbook 2014: Economic, Environmental and Social Statistics*, OECD Publishing, 2014 doi: 10.1787/factbook-2014-en

8. Baxter, Jennifer, 'Parents Working Out Work'

9. http://www.pm.gov.au/media/2013-09-18/remarks-swearing-first-abbott-government, 18 September 2013

Chapter 1: Awful Men, Hopeless Women

1. Workplace Gender Equality Agency, *Gender workplace statistics at a glance,* May 2014, at https://www.wgea.gov.au/sites/default/files/Stats_at_a_glance.pdf

2. Fox, Catherine, *Seven Myths About Women and Work,* NewSouth Publishing, Sydney, 2012, p. 51

3. Barón, Juan D. and Cobb-Clark, Deborah A. 'Occupational Segregation and the Gender Wage Gap in Private- and Public-Sector Employment: A Distributional Analysis', *Economic Record,* vol. 86, no. 273, June, 2010, 227–246 http://www.econstor.eu/bitstream/10419/34818/1/571633919.pdf

4. Fox, Catherine, *Seven Myths About Women and Work*, p. 57

5. Barr, Natalie 'Working women must stop blaming men for their troubles, says *Sunrise* presenter Natalie Barr who has "never been discriminated against"', *Daily Telegraph*, 20 March 2014, at http://www.dailytelegraph.com.au/news/opinion/working-women-must-stop-blaming-men-for-their-troubles-says-sunrise-presenter-natalie-barr-who-has-never-been-discriminated-against/story-fni0cwl5-1226859496003

6. Fagg, Jenny and Hellicar, Meredith and Sanders, Melanie and Zehner, David, 'Creating a positive cycle: critical steps to achieving gender parity in Australia', *Bain Report*, 6 February 2013 at http://www.bain.com/offices/australia/en_us/publications/creating-a-positive-cycle.aspx

7. Fitzsimmons, Terrance William, 'Navigating CEO appointments: do Australia's top male and female CEOs differ in how

they made it to the top?' PhD Thesis, UQ Business School, University of Queensland, p. 2

8. Equal Opportunity for Women in the Workplace Agency (EOWA), 'Australian Census of Women in Leadership', 2012, at https://www.wgea.gov.au/lead/australian-census-women-leadership

9. Toohey, Tim and Colosimo, David and Boak, Andrew and Goldman Sachs JBWere, 'Australia's hidden resource: the economic case for increasing female participation', Goldman Sachs JBWere Investment Research, Melbourne, 2009

10. World Economic Forum, 'The Global Gender Gap Report', 2013, at http://www.weforum.org/reports/global-gender-gap-report-2013

11. Cassells, Rebecca and Duncan, Alan and Abello, Annie and D'Souza, Gabriela and Nepal, Binod, 'AMP.NATSEM Income and Wealth Report Issue 32 – Smart Australians: Education and Innovation in Australia', National Centre for Social and Economic Modelling, University of Canberra, October 2012 at http://www.natsem.canberra.edu.au/publications/?publication=ampnatsem-income-and-wealth-report-issue-32-smart-australians-education-and-innovation-in-australia

12. Summers, Anne, *The Misogyny Factor*, NewSouth Publishing, Sydney, 2013, p. 54

13. Fitzsimmons, Terrance William, 'Navigating CEO appointments', p. 156

14. Biernat, M., Manis, M., and Nelson, T. F. (1991), 'Comparison and expectancy processes in human judgment', *Journal of Personality and Social Psychology, 61*, 203–211

15. Uhlmann, Eric Luis and Cohen, Geoffrey L., 'Constructed Criteria: Redefining Merit to Justify Discrimination', *Psychological Science*, June 2005, 16, pp. 474–480, doi:10.1111/j.0956-7976.2005.01559.x

16. Furnham, Adrian, 'Self-estimates of intelligence: culture and gender difference in self and other estimates of both general (g)

and multiple intelligences', *Personality and Individual Differences*, vol. 31, no. 8, December 2001, 1381–1405 http://www.sciencedirect.com/science/article/pii/S0191886900002324

17. Financial Services Institute of Australasia (FINSIA), 'Significance of the Gender Divide in Financial Services', 2012

18. Sandberg, Sheryl, *Lean In*, Random House, New York, 2013

19. Kay, Katty and Shipman, Claire, 'The Confidence Gap', *The Atlantic*, 14 April 2014 at http://www.theatlantic.com/features/archive/2014/04/the-confidence-gap/359815/

20. Swaine, Jon, 'Hillary Clinton advises women to take criticism "seriously but not personally"', 14 February 2014, at http://www.theguardian.com/world/2014/feb/13/hillary-clinton-melinda-gates-women-criticism

21. Babcock, Linda and Laschever, Sara, *Women Don't Ask: Negotiation and the Gender Divide*, Bantam Books, New York, 2007

22. Frankel, Lois P., *Nice Girls Don't Get the Corner Office: 101 Unconscious Mistakes Women Make That Sabotage Their Careers*, Business Plus, 2004, p. 80

23. Sandberg, Sheryl, *Lean In*, p. 63

24. Galinsky, Ellen and Salmond, Kimberlee and Bond, James T. and Brumit, Marcia Kropf and Moore, Meredith and Harrington, Brad, 'Leaders in a Global Economy: A Study of Executive Women and Men', Families and Work Institute, Catalyst, Boston College Center for Work and Family, 2003 at http://www.catalyst.org/knowledge/leaders-global-economy-study-executive-women-and-men

25. Australian Bureau of Statistics 2011, *Census of Population and Housing*, ABS, Canberra, 2011, analysis provided by Jennifer Baxter, Australian Institute of Family Studies

26. Lindell, Richard, 'Gender pay gap closes for Gen Y but not for long', AM ABC Radio, 1 April 2009, at http://www.abc.net.au/am/content/2008/s2531670.htm

27. Desai, Sreedhari D. and Chugh, Dolly and Brief, Arthur, 'The Organizational Implications of a Traditional Marriage: Can

a Domestic Traditionalist by Night be an Organizational Egalitarian by Day?' UNC Kenan-Flagler Research Paper No. 2013–19, 12 March 2012, at SSRN: http://ssrn.com/abstract=2018259

28. Dahl, Michael S. and Dezső, Cristian L. and Gaddis Ross, David, 'Fatherhood and Managerial Style: How a Male CEO's Children Affect the Wages of His Employees', *Administrative Science Quarterly*, December 2012, 57, pp. 669–693, doi:10.1177/0001839212466521

29. Washington, Ebonya L., 'Female Socialization: How Daughters Affect Their Legislator Fathers,' *American Economic Review*, 2008, vol. 98, no. 1, pp. 311–32

Chapter 2: Looking at Things the Wrong Way Up

1. http://w3.unisa.edu.au/hawkeinstitute/cwl/documents/AWALI2012-National.pdf

2. Baxter, Jennifer, 'Parents Working Out Work', *Australian Family Trends No. 1*, Australian Institute of Family Studies, April 2013, at http://www.aifs.gov.au/institute/pubs/factssheets/2013/familytrends/aft1/

3. Gray, Edith, 'Fatherhood and Men's Involvement in Paid Work in Australia', in Ann Evans and Janeen Baxter (ed.), *Negotiating the Life Course: Stability and Change in Life Pathways*, Springer, Berlin, Heidelberg, Germany, 2013, pp. 161–74

4. Australian Human Rights Commission 'Headline Prevalence Data: National Review on Discrimination Related to Pregnancy, Parental Leave and Return to Work 2014', 2014

5. Morin, Rich, 'Study: More men on the "daddy track"', Pew Research Center, 17 September 2013 at http://www.pewresearch.org/fact-tank/2013/09/17/more-men-on-the-daddy-track/

6. Miller, Sarah, 'New Parenting Study Released', *New Yorker*, 24 March 2014, at http://www.newyorker.com/online/blogs/shouts/2014/03/new-parenting-study-released.html?mobify=0

7. Morin, Rich, 'Study: More men on the "daddy track"'

8. Ibid.

9. Baxter, Jennifer, 'Parents Working Out Work'

10. Russell, Graeme and O'Leary, Jane, 'Men get Flexible!', Diversity Council Australia, 2012, at http://dca.org.au/News/News/Employers-take-note%3A-men-want-flexible-working-too%21/293#sthash.XRvHDsfu.dpuf

11. Sandberg, Sheryl, *Lean In*, p. 100

12. Ibid., p. 20

13. Skinner, Natalie and Hutchinson, Claire and Pocock, Barbara, 'The Big Squeeze: Work, Life and Care in 2012 – The Australian Work and Life Index', Centre for Work and Life, University of South Australia, 2001

14. Wade, Matt, 'Fewer than 20 men a month take paid parental leave', *Sydney Morning Herald*, 1 September 2013, at http://www.smh.com.au/lifestyle/fewer-than-20-men-a-month-take-paid-parental-leave-20130831-2sxf6.html#ixzz33kEdWUVO

15. 'Voluntary paid maternity leave, yes; compulsory paid maternity leave, over this Government's dead body, frankly, it just won't happen under this Government' ABC Radio PM, 22 July 2002 at http://www.abc.net.au/pm/stories/s613611.htm

16. Australian Human Rights Commision, 'Headline Prevalence Data: National Review on Discrimination Related to Pregnancy, Parental Leave and Return to Work 2014', 2014

17. Berdahl, J. L. and Moon, S. H., 'Workplace Mistreatment of Middle Class Workers Based on Sex, Parenthood, and Caregiving', *Journal of Social Issues*, 2013, 69, pp. 341–366. doi: 10.1111/josi.12018

Chapter 3: With This Ring, I Thee Make Redundant

1. Sawer, Marian and University of Canberra Centre for Research in Public Sector Management, *Removal of the Commonwealth marriage bar: a documentary history*, Belconnen, ACT: Centre

for Research in Public Sector Management, University of Canberra, 1996

2. Trotman, Janina, *Girls Becoming Teachers: An Historical Analysis of Western Australian Women Teachers, 1911-1940* (Google eBook), Cambria Press, 2008, p. 349

3. *Hansard*, 4 October 1922, http://parlinfo.aph.gov.au/parlInfo/search/display/display.w3p;db=HANSARD80;id=hansard80%2Fhansardr80%2F1922-10-04%2F0096;query=Id%3A%22hansard80%2Fhansardr80%2F1922-10-04%2F0107%22

4. Ibid.

5. Sawer, Marian, *Removal of the Commonwealth marriage bar*, p. 36

6. Ibid.

7. Sheridan, Tom and Stretton, Pat, 'Mandarins, Ministers and the Bar on Married Women', *Journal of Industrial Relations*, vol. 46, nos 84–101, March 2004. p. 91

8. Ibid., p. 93

9. Ibid., p. 85

10. Sawer, Marian, *Removal of the Commonwealth marriage bar*, p. 24

11. Hewitt, Belinda and Western, Mark and Baxter, Janeen, 'Marriage and money: The impact of marriage on men's and women's earnings', ANU, Negiotiating the Life Course, Discussion Paper 007, July 2002 at http://lifecourse.anu.edu.au/publications/Discussion_papers/NLCDP007.pdf

12. Ginther, Donna and Zavodny, Madeline, 'Is the male marriage premium due to selection? The effect of shotgun weddings on the return to marriage', no. 97–5, Working Paper, Federal Reserve Bank of Atlanta, 1998, at http://EconPapers.repec.org/RePEc:fip:fedawp:97-5.

13. Cassells, Rebecca and Nepal, Binod and Miranti, Riyana and Tanton, Robert, 'AMP.NATSEM Income and Wealth Report Issue 22 – She Works Hard for the Money', National Centre for Social and Economic Modelling, University of Canberra, April 2009, at http://www.natsem.canberra.edu.

au/publications/?publication=ampnatsem-income-and-wealth-report-issue-22-she-works-hard-for-the-money, p. 32

14. J. Correll, Shelley and Benard, Stephen and Paik, In, 'Getting a Job: Is There a Motherhood Penalty?', *American Journal of Sociology*, vol. 112, no. 5, March 2007, pp. 1297–1339

15. Gray, Edith, 'Fatherhood and Men's Involvement in Paid Work in Australia', in Ann Evans and Janeen Baxter (ed.), *Negotiating the Life Course: Stability and Change in Life Pathways*, Springer, Berlin, Heidelberg, Germany, 2013, p. 171

16. Baxter, Jennifer, 'Parents Working Out Work', *Australian Family Trends No. 1*, Australian Institute of Family Studies, April 2013, p. 9, at http://www.aifs.gov.au/institute/pubs/factssheets/2013/familytrends/aft1/

17. van Egmond, Marcel and Baxter, Janeen and Buchler, Sandra and Western, Mark, 'A Stalled Revolution? Gender Role Attitudes in Australia, 1986–2005', *Journal of Population Research*, 2010, vol. 27, no. 3, p. 157

Chapter 4: Meanwhile, on the Home Front

1. www.abs.gov.au/AUSSTATS/abs@.nsf/mediareleasesby Catalogue/51A7251ECB4E4ED5CA257BB2001422FE?Open Document

2. Australian Bureau of Statistics 2013, *Australian Social Trends – The 'average' Australian*, cat. no. 4102.0, ABS, Canberra, April 2013

3. OECD *Factbook 2014: Economic, Environmental and Social Statistics*, OECD Publishing, 2014. doi: 10.1787/factbook-2014-en or http://www.oecdbetterlifeindex.org

4. Burnham, Linda and Theodore, Nik, 'Home Economics: the Invisible and Unregulated World of Domestic Work', National Domestic Workers Alliance Report 2012 at http://www.domesticworkers.org/sites/default/files/HomeEconomics English.pdf

5. OECD *Factbook 2014: Economic, Environmental and Social Statistics*

6. Rampell, Catherine, 'You Don't Work as Hard as You Say You Do', *New York Times*, 19 October 2012 at http://economix. blogs.nytimes.com/2012/10/19/you-dont-work-as-hard-as-you-say-you-do/?_php=trueand_type=blogsand_php=trueand_type=blogsand_r=1

7. Craig, Lyn, 'Does Father Care Mean Fathers Share? A Comparison of How Mothers and Fathers in Intact Families Spend Time with Children', *Gender and Society*, vol. 20, no. 2, April 2006, p. 277

8. Macdonald, Emma, 'Why work on the homefront won't count this year', *Sydney Morning Herald*, 5 March 2013 at http://www.smh.com.au/national/public-service/why-work-on-the-homefront-wont-count-this-year-20130304-2fhbs.html

9. Australian Bureau of Statistics 2009, *Australian Social Trends – Trends In Household Work*, cat. no. 4102.0, ABS, Canberra, March 2009

10. Ibid.

11. Ibid.

12. Ibid.

13. Ibid.

14. Baxter, Janeen, 'Patterns of time use over the lifecourse: what we know and what we need to know', *Time and Gender Seminar*, University of New South Wales, June 2006, p. 5

15. Ibid., p. 6

16. Ibid.

17. Baxter, Janeen and Hewitt, Belinda, 'Negotiating Domestic Labor: Women's Earnings and Housework Time in Australia', *Feminist Economics*, 19.1, 2013, pp. 29–53

18. Ibid., p. 40

19. Bittman, Michael and Paula England and Liana Sayer and Nancy Folbre and George Matheson, 'When Does Gender Trump Money? Bargaining and Time in Household Work,' *American Journal of Sociology*, 109(1), 2013, pp. 186–214

20. Ibid., p. 210

21. Ibid., p. 207

22. Baxter, Jennifer, 'Parents Working Out Work', *Australian Family Trends No. 1*, Australian Institute of Family Studies, April 2013, at http://www.aifs.gov.au/institute/pubs/factssheets/2013/familytrends/aft1/

23. Craig, Lyn and Mullan, Killian, 'How Mothers and Fathers Share Childcare: A Cross-National Time-Use Comparison', *American Sociological Review*, December 2011, vol. 76, no. 6, pp. 834–861 doi: 10.1177/0003122411427673

24. Chait, Jonathan, 'A Really Easy Answer to the Feminist Housework Problem', *New York Magazine*, 21 March 2013 at http://nymag.com/daily/intelligencer/2013/03/really-easy-answer-to-the-housework-problem.html

25. Marche, Stephen 'The Case for Filth', *New York Times*, 7 December 2013 at http://www.nytimes.com/2013/12/08/opinion/sunday/the-case-for-filth.html?_r=0

26. Ibid.

27. Craig and Mullan, 'How Mothers and Fathers Share Childcare: A Cross-National Time-Use Comparison', p. 835

28. Ibid., p. 847

Chapter 5: A Question of Competence

1. *Mere Male: The best from three decades of* New Idea*'s popular column*, Southdown Press, Sydney, 1981

2. Meisenbach, Rebecca J., 'The Female Breadwinner: Phenomenological Experience and Gendered Identity in Work/Family Spaces', *Sex Roles*, January 2010, vol. 62, nos 1–2, p. 16

3. Smith, Stacy L. and Choueiti, Marc and Prescott, Ashley and Pieper, Katherine, 'Gender Roles and Occupations: a look at character attributes and job-related aspirations in film and television', Annenberg School for Communication and Journalism, University of Southern California, 2013, at https://www.seejane.org/downloads/key-findings-gender-roles-2013.pdf

4. Change.org online petition created by Chris Routly, 'We're Dads, Huggies. Not Dummies', March 2012 at http://www.change.org/petitions/we-re-dads-huggies-not-dummies

5. ABC TV, *Q&A*, 'From the Festival of Dangerous Ideas', 4 November 2013 at http://www.abc.net.au/tv/qanda/txt/s3868791.htm

6. Chemin, Anne, 'Norway, The Fatherland', *Guardian Weekly*, 19 July 2011 at http://www.theguardian.com/money/2011/jul/19/norway-dads-peternity-leave-chemin

7. Lindsay, Elizabeth, 'Father's leave still a burning issue' *News in English*, no. 20, September 2013 at http://www.newsinenglish.no/2013/09/20/fathers-leave-still-a-burning-issue/

8. Huerta, M. *et al.*, 'Fathers' Leave, Fathers' Involvement and Child Development: Are They Related? Evidence from Four OECD Countries', *OECD Social, Employment and Migration Working Papers*, No. 140, OECD Publishing, 2013 http://dx.doi.org/10.1787/5k4dlw9w6czq-en

Chapter 6: What's a Wife Worth?

1. Cowan, Peter, *A Unique Position: A Biography of Edith Dircksey Cowan 1861–1832*, University of Western Australia Press, Perth, 1978

2. Cartoon, 'The New "House"-Wife', *Bulletin*, 31 March 1921

3. Cowan, Peter, *A Unique Position*, p. 191

4. Western Australian Legislative Assembly, Parliamentary Debates (1921–1922), 16 November 1921, vol. 65, p. 1730

5. 'Death of Mr F. W. Teesdale', *West Australian*, Perth, WA, 15 December 1931, p. 12. Retrieved 8 June 2014, from http://nla.gov.au/nla.news-article32392893

6. Western Australian Legislative Assembly, Parliamentary Debates, p. 1731

7. Ibid.

8. Traikovski, Louie, 'The Housewives' Wages Debate in the 1920s Australian Press' published in Richard Nile (ed), *Grit: Journal of Australian Studies*, no. 78, St Lucia, UQP, 2003 – cites *Australian Woman's Mirror*, 3 February 1925, p. 24

9. Ibid., cites *Leader*, 24 January 1920, p. 43

10. Ibid., cites *Herald*, 12 April 1922, p. 4

11. Ibid, cites *Australian Woman's Mirror*, 3 February 1925, p. 24

12. Cowan, Peter, *A Unique Position*, p. 190

13. Wright, Clare, *The Forgotten Rebels of Eureka*, Text Publishing, 2013, p.164–65

14. Ibid., p. 165

15. Ibid., p. 168

16. Ibid., p. 169

17. Australian Bureau of Statistics 2009, *Australian Social Trends – Trends in Household Work*, cat. no. 4102.0, ABS, Canberra, March 2009

18. Miniclier, Christopher, 'Survey Says Average Wife Worth $8,300' *Gettysburg Times*, 19 May 1967

19. '2013 What's a Mom Worth Infographics', salary.com, at http://www.salary.com/2013-mom-infographics/

20. *Burnicle v Cutelli*, 1982, 2 NSWLR 26 (CA), p. 28

21. Graycar, Reg, 'Sex, Golf and Stereotypes: Measuring, valuing and imagining the body in court', *Torts Law Journal*, 2002, 10(2), 205–21

22. Finlay, Henry, 'Divorce and the Status of Women: Beginnings in Nineteenth Century Australia', University of Tasmania. Discussion Paper presented to the Australian Institute of Family Studies seminar, 20 September 2001 at http://www.aifs.gov.au/institute/seminars/finlay.html

23. Ibid.

24. Ibid.

25. Howard, John, *Lazarus Rising: A Personal and Political Autobiography*, HarperCollins, Sydney, 2010, p. 73

26. Australian Parliament House, *Hansard*, Family Law Bill (Second Reading), 28 February 1975 http://parlinfo.aph.gov.au/parlInfo/search/display/display.w3p;db=HANSARD80;id=hansard80%2Fhansardr80%2F1975-02-28%2F0003;query=Id%3A%22hansard80%2Fhansardr80%2F1975-02-28%2F0021%22

27. Australian Parliament House, *Hansard*, 9 April 1975, http://parlinfo.aph.gov.au/parlInfo/search/display/display.w3p;query=Id%3A%22hansard80%2Fhansardr80%2F1975-04-09%2F0121%22

28. Justice Nygh, 1987, as quoted in Parkinson, Patrick, 'Quantifying the Homemaker Contribution in Family Property Law', *Fed. L. Rev.* 31 (2003): 1. p. 37

29. (1984) 156 CLR 605, 646

30. *Whiteley and Whiteley* (1992) FLC 92-304 at p. 79, 299. For a broad discussion of homemaker entitlements read Guest, Paul, 'An Australian Perspective on the Evolution of the Law in Relation to the Assessment of Special Contributions in "Big Money" Cases: Never Mind the Law, Feel the Politics', *International Journal of Law, Policy and the Family* 19.2 (2005): 148–62

31. *Ferraro and Ferraro* (1993) FLC 92–335, p. 79

32. Carnegie, Mrs Dale, *How to Help Your Husband Get Ahead In His Social and Business Life*, Greystone Books, Vancouver, 1953

Chapter 7: Public Life? Need a Wife!

1. Baird, Julia, *Media Tarts: How the Australian Press Frames Female Politicians,* Scribe Publications, Melbourne, 2004, p. 79

2. Hinch, Derryn, 'Hinch Hits', *Sydney Morning Herald,* 28 August 1983

3. *Age*, 24 August 1983, p. 11 as cited in Jenkins, Cathy, 'Women in Australian politics: mothers only need apply', Griffith University, 2006

4. Leigh, Andrew, *The Luck of Politics,* unpublished ms

5. Ibid.

6. Campbell, Rosie and Childs, Sarah, 'This Ludicrous Obsession, Parents in Parliament: The Motherhood Trap', *Huffington Post UK*, 16 January 2014 at http://www.huffingtonpost.co.uk/dr-rosie-campbell/women-in-politics_b_4608418.html?utm_hp_ref=uk-politicsandir=UK+Politics

7. Leigh, Andrew, *The Luck of Politics*

8. Campbell, Rosie and Childs, Sarah, 'This Ludicrous Obsession, Parents in Parliament: The Motherhood Trap', *Huffington Post UK*, 16 January 2014

9. Lyons, John, 'Bill & Lachlan's Excellent Adventure', *Bulletin with Newsweek*, 8 May 2007, vol. 125, no. 6568

10. Transcript, ABC TV, *Australian Story*, 'Julia Gillard', 6 March 2006 at http://www.abc.net.au/austory/content/2006/s1585300.htm

11. Crabb, Annabel, 'Latham's cheap shot fails to wound', *Sydney Morning Herald*, 22 August 2009 at http://www.smh.com.au/federal-politics/lathams-cheap-shot-fails-to-wound-20090821-etpn.html

12. Silkstone, Dan and Gray, Darren, 'Playing Personal Politics', *Age*, 10 January 2004 at http://www.theage.com.au/articles/2004/01/09/1073437471553.html?from=storyrhs

13. Ibid.

14. Clennell, Andrew and Pearlman, Jonathan, 'Iemma lacks ticker to be premier, taunts Brogden', *Sydney Morning Herald*, 2 August 2005 at http://www.smh.com.au/news/national/iemma-lacks-ticker-to-be-premier-taunts-brogden/2005/08/01/1122748579443.html?oneclick=true

15. Roxon, Nicola, 'Goodbye to All That – Why I Resigned', *The Monthly*, March 2013 at http://www.themonthly.com.au/issue/2013/march/1366758466/nicola-roxon/goodbye-all

16. Harbutt, Karen, 'Wounded Janine Haines Parries Siddons' Sword', *Canberra Times*, 18 January 1987, cited in Baird, Julia, *Media Tarts*, p. 83

17. Ibid.

18. Waters, Larissa, 'Does every working mum feel like this?', *Mamamia*, 17 May 2013 at http://www.mamamia.com.au/parenting/failing-at-motherhood/#Kgwl6K37qvyVgjHI.97

19. *Age*, 15 March 1921, p. 6

Chapter 8: Role Reversal

1. Grose, Jessica, 'Questions for Louis CK', salon.com, 17 June 2011 at http://www.slate.com/articles/news_and_politics/inter rogation/2011/06/questions_for_louis_ck.html

2. Robertson, John and Fitzgerald, Louise, 'The (Mis)Treatment of Men: Effects of Client Gender Role and Life-Style on Diagnosis and Attribution of Pathology', *Journal of Counseling Psychology*, vol. 37, no. 1, January 1990, pp. 3–9, cited in Warren Farrell, *Father and Child Reunion*, Finch Publishing, 2001, p. 108

3. Cassells, Rebecca and Toohey, Matthew and Keegan, Marcia and Mohanty, Itismita, 'AMP.NATSEM Income and Wealth Report Issue 34 – Modern Family; The Changing Shape of Australian Families', National Centre for Social and Economic Modelling, University of Canberra, October 2013, p. 25 at http://www.natsem.canberra.edu.au/publications/?publication= modern-family-the-changing-shape-of-australian-families

4. Reeves, Karen, 'Female Breadwinners: a subtle but significant shift in women's paid employment in the 21st Century', PhD Thesis, University of Sydney, March 2013, p. 1

5. Australian Bureau of Statistics 2011, *Census of Population and Housing*, ABS, Canberra analysis provided by Jennifer Baxter, Australian Institute of Family Studies

6. Baxter, Jennifer, 'Parents Working Out Work', *Australian Family Trends No. 1*, Australian Institute of Family Studies, April 2013, at http://www.aifs.gov.au/institute/pubs/factssheets/2013/familytrends/aft1/

7. Reeves, Karen, 'Female Breadwinners'

8. Ibid., p. 147

9. Ibid., p. 148

10. Ibid., p. 85

11. Ibid., p. 151

12. Ibid.

13. Ibid., p. 146

14. Ibid., p. 149
15. Ibid., p. 153
16. Kabeer, Naila, 'Marriage, Motherhood and Masculinity in the Global Economy: Reconfigurations of Personal and Economic Life', UC Santa Cruz: Center for Global, International and Regional Studies, 2007
17. Ibid., p. 18
18. Stuart, H. Colleen and Moon, Sue and Casciaro, Tiziana, 'The Oscar Curse: Status Dynamics and Gender Differences in Marital Survival', *Social Sciences Research Network*, 27 January 2011
19. Ibid.
20. Kraft, Kornelius and Neimann, Stefanie, 'Effect of Labor Division between Wife and Husband on the Risk of Divorce: Evidence from German Data', Institute for the Study of Labor, IZA DP, no. 4515, October 2009
21. Kalmijn, Matthijs and Loeve, Anneke and Manting, Dorien, 'Income Dynamics in Couples and the Dissolution of Marriage and Cohabitation', *Demography*, vol. 44, no. 1, February 2007

Conclusion

1. http://data.worldbank.org/indicator/NV.IND.MANF.ZS? page=4
2. Bianchi, Suzanne and Robinson, John and Milkie, Melissa, *Changing Rhythms of American Family Life*, 2006, cited on pp. 52–53 of Eagly/Carli, 2007
3. Reese, Hope, 'Studying US Families: 'Men Are Where Women Were 30 Years Ago', *Atlantic Monthly*, 27 March 2014 at http://www.theatlantic.com/education/archive/2014/03/ studying-us-families-men-are-where-women-were-30-years-ago/284515/

ACKNOWLEDGEMENTS

The first thing to say about this book – written at warp-speed, much of the time either late at night or with one small person or other sitting under the desk – is that it would never have been written without the help of Madeleine Hawcroft. Madeleine, a brilliant young woman who as series producer for *Kitchen Cabinet* has done everything from wrangling prime ministers to procuring weird ingredients, proved equally invaluable to this book – and its grateful author – as ace researcher, proofreader and dispenser of wise counsel. One day, Madeleine will be the boss of everything; to exploit her in the meantime has been one of my great professional pieces of good fortune.

The second thing to say is that neither would this book have happened without the small people under the desk. You little varmints are, above everything, the delight of my life.

To my regular employers who allowed me to take leave and write the thing – Mark Scott, Kate Torney and Gaven Morris at the ABC, and the Fairfax Sunday editors – thank you for your patience.

I have been assisted mightily by individuals far more expert than I in the field of gender, family and work. Some patiently endured phone calls: Elizabeth Broderick and her staff, Lisa Annese, Terrance Fitzsimmons, Marian Baird, Kaz Cooke, Graeme Russell and – of course – the redoubtable Jennifer Baxter. Others too numerous to mention here wrote books, articles and theses to which I am heavily indebted. Especially those who did the kooky social experiments – you are excellent.

I asked a lot of people some very nosy questions in the course of writing the book, and from politicians to political spouses to businesspeople to stay-at-home mums and dads and people I met on Twitter, I encountered so many interesting and thoughtful responses. These are not always easy issues to discuss publicly, and I thank you all very much for being so helpful.

Leigh Sales, Julia Baird, Miranda Murphy, Samantha Maiden, Rachel Healy, Helen McCabe and Maria O'Brien maintained enthusiasm in the face of repeated harangues, and offered valuable insights and ideas, for which many thanks. Lisa Wilkinson's support for the book was immediate, generous, and vastly appreciated.

Nikki Christer at Random House deployed her customary charm and enthusiasm to get this project on the way. My debt to her goes back a decade to when she rescued my first book, an act of faith I have never forgotten. I would also like to thank Catherine Hill, Deonie Fiford, Sophie Ambrose, Josh Durham and Peri Wilson for variously belting the thing into shape, making it look good and organising the author. Additional thanks on this front to Fiona Inglis, an author-organiser from way back.

I am constantly aware of how fortunate I am, not only to have and love a job that allows a measure of flexibility, but also to have the kind of help without which a sustainable juggle would be impossible. As would (to state the arterially-bleeding obvious) an entire book.

So many people have made my life easier in one way or another over the course of this book's genesis. They include Jodi Fleming, Deb Claxton, Sue Bath, Anja Seidel, Nico de Soleil, Lisa Whitby, and of course Madeleine. Not to mention the entire Storer family (Jen, Brian, Margot and Rob, Joseph, Uncle Mark, Damien and Anisa, Tim and Belinda), who provide a sophisticated child-entertainment network incorporating books, Scalextric and model aeronautics, stretching all the way from Adelaide to Sydney; my parents (of whom more in a moment) and my brothers James and Tom.

Special thanks to Miranda Murphy and Fiona Hughes, for all the times you've generously complicated your own juggles by accommodating an extra ball or two from my place.

I owe a lot to mothers. My own, for starters – Christobel. Her good humour, unflappability and unfailing generosity (not to mention her preparedness to run rescue missions from rural South Australia) have meant the difference between failure and success to many of my more ambitious enterprises, from Canberra sitting weeks with newborns to white-knuckle rides between *Kitchen Cabinet* shoots. Her sister, Elizabeth Coles, is also an astounding mother and continuing world standard-bearer for cheerfulness in the face of life's intricate challenges; as is their mother – my Granny, Sheila Riggs, now in her late nineties – whose love of reading I inherited, and whose potent combination of charm and fearsomeness I still hope some day to develop. And my oldest friend Wendy Sharpe is an inspiration to me in the art of mothering, among so many other things.

I owe a lot to fathers, too: I thank mine, MacDonald, for his love, adventurism and support, and for his impeccable foresight in buying a hovercraft before they were fashionable. To all those fathers who push, every day, to exceed rather than fulfil the expectations of them as parents, I say: good on you, chaps.

And to Jeremy, most importantly of all: thank you for your love and attention and for three beautiful children and for never thinking anything is impossible, even when it really just about is. Thank you for your patience with me over the writing of this book. And thank you for – when faced with a choice between more involved and less involved – always going for the former. You are a great man, and I love you.

INDEX